KIDS LOVE Pennsylvania

A PARENT'S GUIDE TO EXPLORING FUN PLACES IN PENNSYLVANIA WITH CHILDREN. . .YEAR ROUND!

Kids Love Publications
7438 Sawmill Road, PMB 500
Columbus, OH 43235

Dedicated to the Families of Pennsylvania

© Copyright 2000, Kids Love Publications

For the latest updates corresponding to the pages in this book visit our website:

www.kidslovepublications.com

All rights reserved. No part of this book may be reproduced or transmitted in any form or by any means, electronic or mechanical, including photocopying, recording or by any information storage and retrieval system without the written permission from the authors, except for the inclusion of brief quotations in a review.

Although the authors have exhaustively researched all sources to ensure accuracy and completeness of the information contained in this book, we assume no responsibility for errors, inaccuracies, omissions or any other inconsistency herein. Any slights against any entries or organizations are unintentional.

ISBN: 09663457-2-X

KIDS ♥ PENNSYLVANIA ™ Kids Love Publications

MISSION STATEMENT

At first glance, you may think that this is a book that just lists hundreds of places to travel. While it is true that we've invested thousands of hours of exhaustive research (*and drove over 4000 miles in Pennsylvania*) to prepare this travel resource...just listing places to travel is <u>not</u> the mission statement of these projects.

As children, Michele and I were able to travel extensively throughout the United States. We consider these family times some of the greatest memories we cherish today. We, quite frankly, felt that most children had this opportunity to travel with their family as we did. However, as we became adults and started our own family, we found that this wasn't necessarily the case. We continually heard friends express several concerns when deciding how to spend "quality" and "quantity" family time. 1) What to do? 2) Where to do it? 3) How much will it cost? 4) How do I know that my kids will enjoy it?

Interestingly enough, as we compare our experiences with our families when we were kids, many of our fondest memories were not made at an expensive attraction, but rather when it was least expected.

It is our belief and mission statement that if you as a family will study and <u>use</u> the contained information <u>to create family memories</u>, these memories will grow a stronger, tighter family. Our ultimate mission statement is, that your children will develop a love and a passion for quality family experiences that they can pass to another generation of family travelers.

We thank you for purchasing this book, and we hope to see you on the road (*and hearing your travel stories!*) God bless your journeys and happy exploring!

George, Michele, Jenny and Daniel

INTRODUCTION

HOW TO USE THIS BOOK

If you are excited about discovering Pennsylvania, this is the book for you and your family! We've spent over a thousand hours doing all the scouting, collecting and compiling (*and most often visiting!*) so that you could spend less time searching and more time having fun.

<u>Here are a few hints to make your adventures run smoothly</u>:

❑ Consider the **child's age** before deciding to take a visit.

❑ Know **directions** and parking. Call ahead (or visit the company's website) if you have questions *and* bring this book. Also, don't forget your camera! *(please honor rules regarding use)*

❑ **Estimate the duration** of the trip. Bring small surprises (favorite juice boxes) and travel books and toys.

❑ Call ahead for **reservations** or details, if necessary.

❑ Most listings are **closed major holidays** unless noted.

❑ Make a **family "treasure chest"**. Decorate a big box or use an old popcorn tin. Store memorabilia from a fun outing, journals, pictures, brochures and souvenirs. Once a year, look through the "treasure chest" and reminisce.

❑ Plan **picnics** along the way. Many Historical Society sites and state parks are scattered throughout Pennsylvania. Allow time for a rural/scenic route to take advantage of these free picnic facilities.

❑ Some activities, especially tours, require **groups** of 10 or more. To participate, you may either ask to be part of another tour group or get a group together yourself (neighbors, friends, school organizations). If you arrange a group outing most places offer discounts.

- ❑ Each chapter is an area of the state (*see map below*), then by city, zip code, and place/event name. **The front index lists places by Activity Heading (i.e. Pennsylvania History, Tours, Outdoors, Museums, etc.), the back index is alphabetical.**
- ❑ For the latest updates corresponding to the pages in this book, visit our website: **www.kidslovepublications.com**.

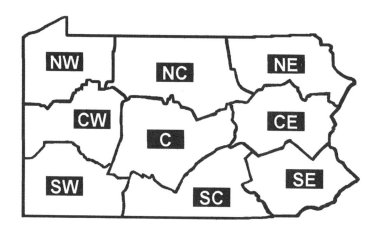

In a Hundred Years...

It will not matter,
The size of my bank account...
The kind of house that I lived in...
The kind of car that I drove...
But what will matter is...
That the world may be different
Because I was important in the life of a child.

- author unknown

Acknowledgements

*Special feelings while researching and writing this book are
dedicated to my Dad, Edwin Darrall. Being raised in Pittsburgh
and loving to visit and travel his home state, I feel his heart in this
project all the time. Parents... you do leave priceless memories
with your kids when you take the <u>time</u> to plan trips and are
passionate about family time! - Michele*

We are most thankful to be blessed with our parents, Barbara
Darrall and George and Catherine Zavatsky who helped us every
way they could – researching, typesetting, proofing and
babysitting. More importantly, they were great sounding boards
and offered loving, unconditional support.

Our own young kids, Jenny and Daniel, were delightful and fun
children during all of our trips across the state.

We both sincerely thank each other – our partnership has
created a great "marriage of minds" with lots of exciting moments
and laughs woven throughout.

Above all, we praise the Lord for His many answered prayers
and special blessings throughout the completion of this project.

We think Pennsylvania is a wonderful, friendly area of the
country with more activities than you could imagine! Our sincere
wish is that this book will help everyone "fall in love" with
Pennsylvania!

\- *George & Michele*

"Where to go?, What to do?, and How much will it cost?", are all questions that they have heard throughout the years from friends and family. These questions are one of the inspirations for motivating them to research, write and publish the "Kids Love" travel series.

This adventure of writing and publishing family travel books has taken them on a journey of experiences that they never could have imagined. They have appeared as guests on over 50 radio and television shows, had featured articles in statewide newspapers and magazines, spoken to thousands of people at schools and conventions, and write monthly columns in many publications talking about "family friendly" places to travel.

George Zavatsky and Michele (Darrall) Zavatsky were born in the Pittsburgh area. Although currently residing in Columbus, Ohio they maintain their strong affection for Pennsylvania since they have numerous family members living in the state. Along with writing and publishing a series of best-selling kids' travel books, each of them also own and operate a courier business and an internet marketing company. Besides the wonderful adventure of marriage, they place great importance on being loving parents to Jenny and Daniel.

GENERAL INFORMATION

- ❑ Biking Directory of Pennsylvania – (717) 878-6746. Free through Pennsylvania Department of Transportation.
- ❑ Council of The Arts – (717) 787-6883.
- ❑ National Park Service – (215) 597-7018.
- ❑ Pennsylvania Agricultural Fairs – (717) 787-5342. Department of Agriculture.
- ❑ PCOA – Pennsylvania Campground Owners Association Directory. (888) 660-7262.
- ❑ Pennsylvania Fish and Boat Commission – (717) 657-4518.

Fish Farms Information

- Arrowhead Springs Trout Hatchery, Newmanstown. (610) 589-4830.
- Federal Fish Hatchery, Warren. (814) 726-0164.
- Fisherman's Paradise, Bellefonte. (814) 355-4159.
- Laurel Hill Trout Farm, Somerset. (724) 593-7101.
- Reynoldsdale Fish Cultural Station, Bedford. (814) 839-2211.
- Tionesta Fish Hatchery, Tionesta. (814) 437-5774.

- ❑ Pennsylvania Snowmobile Hotline – (717) 787-5651.
- ❑ Pennsylvania State Forests – (717) 783-7941.
- ❑ Pennsylvania State Parks – (888) PA-PARKS. Junior Naturalists Program.
- ❑ Pennsylvania Visitor's Bureau, (800) VISIT-PA. www.state.pa.us/visit
- ❑ Statewide Fall Foliage Hotline – (800) FALL-IN-PA.
- ❑ U.S. Army Corps of Engineers. Susquehanna River Basin, (410) 962-3693. Ohio Basin, (412) 644-4130.

Listed by Area

- ❑ C – Cambria County Conservation District – (814) 472-2120.
- ❑ C – Centre County Region Parks & Recreation – (814) 231-3071.
- ❑ CE – Dam Releases. LeHigh River Area – (717) 424-6050. Releases create whitewater rapids. Call for rafting outfitters. Late Spring and early Fall.
- ❑ NC – Pennsylvania Canyon Country, Wellsboro. (717) 724-1926.
- ❑ NE – Christmas Tree Farms, Endless Mountains. (800) 769-8999.
- ❑ NE – Poconos Tourist Information – (800) POCONOS. Ask about selection of whitewater rafting, canoeing, and riding stables.
- ❑ NW – Venango County Parks – (814) 676-6116.
- ❑ SC – York County Parks, York. (717) 840-7440. www.york-county.org.
- ❑ SE – Berk's County Parks and Recreation Department, Wyomissing. (610) 372-8939.
- ❑ SW – Allegheny County Parks Department – (412) 350-PARK.
- ❑ SW – Washington County Department of Parks and Recreation – (724) 228-6867.

*Check out these businesses / services in
your area for tour ideas:*

AIRPORTS

Understand all the jobs it takes to run an airport. Tour the terminal, baggage claim, gates and security / currency exchange. Maybe you'll even get to board a plane.

ANIMAL SHELTERS

Great for the would-be pet owner.

BANKS

Take a "behind the scenes" look at automated teller machines, bank vaults and drive-thru window chutes. You may want to take this tour and then open a savings account for your child.

ELECTRIC COMPANY / POWER PLANTS

Coal furnaces heat water, which produces steam, that propels turbines, that drive generators, that make electricity.

FIRE STATIONS

Many Open Houses in October, Fire Prevention Month. Take a look into the life of the firefighters servicing your area and try on their gear. See where they hang out, sleep and eat.

HOSPITALS

Some Children's Hospitals offer pre-surgery and general tours.

NEWSPAPERS

You'll be amazed at all the new technology. See monster printers and robotics. See samples in the layout department and maybe try to put together your own page. National Newspaper Week is in October.

RESTAURANTS

DOMINO'S PIZZA

❑   Various locations

Telephone your local shop for tour status. Free. Usually ages 4+. Takes 15 – 20 minutes. Your children can be pizza bakers! While the group is instructed on ingredients and pizza secrets, they will get to make their own special pizza. After the custom made pizza bakes, your tour guide will take it out of the special oven, box it up and you get to take it home.

PIZZA HUT

❑   Many participating restaurants

Telephone the store manager. Best days are Monday, Tuesday and Wednesday mid-afternoon. Minimum of 10 people. $3.50 per person. All children love pizza – especially when they can create their own! As the children tour the kitchen, they learn how to make a pizza, bake it, and then eat it. The admission charge includes lots of creatively make pizzas, beverage and coloring book.

MCDONALD'S RESTAURANTS

❑   Participating locations

Telephone the store manager. They prefer Monday or Tuesday. Free. What child doesn't love McDonald's food? This is your child's chance to go behind the counter and look at the machines that make all the fun food. You will be shown the freezer and it's alarm, the fryer and hamburger flipping on the grills. There is a free snack at the end of the tour.

SUPERMARKETS

Kids are fascinated to go behind the scenes of the same store where Mom and Dad shop. Usually you will see them grind meat, walk into large freezer rooms, watch cakes and bread bake and receive free samples along the way. Maybe you'll even get to pet a live lobster!

TV / RADIO STATIONS

Studios, newsrooms, Fox kids clubs. Why do weathermen never wear blue clothes on TV?

WATER TREATMENT PLANTS

A giant science experiment! You can watch seven stages of water treatment. The favorite is usually the wall of bright buttons flashing as workers monitor the different processes.

U.S. MAIN POST OFFICES

Did you know Ben Franklin was the first Postmaster General (over 200 years ago)? Most interesting is the high-speed automated mail processing equipment. Learn how to address envelopes so they will be sent quicker (there are secrets). To make your tour more interesting, have your children write a letter to themselves and address it with colorful markers. Mail it earlier that day and they will stay interested trying to locate their letter in all the high-speed machinery.

Index by Activity Heading

MUSEUMS *(cont.)*

Index by Activity Heading

OUTDOORS

Index by Activity Heading

OUTDOORS (*cont.*)

Index by Activity Heading

OUTDOORS (cont.)

PENNSYLVANIA HISTORY

Index by Activity Heading

SPORTS

THE ARTS

Index by Activity Heading

TOURS (cont.)

Table of Contents

AREA "C"

Clearfield

State College   Mifflinburg

Patton

Altoona

Raystown Lake

Johnstown

Our Favorites...

1) Caverns
2) Horseshoe Curve
3) Boal Mansion/Columbus Chapel
4) Johnstown Inclined Plane
5) Benzel Bakery
6) Allegheny Portage Railroad
7) Johnstown Flood Museum
8) Happy Valley Friendly Farm
9) Raystown Lake Area
10)Railroader's Memorial

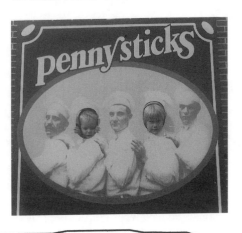

QUAINT CORNER CHILDREN'S MUSEUM

Altoona - 2000 Union Avenue (Downtown SR36), 16601. *Activity: Museums.* (814) 944-6830. *Hours:* Thursday - Saturday, 1:00 - 5:00 pm. *Admission:* Adults $1.50, Children $1.00. This is a real Victorian home that kids are allowed to explore - in fact, they're encouraged to snoop around. Probably the cutest and most popular areas are the closets and climbing the ladder into Grandma's Attic at the very top of the house. The kitchen is set up as the craft center of the house and the Dinosaur Room (complete with sandbox) is in the basement.

SOUTHERN ALLEGHENIES MUSEUM OF ART

Altoona - 1210 - 11th Avenue, 16601. *Activity: The Arts.* (814) 946-4464. *Hours:* Monday - Friday, 10:00 am - 4:00 pm. Saturday, 11:00 am - 3:00 pm. Summer Sundays, Noon - 4:00 pm. Exhibits, tours, classes. Outstanding photography and paintings---especially, railroads.

BENZEL'S PRETZEL BAKERY

5200 Sixth Avenue, **Altoona** 16602

- ❑ Activity: Tours
- ❑ Telephone: (814) 942-5062, **www.benzels.com**
- ❑ Hours: Monday - Friday, 9:00 am - 5:00 pm., Saturday 9:00 am - 1:00 pm
- ❑ Admission: Free
- ❑ Tours: Self-guided viewing through windows and monitors

Third generation family members operate a bakery that makes approximately 5,000,000 pretzels per day. Cute signs and displays lead you through a hallway running parallel to the factory. The pretzels, which were originally made by hand, are now extruded through a machine. Before you leave, get a fresh, warm free sample and have your family "pop" their heads into a life-size picture of the Benzel brothers for a great souvenir photo opportunity.

HORSESHOE CURVE NATIONAL HISTORIC LANDMARK

Horseshoe Curve Road (6 miles West of Altoona), **Altoona** 16602

- ❑   Activity: Pennsylvania History
- ❑   Telephone: (888) 4-ALTOONA
     www.railroadcity.com/railroad/HSCpreview99.htm
- ❑   Hours: Daily, 10:00 am - 7:00 pm (April - October), 10:00 am - 3:30 pm (November - March)
- ❑   Admission: Adults $3.50, Seniors $3.00, Children $1.75 (3-12)
- ❑   Miscellaneous: Gift shop.

Developed in 1854, the Penn Railroad needed to expand west, but through the mountainous terrain. This curve was developed, because, even if a bridge could be built, no locomotive could climb the steep grade. To solve this crossing problem, they built a track around the inside curves of the large mountain range. Inside the Interpretive Center, you can view a video of the curve's history and see a model of what the land looked like before the railroad changed the landscape. Kids like the push button display of sounds of trains as they make the turn (gaining speed, upgrade and downgrade). The highlight is the funicular ride up to the elevation area (or you can walk up - 200 steps) where you can look out onto the horseshoe track. There's a good chance a train (the railroad still uses this curve) will pass through while you are visiting.

LAKEMONT PARK

700 Park Avenue (I-99 to Frankstown Road), **Altoona** 16602

- ❑   Activity: Amusements
- ❑   Telephone: (814) 949-PARK or (800) 434- 8006,
     http://members.tripod.com/ntl111/doc/lkmont.html
- ❑   Hours: Daily, 11:00 am - 9:00 pm, Summers. Weekends only in May and September, Noon-8:00 pm
- ❑   Admission: Free. Buy individual or package tickets.

Over 30 rides and attractions. Island Waterpark. Go-Kart tracks, mini-golf, picnic areas and arcade. Kids Mini-Indy & Kiddie Lane.

RAILROADER'S MEMORIAL MUSEUM

1300 Ninth Ave.(off I-99 exit 17th Street, next to Station Mall)
Altoona 16602

- ❑ Activity: Museums
- ❑ Telephone: (814) 946-0834, **www.railroadcity.com**
- ❑ Hours: Daily, 10:00 am - 6:00 pm (April - October). 10:00 am - 5:00 pm (November - March - Closed Mondays)
- ❑ Admission: Adults $8.50, Seniors $7.75 (62+), Children $5.00 (3-12)
- ❑ Miscellaneous: Museum store.

B est put by the cover of their exhibit guide... "Here in Altoona an army of railroaders designed, built, maintained, and moved the Pennsylvania Railroad, the largest railroad in the world...in so doing, they changed the face of America...this is their story!" Why was Altoona chosen to be the heart of construction? (watch a 27 minute film to find out). Listen to the folks talk about their life at local scenes depicting a home, church, newsstand, and clubs. The "News Boy" is funny to listen to. Learn how railroads worked - laid the tracks, work in shops (the test lab is pretty eye opening) and design and build locomotives. This museum has less focus on displays of trains and more on the lives and work habits of people involved. Nice change.

ALTOONA COMMUNITY THEATER

Altoona - 1213 12th Avenue (Historic Mishler Theatre), 16603. *Activity: The Arts.* (812) 943-4357. Produces 4 shows a year. Youth workshops.

ALTOONA SYMPHONY ORCHESTRA

Altoona - 1331 12th Avenue (Office) #107, 16603. *Activity: The Arts.* (814) 943-2500. Features classical, pops and children's concerts.

BLAIR COUNTY MUSEUM

Altoona - Oak Lane off Logan Blvd. - P O Box 1083 (US 220 to Logan Blvd), 16603. *Activity: Pennsylvania History.* (814) 942-3916. *Hours:* Tuesday - Sunday, 1:00 - 4:30 pm (June - Labor Day). Weekends only (April, May, September, October). *Admission:* Adults $3.00, Seniors $2.50, Children $1.50 (4-12). *Tours:* 1 hour long. Historic Baker Mansion. Interprets local transportation and industrial history (iron, railroads). Civil War, elaborate home furnishings. Check out the tubes used to send orders to servants.

FORT ROBERDEAU HISTORIC SITE

Altoona (Sinking Valley) - RD #3 Box 391 (I-99, Bellwood Exit). 16601. *Activity: Pennsylvania History.* (814) 946-0048. *Hours:* Tuesday - Saturday, 11:00 am - 5:00 pm., Sunday, 1:00 - 5:00 pm (mid-May - September). *Admission:* $1-3.00. Living history reenactments. (Summer). A reconstructed 1778 fort with exhibits. Original site of a Revolutionary War fort established to mine lead for the army. Includes miners quarters, officers quarters, barracks and blacksmith.

BELLEFONTE HISTORICAL RAILROAD

Bellefonte - The Train Station (High Street in Talleyrand Park), 16823. *Activity: Tours.* (814) 355-0311, **www.vicon.net/~bhrs**. *Hours:* Weekends (Memorial Day - Labor Day weekends). Also, May and October excursions. *Admission:* Adults $8.00+, Children $4.00+. Trips to Curtain Village (restored iron furnace - small village) or Sayers Dam and various small towns. Picnic spots available along the way.

CENTRE COUNTY MUSEUM

Bellefonte - 203 North Allegheny Street, 16823. *Activity: Pennsylvania History.* (814) 355-1516, *Hours:* Monday - Friday, 9:00 am - 5:00 pm., Saturday, 9:00 am - Noon and 1:00 - 5:00 pm. **http://bellefonte.com/bellorg/bmuseum.html**. Housed in the

historic Miles-Humes Home.   Centre Furnace Mansion in State
College began the charcoal iron-making industry in this region.
Mansion open Sunday, Monday, Wednesday,Friday, 1:00-4:00 pm.

BOAL MANSION MUSEUM / COLUMBUS CHAPEL

300 Old Boalsburg Road (US322 - Business Route), **Boalsburg**
16827

- ❑ Activity: Museums
- ❑ Telephone: (814) 466-6210, **www.vicon.net/~boalmus**
- ❑ Hours: Tuesday - Sunday, 10:00 am - 5:00 pm (May - October).
  1:30 - 5:00 pm - Late Spring and Early Fall.
- ❑ Admission: Adults $10.00, Seniors $8.00 (59+), Children $6.00
  (7-16).
- ❑ Miscellaneous: Still privately owned.

Want to see a real part of Christopher Columbus? On the
grounds of the originally furnished mansion is the
Columbus Chapel that was brought here from Spain in 1909. They
actually have a sea desk once owned by Columbus and many
Columbus family heirlooms dating back to the 1400's.   The
highlight of this place begins with your first step inside the chapel.
If you're like us...your mouth will drop wide open in disbelief as
you begin to notice the centuries-old heirloom pieces. Many of the
artifacts look like movie props (the natural way they have aged
makes it hard to believe they are real!) Actual parchment family
documents, the family cross, a copy of the family tree and 2 actual
pieces of the "true" cross are awesome to see up close.   It's just
incredible that all of this history is in a small town museum!
Hearing stories about the Boal family and their home can be
interesting too!

PENNSYLVANIA MILITARY MUSEUM

P.O. Box 160A (US322), **Boalsburg** 16827

❑ Activity: Museums
❑ Telephone: (814) 466-6263
   www.psu.edu/dept/aerospace/museum
❑ Hours: Tuesday - Saturday, 9:00 am - 5:00 pm., Sunday, Noon - 5:00 pm.
❑ Admission: Adults $3.50, Seniors $3.00 (59+), Children $1.50 (6-12). Family $8.50

Honoring Pennsylvania's soldiers from Benjamin Franklin's first volunteer unit to Operation Desert Storm. Younger children enjoy climbing on tanks and cannons outside in the park, but it takes older kids to enjoy the museum. As they study American History this place brings it to life, especially the World War I trench scene, complete with sound and light effects. The museum only focuses on citizen soldiers - "the men and women of Pennsylvania who served their country in time of war."

TUSSEY MOUNTAIN SKI AREA

Boalsburg - Bear Meadow Road - Route 322, 16827. *Activity: Outdoors.* (814) 466-6266. Snow Report: (814) 466-6810, **www.tusseymountain.com**. Longest Run: 2700 ft.; 8 Slopes & Trails.

PENN'S CAVES

R.R. 2, Box 165A (SR 192 East, Near I-80, Exit 14), **Centre Hall** 16828

❑ Activity: Outdoors
❑ Telephone: (814) 364-1664, **www.pennscave.com**
❑ Hours: Daily, 9:00 am - 5:00 pm, (February 15 - May 31). Daily, 9:00 am - 7:00 pm (June 1 - August 31). Daily, 9:00 am - 5:00 pm. (September 1 - November 30). Weekends Only, 11:00 am - 5:00 pm (December) Closed Thanksgiving and Christmas Day.
❑ Admission: Adults $9.50, Seniors $8.50, Children $4.50 (2-12)

❑   Tours: 1 mile guided tour by motorboat - approximately 1 hour long

America's only all-water cavern and wildlife (1000 acre) sanctuary. Colored lights enhance "The Statue of Liberty", "The Garden of Gods" and "Niagara Falls".

ROHNEYMEADE ARBORETUM SCULPTURE GARDEN

Centre Hall - Route 1, 16828. *Activity: Outdoors.* (814) 364-1527. Arts and nature garden.

WHISTLE STOP RESTAURANT

Centre Hall - SR144 - Old Pennsylvania Avenue, 16828. *Activity: Theme Restaurants.* (814) 364-2544. Hours: Lunch and Dinner daily. Look for the train cars parked outside and then park and enter a restored 1886 Victorian railroad station. Casual dress. Moderate pricing. Children's menu.

BLUE KNOB SKI AREA

Claysburg - P.O. Box 247, 16625. *Activity: Outdoors.* (814) 239-5111. Snow Report: (800) 822-3045 (In PA), (800) 458-3403 (Outside PA), **www.blueknob.com**. Longest Run : 2 miles; 34 Slopes & Trails.

MOSHANNON STATE FOREST

Clearfield - P.O. Box 952, 16830. *Activity: Outdoors.* (814) 765-0821. **http://parec.com/forests/moshanon.htm**.   188,885 acres of Fishing, Rugged Camping, Hiking, Bike and Horse Trails, and Winter Sports.

CAMBRIA COUNTY MUSEUM

Ebensburg - 615 North Center Street, 15931. *Activity: Pennsylvania History.* (814) 472-6674. *Hours:* Tuesday - Friday, 10:00 am - 4:30 pm., Saturday, 9:00 am - 1:00 pm. Large map collection, relics including military, industrial and household, extensive photograph collection.

PROUD MARY TOURBOAT

Entriken - 100 Chipmunk Crossing (Lake Raystown Resort & Lodge - Route 994), 16638. *Activity: Tours.* (814) 658-3500, **www.raystownresort.com**. *Hours:* Scheduled departures by season (April - October). *Admission:* Adults $6.50+, Children 50% off Adult pricing (under 12). Sightseeing cruises. Food available.

WILDRIVER WATER PARK

Entriken - Route 994 (Lake Raystown Resort and Lodge), 16638. *Activity: Amusements.* **www.raystownresort.com**. (814) 658-3500. Speed slides, twisting slides, whitewater tubing slides, Children's splash pool and mini-golf.

ALLEGHENY PORTAGE RAILROAD & NATIONAL HISTORIC SITE

110 Federal Park Road (US22, Gallitzin exit - follow signs),
Gallitzin 16641

❑ Activity: Pennsylvania History
❑ Telephone: (814) 886-6150, **www.nps.gov/alpo/welpo.htm**
❑ Hours: Daily, 9:00 am - 6:00 pm (Summer), Daily, 9:00 am - 5:00 pm (rest of year), Closed Christmas only.
❑ Admission: Adults $3.50, Seniors $3.00 (62+), Children $1.75 (3-12)
❑ Miscellaneous: Visitor Center with 20 minute film. Costumed presentations during the summer. Lemon House - restored tavern and business office on premises and open to the public.

Y ou'll be amazed at the ingenuity of railroad engineers back
then! The problem was the Allegheny Mountains. No trains
or canals could get through them before the idea of the "incline"
was introduced. Called "an engineering marvel" at its opening,
travel that took three weeks by wagon took only four days by
railroad and canal. It used a combination of 10 inclines and horses
on steam locomotives pulling cars on levels in between. It's
difficult to visualize until you see the working small-scale model in
the center of the museum - then it all makes sense (still in
amazement of course!). With a hands-on demonstration, you can
personally try turning a wheel hooked to balanced and unbalanced
weights. This clearly demonstrates the need for balanced (one car
up - one car down at the same time) inclines.

TUNNELS PARK

Gallitzin - 702 Jackson Street (off Route 22 - Follow signs),
16641. *Activity:* *Outdoors.* (814) 886-8871,
www.visitjohnstownpa.com/attractions.html. *Hours:* Daily,
daylight hours. Free Admission. See and feel the awesome power
of the trains passing through the Allegheny Tunnel (modified
1854). Also on site is a PRR walkway and railroad signal and a
restored PRR caboose - climb aboard to see the sleeping quarters
and pot-bellied stove. Three tunnels to view that were built with
picks and shovels using over 300 immigrants to complete it. This is
a cute side trip between visits to the Allegheny Portage Railroad
and Horseshoe Curve.

RAYSTOWN BELLE AND QUEEN LINES

RD #1 (Rt. 26 - Seven Points Marina), **Hesston** 16647

- ❑ Activity: Tours
- ❑ Telephone: (814) 658-3074
  www.7pointsmarina.com/cruises1.htm
- ❑ Hours: May - mid-October. Summers usually have 3 cruises
  daily.
- ❑ Admission: Adults $8.00+, Seniors $7.00+, Children $3.00+
  (under 12). (10 passenger minimum on all cruises)

❑   Tours: 90 minutes, 23 miles

Public sightseeing boat cruises where you can view wooded shoreline (esp. cedar trees), wild turkey, deer, beaver, bald eagles, and ravens. Close to Lake Raystown Resort (waterpark and activities). Ask for the "Kids Kruz" that includes tour, box lunch, fish feeding, and demonstration of "rack storage" of 200+ boats in a warehouse (real neat if you're not a boater and already familiar with this).

CANOE CREEK STATE PARK

Holidaysburg - RR 2, Box 560 (US 22), 16648. *Activity: Outdoors.* **http://parec.com/state_parks/canostpk.htm**. (814) 695-6807 Beach, Visitor Center, Year-round Education & Interpretation Center, Boat Rentals, Horseback Riding, Sledding, Limestone kilns, Modern Cabins, Trails, Cross-Country Skiing.

BALD EAGLE STATE PARK

Howard - 149 Main Park Road, 16841. *Activity: Outdoors.* (814) 625-2775, **http://parec.com/state_parks/baldstpk.htm**. Beach, Boat Rentals, Year-round Education & Interpretation Center, Sledding, Campsites, Hiking, Fishing.

GREENWOOD FURNACE STATE PARK

Huntingdon - RR 2, Box 118 (SR 305 North), 16652. *Activity: Outdoors.* **http://parec.com/state_parks/grnfstpk.htm**. (814) 667-1800, Beach, Historical Center, Year-round Education & Interpretation Center, Campsites, Last charcoal-fired furnace.

LINCOLN CAVERNS

R.R.#1 Box 280 (I-76 to US 522 North to US 22 West),
Huntingdon 16652

❑   Activity: Outdoors
❑   Telephone: (814) 643-0268, **www.lincolncaverns.com**

❏ Hours: Daily, 9:00 am - 7:00 pm (July 1 - Labor Day). Daily, 9:00 am - 6:00 pm (Memorial Day Weekend - June 30), Daily, 9:00 am - 5:00 pm (April, May, September and October), Daily, 9:00 am - 4:00 pm (March and November, December - Weekends only)

❏ Admission: Adults $8.50, Seniors $7.50 (65+), Children $4.50 (4-14)

❏ Miscellaneous: Gift shop, nature trails, gem panning.

Close to Raystown Lake. 2 crystal caverns - Lincoln and Whisper Rock. Winding passages, large "rooms" with massive and delicate flowstones, pure white calcite and crystals.

SWIGART ANTIQUE AUTO MUSEUM

Huntingdon - P.O. Box 214 (US22 East), 16652. *Activity: Museums.* (814) 643-0885. *Hours:* Daily, 9:00 am - 5:00 pm (Summer). Weekends only (May, September, October). *Admission:* Adults $4.00, Seniors $3.50 (65+), Children $2.00 (6-12). See over 40 cars on display and the world's largest collection of cars, toys, license plates, bicycles and clothing. There's a special focus on cars made by smaller companies.

ROTHROCK STATE FOREST

Huntingdon - Rothrock Lane - Box 403, 16652. *Activity: Outdoors.*(814) 643-2340. **http://parec.com/forests/rothrock.htm** 93,349 acres of Fishing, Camping, Hiking, Cross-Country Skiing, Snowmobile and Bike Trails, Picnic Areas.

TROUGH CREEK STATE PARK

James Creek - RR 1, Box 211 (PA Route 994), 16657. *Activity: Outdoors.* **http://parec.com/state_parks/trghstpk.htm**. (814) 658-3847, Campsites, Modern Cabins, Fishing and Hiking.

WARRIORS PATH STATE PARK

James Creek - RD #1 (c/o Trough Creek), 16657. *Activity: Outdoors.* **http://parec.com/state_parks/warrstpk.htm**. (814) 658-3847.

JOHNSTOWN SYMPHONY ORCHESTRA

Johnstown - 227 Franklin Street, Suite 302, 15547. *Activity: The Arts.* (814) 535-6738.

JOHNSTOWN CHIEFS HOCKEY

Johnstown - 326 Napoleon St (Cambria County War Memorial Arena), 15901. *Activity: Sports.* **www.johnstownchiefs.com**. (800) 243-8499, Admission: $7 - $10.00.

JOHNSTOWN JOHNNIES BASEBALL

Johnstown - 345 Main Street (Point Stadium), 15901. *Activity: Sports.* **www.johnniesbaseball.com**. (814) 536-8326 or (877) 536-TEAM. Admission: $3.00 - $4.00.

INCLINE STATION RESTAURANT

Johnstown - 709 Edgehill Drive, 15905. *Activity: Theme Restaurants.* (814) 536-7550. **www.inclinedplane.com**. Lunch and Dinner. Ride on the incline and then dine at the top. Spectacular views of the valley and see the largest American flag in the country.

INCLINED PLANE

711 Edgehill Drive (off SR56, 403 or 271 & Johns Street)

Johnstown 15905

- ❑ Activity: Tours
- ❑ Telephone: (814) 536-1816, **www.inclinedplane.com**
- ❑ Hours: Weekdays, 6:30 am - 10:00 pm, Saturday, 7:30 am - Midnight, Sunday, 9:00 am - 10:00 pm.

❑   Admission: Adults $3.00, Seniors FREE (65+), Children $1.75
    (6-12)
❑   Miscellaneous: Gift shop. Visitor's center. Laser light sculptures
    lit on weekend nights. Observation deck on top.

B rightly lit, it is the world's steepest vehicular inclined plane
(72 % grade) with a panoramic view of the city through
viewing windows. After the flood, many residents wanted to live
up on the hill...but they needed a way to commute. It was also
used as an escape route during subsequent floods. A viewing
window looking into the motor room explains the "physics" behind
the scenes. Hang on tight to those little ones!

JAMES WOLFE SCULPTURE TRAIL

Johnstown - SR56 or SR403 (Bottom of the incline), 15905.
Activity: Outdoors. Hours: Dawn to Dusk. The first nature trail
with sculptures made from steel. It honors the city's steel heritage
with ten pieces, eight on the trail. Most photographed and visible is
"Steel Floats".

JOHNSTOWN FLOOD MUSEUM
304 Washington Street (off SR56 West to Walnut Street Exit)
Johnstown 15907

❑   Activity: Museums
❑   Telephone: (888) 222-1889
    www.visitjohnstownpa.com/attractions.html
❑   Hours: Sunday - Thursday, 10:00 am - 5:00 pm, Friday &
    Saturday, 10:00 am - 7:00 pm (May - October). Daily, 10:00 am -
    5:00 pm (November - April).
❑   Admission: Adults $4.00, Seniors $3.25 (62+), Children $2.50
    (6-18)
❑   Miscellaneous: Museum store. Film shown hourly (25 minutes)

H ear and see the story of the infamous disaster of 1889
focusing on both the tragedy and triumph of the human spirit.
View the Academy Award Winning "The Johnstown Flood"

documentary film (shown hourly) with multi-media exhibits including an animated map with sound and light effects showing water movement. On May 31, 1889, a phenomenal storm and a neglected dam led to the natural disaster in which 2209 people died. It turned a thriving town into a wasteland..."it was a roar and a crash and a smash...". Other exhibits include: A Quilt - used as a rescue rope, A Wall of Wreckage in 3-D (17 feet tall - flood wall was actually 40 feet tall). It really captures the horror of the moment, yet is subtle enough to not scare school-aged children.

JOHNSTOWN FLOOD NATIONAL MEMORIAL

Box 355 (US219 to St. Michael Exit - SR869), **Johnstown (St. Michael)** 15951

- ❑ Activity: Museums
- ❑ Telephone: (814) 495-4643, **www.nps.gov/jofl/home.htm**
- ❑ Hours: Daily, 9:00 am - 6:00 pm (Summer). Daily, rest of year - closes at 5:00 pm.
- ❑ Admission: Adults $2.00

The flood began here - see what little is left of South Fork Dam. A documentary - "Black Friday" - a 35 minute film puts you in the middle of the terror - a little frightening for youngsters. Remember over 2200 people died in about 10 minutes.

MINERS MEMORIAL MUSEUM

Johnstown (St. Michael) - SR869 @ 242 Lake Road (off US219), 15951. *Activity: Museums.* (814) 495-7281. *Hours:* Daily, 12:30 - 4:00 pm (April - October). *Admission:* Small fee. Replica of a coal mine interior. Exhibits feature mining tools and rescue equipment. Coal gift shop.

BALD EAGLE STATE FOREST

Laurelton - P.O. Box 147, 17835. *Activity: Outdoors.* (717) 922-3344. **http://parec.com/forests/bald.htm**. ATV Trails. (7 miles), Winter Sports, Trails, Fishing, Camping.

PLAYHOUSE

McConnellstown - P.O. Box 115 (Rt. 26, five miles South of Huntingdon), 16660. *Activity: The Arts.* (814) 627-0311, **www.vicon.net/~danwest/gowest.html**. Community theatre including original plays, musicals, and children's shows in an intimate 76 seat theatre.

R.B. WINTER STATE PARK

Mifflinburg - RR 2, Box 314, 17844. *Activity: Outdoors.* (717) 966-1455, **http://parec.com/state_parks/rbwnstpk.htm**. Beach, Visitor Center, Year-round Education & Interpretation Center, Campsites, Modern Cabins, Trails, Winter Sports.

RAVENSBURG STATE PARK

Mifflinburg - R.D. 2, Box 377 (c/o R.B. Winter State Park), 17844. *Activity: Outdoors.* (717) 745-7700. **http://parec. com/state_parks /rvnsstpk.htm**

POE PADDY STATE PARK

Milroy - 1405 New Lancaster Valley Road (c/o Reed's Gap), 17063. *Activity: Outdoors.* (717) 667-3622, **http://parec.com /state_parks/poepstpk.htm**

POE VALLEY STATE PARK

Milroy - R.R. 1, Box 276-A (c/o Reeds Gap), 17063. *Activity: Outdoors.* **http://parec.com/state_parks/poevstpk.htm**. (814) 349-8778.

REEDS GAP STATE PARK

Milroy - 1405 New Lancaster Valley Road, 17063. *Activity: Outdoors.* **http://parec.com/state_parks/rdsgstpk.htm** (717) 667-3622. Pool, Sledding, Campsites, Fishing, Winter Sports.

PRINCE GALLITZIN STATE PARK

Patton - 966 Marina Road, 16668. *Activity: Outdoors.* (814) 674-1000.   **http://parec.com/state_parks/prncstpk.htm**.   Beach, Visitor Center, Boat Rentals, Horseback Riding, Sledding, Campsites, Modern Cabins, Fishing, Trails, Cross-Country Skiing.

SELDOM SEEN TOURIST COAL MINE

P.O. Box 83 (I-76 to US219 to US22 East to Patton – Rt. 36)
Patton 16668

❑   Activity: Tours
❑   Telephone: (814) 247-6305 (in season) or (800) 237-8590
     www.visitjohnstownpa.com/attractions.html
❑   Hours: Thursday – Sunday, 11:00 am - 6:00 pm (Memorial Day
     Weekend - September), Weekends only (June & September)
❑   Admission: Adults $6.00, Children $3.50 (3-12)
❑   Tours: Hour long beginning at noon. Last tour at 6:00 pm.

Go underground to learn first hand the lives and working conditions of coal miners from the past to the present. Family run operations, so tours are given by miners or descendants. You'll learn that coal was dug by hand, loaded on cars and hauled from the mine by mules - for as little as 25 cents per ton!

PARKER DAM STATE PARK

Penfield - R.D. 1, Box 165, 15849. *Activity: Outdoors.* (814) 765-0630,   **http://parec.com/state_parks/parkstpk.htm**.   Beach, Visitor Center, Year-round Education & Interpretation Center, Boat Rentals, Sledding, Campsites, Rustic Cabins, Hiking Trails, Cross-Country Skiing.

S. B. ELLIOTT STATE PARK

Penfield - R.D. 1, Box 165 (c/o Parker Dam), 15849. *Activity: Outdoors.* **http://parec.com/state_parks/sbelstpk.htm**.   (814) 765-7271.

WALNUT ACRES ORGANIC FARMS

Penns Creek - Walnut Acres Road (SR104), 17862. *Activity: Farms.* (800) 433-3998. **www.walnutacres.com** *Hours:* Monday - Friday, 9:30 am, 11:00 am, 1:00 pm. Observe "chemical free" foods produced as you watch the cannery, bakery and mill. Snack Bar (11:00 am - 2:00 pm). Picnic areas.

BLACK MOSHANNON STATE PARK

Philipsburg - R.R. 1, Box 185, 16866. *Activity: Outdoors.* (814) 342-5960. **http://parec.com/state_parks/bmosstpk.htm**. Beach, Mountain Biking, Boat Rentals, Campsites, Modern Cabins, Trails, Cross-Country Skiing, Known for bogs.

EAST BROAD TOP RAILROAD

Rockhill Furnace - P.O. Box 158 (I-76, exit 13 to US522 North), 17249. *Activity: Tours.* **www.spikesys.com/ebt.html**. (814) 447-3011. *Hours:* Weekends at 11:00 am, 1:00 & 3:00 pm. (June - October). *Admission:* Adults $9.00, Children $6.00 (2-12). Tours: 50 minutes, 10 mile trip. Ride an authentic steam powered train through a valley as you learn railroad history. Station gift shop.

ROCKHILL TROLLEY MUSEUM

P.O. Box 203 (PA Turnpike, exit 13 to US522 North to Route 994 - Meadow Street), **Rockhill Furnace** 17249

- ❑ Activity: Museums
- ❑ Telephone: (814) 447-9576 (weekends only) (610) 437-0448 **www.vicon.net/~trolley**
- ❑ Hours: Weekends and Holidays, 10:30 am to 5:00 pm, Sundays until 4:00 pm (Memorial Day - October)
- ❑ Admission: Adults $3.00, Children $1.00 (2-12)
- ❑ Tours: Every 1/2 hour service (Noon- 4:30 pm)
- ❑ Miscellaneous: Pennsylvania Transportation Museum and restoration shop where volunteers are always working on new projects.

Take the 2 1/2 mile trolley rides along with a motorman on an antique streetcar - unlimited rides on many different varieties of streetcars. Even though they run on a standard railroad track, streetcars or interurbans (city to city) are powered by electricity. Wires running along the length of main streets were connected to rods moving along a set track. The grandparents will remember this form of transport and have fun memories to share of the friendships that freely developed on the way to work or to the movies.

HAPPY VALLEY FRIENDLY FARMS

US 322 (12 miles east of State College) **Spring Mills** 16875

- ❑ Activity: Animals & Farms
- ❑ Telephone: (814) 364-1902
- ❑ Hours: Tuesday - Saturday, 10:00 am - 5:00 pm., Sunday, Noon-5:00 pm. (May - October)
- ❑ Admission: Adults $5.75, Children $5.00 (1-12)
- ❑ Miscellaneous: Gift Shop. Picnic Areas. Ice cream shop. Hayrides.

First watch goats being milked, then see how they take that product to their fudge factory to use in yummy treats that you can buy. Whenever could you get kids to try goat's milk (unless it was in candy)? Younger kids seem to really enjoy the (not overly crowded) petting area where they can feed and touch baby goats, lambs, baby chicks, and llamas. You'll get some great photographs of your children cuddling newborn lambs or goats. The entire farm is well maintained and divided into areas (each with their own little barn). There's the Chicken Coop, Maternity and Nursery Center, Bunny Barn, and Reptile Room. Their Activity Center is full of farm toys and games that educate as the kids play. Because the admission is priced comparable to many full-sized zoos (but this is one of the best petting zoos we have seen), plan on spending at least a couple of hours here.

INDIAN CAVERNS

US 22 to SR 45 North, **Spruce Creek** 16683

❑ Activity: Outdoors
❑ Telephone: (814) 632-7578,
    http://parec.com/parec/caves/indian.htm
❑ Hours: Daily 9:00 am - 6:00 pm. (Summers) 9:00 am-4:00 pm.
    (April, May, September, October)
❑ Admission: $4.00 - $8.00

K nown for their massive formations. Authentic Indian history - 400 relics and tablet of picture writing found in cave. A mile of lighted walkways - includes a one-of-a-kind "Star Room" grotto and "Frozen Niagara".

PENN STATE UNIVERSITY PARK CAMPUS

(Hetzel Union Building - off US322), **State College** 16801

❑ Activity: Tours
❑ Telephone: (800) PSU-TODAY, **www.psu.edu**
❑ Hours: Mostly weekdays. Some museums also open Sat. & Sun.
❑ Tours: Call for reservations. Things you can see:
    • NITTANY LION SHRINE - The 13 ton block of Indiana
      limestone shaped like the mascot, Nittany Lion.
    • FOOTBALL HALL OF FAME - Greensburg Sports
      Complex, (814) 865-0411. Nittany Lion football greats.
    • MUSEUM OF ANTHROPOLOGY - (814) 865-3853.
      Ethnographic and archeological collection.
    • FROST ENTOMOLOGICAL MUSEUM - (814) 865-
      2865. 250,000 insects!
    • EARTH & MINERAL SCIENCES MUSEUM - (814)
      865-6427. Minerals and paintings depicting
      Pennsylvania's mineral industries.
    • PALSNER MUSEUM OF ART - (814) 865-7672.
    • PENN STATE BOOKSTORE - (814) 863-0205.
    • COLLEGE OF AGRICULTURAL SCIENCES - Dairy,
      beef and sheep research center, deer pens.

STONE VALLEY RECREATION AREA

State College - (CR1029 - off SR26 South), 16801. *Activity: Outdoors.* (814) 863-1164. Center - (814) 863-2000. **http://tips.libraries.psu.edu/text/708.html**. *Hours:* Dawn – Dusk. Free Admission. Boating, fishing, hayrides, ice skating, sledding, cross-country skiing, hiking and equipment rental. Cabins, Shauer's Creek Environmental Center - Raptor Center (rehabilitate injured large birds) and Day Camps.

PENN STATE INTERCOLLEGIATE ATHLETICS

State College - 16803. *Activity: Sports.* (800) 833-5533. (800) 863-1000 (tickets). PSU's 29 - sport intercollegiate athletics for men and women including baseball, basketball, fencing, field hockey, football, golf, gymnastics, la Crosse soccer, softball, swimming, tennis, track, volleyball, and wrestling.

SHIKELLAMY STATE PARK

Sunbury - Bridge Avenue, 17801. *Activity: Outdoors.* (717) 988-5557. **http://parec.com/state_parks/shikstpk.htm**. Boat Rentals. Largest inflatable dam / Lake Augusta.

BLAND'S PARK
Old Route 220 (I-99 North, Exit Grazierville or Bellwood), **Tipton 16684**

- ❑ Activity: Amusements
- ❑ Telephone: (814) 684-3538, **www.blandspark.com**
- ❑ Hours: Tuesday - Sunday, Summer. Weekends in May and September. Open at Noon
- ❑ Admission: Free. (All-day passes and individual ride prices available).

30 rides and attractions. Mini-golf - (18 holes with lakes and waterfalls), Go-Karts, mini-train rides and an Interactive water park. Free concert series during the summer.

CANDYLAND

Tyrone - 30 West 10th Street (I-99 to SR453 or SR220), 16686. *Activity: Museums.* (814) 684-0857, **www.gardnerscandies.com**. *Hours:* Monday - Saturday, 9:30 am - 9:00 pm., Sunday, 1:00 - 9:00 pm. Free admission. Nostalgic walk through a penny candy store. Big candy counters with large jars of candy. Also stop in the Candy Kitchen where old-time (mostly brass) equipment is displayed. Take a look at their giant Taffy Hook. Mr. Gardner started "the sweetest place in town" in 1897 and still has licorice whips and candy buttons for sale.

PSU CENTER FOR THE PERFORMING ARTS

University Park - Eisenhower Auditorium, 16802. *Activity: The Arts.* (814) 863-0255. **www.psu.org.** World class symphonies, ballet and Broadway shows.

WINDBER COAL HERITAGE CENTER

Windber - 501 15th Street (off SR56), 15963.   *Activity: Museums.* **www.allegheny.org/windber/center.htm**.   (814) 467-6680. *Hours:* Daily, 10:00 am – 5:00 pm (May – October) *Admission:* $1.50 - 3.50. Mine #40 Scenic Overlook has 3 floors of exhibits, videos, and interactive maps. A working mine seam exhibit is interesting and other exhibits help you to experience the life of a miner and his family. See working and living conditions - "The Underground Farmer" as they were called. Cities were created overnight by mining companies - Windber being a model town. Unique coal gift shop.

WOODWARD CAVE
SR 45, **Woodward** 16882

❑ Activity: Outdoors
❑ Telephone: (814) 349-9800, **www.woodwardcave.com**
❑ Hours: 9:00 am - 7:00 pm (Summer) 10:00 am - 5:00 pm (Spring, Fall)

❑   Admission: $5.00 - $10.00

❑   Tours: 50 - 60 minutes, guided

Five big, well-lit rooms include the "Ball Room", "Square Room". "Hanging Forest" , "Hall of Statues" (largest stalagmites in U.S.), "Tower of Babel" and "Upper Room" (cathedral ceiling). Indian burial room and the passageways are wide and flat.

GALLITZEN STATE FOREST

Ebensburg - 155 Hillcrest Drive, 15931. *Activity: Outdoors.* (814) 472-1862. **http://parec.com/forests/gallit.htm**.   15,337 acres of Fishing, Camping, Trails, Winter Sports.

SPROUL STATE FOREST

Renovo - HCR 62 Box 90, 17764. *Activity: Outdoors.* (717) 923-6011. **http://parec.com/forests/sproul.htm**. Horse Trails, ATV Trails (32 miles). 279,636 acres of Fishing, Camping, Winter Sports.

AREA "CE"

Our Favorites...

1) Pioneer Tunnel Coal Mine
2) Water Gap Trolley
3) Crayola Factory
4) National Canal Museum
5) Hugh Moore Canal Ride
6) Martin Guitar Company
7) Whitewater Rafting
8) Mrs. T's Pierogies Tour
9) Quiet Valley Living Farm
10) Eckley's Miner's Village

CLYDE PEELING'S REPTILAND

R.R. 1, Box 388 (I-80 exit 30B), **Allenwood** (Williamsport Area)
17810

- ❑ Activity: Animals & Farms
- ❑ Telephone: (570) 538-1869 or (800) REPTILAND,
  www.reptiland.com
- ❑ Hours: Daily, 9:00 am - 7:00 pm. (May - September). Daily,
  10:00 am - 5:00 pm (October - April)
- ❑ Admission: Adults $7.00, Children $5.00 (4-11)
- ❑ Shows: Summers, every 90 minutes beginning at 10:30 am.
  Demonstrations and multi-image shows.

Cobras, alligators, pythons, vipers, are all slithering around in a
tropical garden setting. You even get to touch a real snake! Meet
"Big Boy" the alligator or poison dart frogs.

ALLENTOWN ART MUSEUM

Allentown - 31 North Fifth Street (5th & Court Streets), 18101.
Activity: The Arts. **www.allentownartmuseum.org**. (610) 432-
4333. *Hours:* Tuesday - Saturday, 11:00 am - 5:00 pm Sunday,
Noon - 5:00 pm. *Admission:* $2 – 4.00 (over 12). European to
architecture of Frank Lloyd Wright to American art. Fuller Gem
Collection, photography, textiles, museum shop. Junior Gallery
with hands-on and touchable art.

LEHIGH COUNTY MUSEUM

501 Hamilton Street - P O Box 1548 (Old Courthouse)
Allentown 18101

- ❑ Activity: Pennsylvania History·
- ❑ Telephone: (610) 435-4664, **http://pavisnet.com/lehigh**
- ❑ Hours: Monday - Friday, 9:00 am - 4:00 pm., Saturday, 10:00 am
  - 4:00 pm., Sunday, 1:00 - 4:00 pm
- ❑ Admission: Free
- ❑ Miscellaneous: Original Indian inhabitants, Pennsylvania German
  and local historians. Geology Garden adjacent.

Other properties worth a look in this county are:

- CLARISVILLE ONE-ROOM SCHOOLHOUSE (May - September weekends)
- SAYLOR CEMENT INDUSTRY MUSEUM - On site, 9 cement kilns from beginnings of cement industry (May - September weekends)
- HAINES MILL MUSEUM - Operating gristmill built in 1760 shows milling techniques (May - September weekends)
- LOCH RIDGE FURNACE MUSEUM (Alburtis) - Iron furnaces, industry park (May - September)

TRAINS AND MORE

Allentown - 1901 South 12th Street, 18102. *Activity: Amusements.* (610) 791-9397. *Hours:* Friday, 4-9:00 pm. Saturday, 10:00 am - 7:00 pm. Sunday, 10:00 am - 5:00 pm. Shows every half hour. *Admission:* Adults $3.00. Children $2.50. Little Village Train Display features over 30 operating trains, waterfalls and amusement park.

MUSEUM OF INDIAN CULTURE & LENNI LENAPE

Allentown - 2825 Fish Hatchery Road, 18103. *Activity: Museums.* (610) 797-2121. **www.lenape.org.** *Hours:* Thursday - Sunday, Noon- 3:00 pm. *Admission:* Adults $3.00, Seniors $2.00, Children $2.00 (12 and under). Hands-on exhibits enhance the learning of the Native American culture. Pretend you're walking in an Indian's moccasins and head dress as you look at exhibits of their crafts and tools. Special events include corn planting in May and Time of Thanksgiving in October.

DORNEY PARK AND WILDWATER KINGDOM

3830 Dorney Park Road (I-78 West to Exit 16 B)
Allentown 18104

- ❑ Activity: Amusements
- ❑ Telephone: (800) FUN-TIME or (610) 395-3724
  www.dorneypark.com
- ❑ Hours: Daily, (Memorial Day - Labor Day) Weekends, May and September
- ❑ Admission: $6 - $28.00 (ages 4+)

Over 100 rides and attractions. Includes 11 water slides, dozens of rides, a giant wavepool and Berenstain Bear Country for little kids. Steel Force is the longest, tallest, fastest coaster in the East. Hang Time - "hang out" thrill ride and Water Works interactive aquatic play ride. Also, high energy live shows. Aquablast is the longest elevated water slide (701ft.) in the world.

GAME PRESERVE

5150 Game Preserve Road (off SR309)
Allentown (Schnecksville) 18078

- ❑ Activity: Animals & Farms
- ❑ Telephone: (610) 799-4171, **www.lehighvalleyzoo.org**
- ❑ Hours: Daily, 10:00 am - 5:00 pm (Late April - October)
- ❑ Admission: Adults $5.00, Seniors $3.00 (65+), Children $3.00 (2-12)

Native, exotic birds, and petting zoo inhabit a 25 acre zoo. "Where in the zoo is Carmen Sandiego"? Become an Investigative Agent and solve eco-crimes, catch evil-doers or solve the earth.

ALPINE MOUNTAIN

Analomink - Route 447, 18320. *Activity: Outdoors.* (717) 595-2150. (800) 233-8240 (Lodging). Snow Report: (800) 233-8100, **www.alpinemountain.com**. Longest Run: 2640 ft.; 20 Slopes & Trails.

MUSEUM OF ANTHRACITE MINING

17th and Pine Streets (off SR61), **Ashland** 17921

❑ Activity: Museums
❑ Telephone: (570) 875-4708
  www.state.pa.us/PA_Exec/Historical_Museum/BHSM/toh/ant hmining/anthracite.htm
❑ Hours: Monday - Saturday, 10:00 am - 6:00 pm, Sunday, Noon - 6:00 pm. (May - October), Tuesday - Saturday, 9:00 am - 5:00 pm., Sunday, Noon - 5:00 pm (November - April - Closed Winter holidays)
❑ Admission: Adults $3.50, Seniors $3.00 (60+), Children $1.50 (6-12), Families $8.50
❑ Miscellaneous: Pioneer Tunnel Coal Mine next door.

The focus is on tools and machinery used to mine hard coal by hand up to the surface mining operations of today. A good place to quick stop for background information on underground and strip mining. Then, to see it in person, go next door to the Coal Mine Tour. (Kids seem to get more out of actual mining site than pictures and displays)

PIONEER TUNNEL COAL MINE

19th & Oak Streets (SR61 North to Downtown Area - Follow signs off Center Street SR61), **Ashland** 17921

❑ Activity: Tours
❑ Telephone: (570) 875-3850, **www.easternpa.com/pioneertunnel**
❑ Daily, 10:00 am - 6:00 pm (Summer) Weekdays, 11:00 am, 12:30 pm, 2:00 pm (May, September, October). 10:00 am - 6:00 pm (Weekends)
❑ Admission: Adults, $3.50 - $6.00 Children, $2.00 - $3.50 (each activity)
❑ Tours: Approximately 35 minutes given by real coal miner guides.
❑ Miscellaneous: Snack bar, Gift shop where most novelties are made from coal. Wooden "train" playground

Two tour options are available and we highly recommend both. (Pre-schoolers may find the mine tour frightening due to darkness, dampness, and confined areas).

PIONEER TUNNEL COAL MINE TOUR

Watch you children's eyes light up with fascination as you enter and travel 400' deep into a real working coal mine! Though closed in 1931 (because of the Great Depression), you will see and have explained all the features of a real mine. Learn how and why tunnels were built to access the coal. See the Mammoth Vein (the largest in Pennsylvania) and learn why all miners carried a safety lamp (not for light, but for safety from dangerous gasses). Our guide was a real miner who carefully explained what we were seeing. He even turned out all of the lights to show how dark a real mine is! If you're concerned, the mine is inspected regularly by the state to insure it its safety. If your parents or grandparents were miners this will surely bring their stories to life. A top 10 Pennsylvania tour and we definitely agree!

TRAIN RIDE - OPEN COAL FIELD TOUR

A "lokie" (steam locomotive) called the "Henry Clay" takes real mine cars to show you strip mining - where a "vein" of coal is discovered and dug out of the side of a mountain. Also stop by a relic "bootleg" coal mine where men risked life and the law during the Great Depression. They used these small illegal mines to get bags of coal to sell and heat their homes.

TUSCARORA & LOCUST LAKE STATE PARK

Barnesville - R.D. 1, Box 1051 (Off I-81, exit 37), 18214. *Activity: Outdoors.* **http://parec.com/state_parks/tuscstpk.htm**. (717) 467-2404, Beach, Boat Rentals, Campsites, Trails.

RICKETTS GLEN STATE PARK

Benton - R.R. 2, Box 130 (PA Route 487), 17814. *Activity: Outdoors.* **http://parec.com/state_parks/rickstpk.htm**. (717) 477-5675. Beach, Boat Rentals, Horseback Riding, Campsites, Modern Cabins, 21 Waterfalls.

PENNSYLVANIA YOUTH THEATRE

Bethlehem - 211 Plymouth Street, 18015. *Activity: The Arts.* (610) 332-1400 or 865-9188.

BETHLEHEM HISTORIC AREA

52 West Broad Street (off SR378 - Historic area),
Bethlehem 18018

- ❑ Activity: Museums
- ❑ Telephone: (800) 360-8687, **http://pavisnet.com/northampton**
- ❑ Hours: Daily, except Christmas
- ❑ Admission: Free (Walking self-guided tours). Pre-arranged building tours are $3-6/person.
- ❑ Miscellaneous: Best to visit during re-enacted history festivals around Christmas, Bach Festival in May, Celtic Festival in September or Musikfest in August.

  - • VISITORS CENTER - Learn about Moravian Missionaries who first developed this town using pre-Revolutionary German architecture. Watch a video before you take a self-guided walking tour.
  - • GERMAN HAUS - 66 West Church Street. Can you imagine a 5 story log cabin, built without nails? Once used as a church, dorm and workshop, now it is a Moravian historical museum.
  - • INDUSTRIAL QUARTER - 459 Old York Road. Start at the Luchenbach Mill, stop at a 1761 tannery or 1762 waterworks - the first pumped municipal water system in the colonies.

- <u>SUN INN RESTAURANT</u>: Hours: Tuesday - Saturday, Lunch & Dinner, Sunday, Dinner. We recommend to go for lunch for the best kids' value. A stop of famous Colonial statesmen like George Washington, the Marquis de Lafayette, and John Adams. Colonial furnishings. Guided tours (small admission), Tuesday - Saturday (daytime) of museum downstairs. Kids menu. (610) 974-9451.

BIG BOULDER SKI AREA

Blakeslee - P.O. Box 707, 18610. *Activity: Outdoors.* (717) 722-0100. (800) 468-BIG 2 (Lodging). Snow Report: (800) 475-SNOW, **www.big2resorts.com.** Longest Run: 2900 ft.; 14 Slopes & Trails.

JACK FROST MOUNTAIN
P.O. Box 707, **Blakeslee** 18610

- ❏ Activity: Amusements
- ❏ (800) 468-2442, **www.big2resorts.com**
- ❏ Admission: per activity
- ❏ Miscellaneous: Baby sitting provided.
    - <u>RIDE ATV PARK</u> - 4 wheeler vehicle park with curves, hill, whoop-de-doos, mud pits. Smaller course and ATV's for youngsters. Fee includes rentals.
    - <u>SPLATTER</u> - 2500 acres of paintball fields (many with special themes). Year round.
    - <u>WHEELS SKATE PARK</u> - Inline skate and board park with half pipes, quarter pipes, rail slides and pyramids. Kids area. Rentals. Daily (April - October).

JACK FROST MOUNTAIN SKI AREA

Blakeslee - P.O. Box 707, 18610. *Activity: Outdoors.* (717) 443-8425. (800) 468-BIG 2 (Lodging). Snow Report: (800) 475-SNOW. **www.big2resorts.com.** Longest Run: 2700 ft.; 21 Slopes & Trails.

WEISER STATE FOREST

Cressona - Box 99, 17929. *Activity: Outdoors.* (717) 385-7800.
http://parec.com/forests/weiser.htm.   Fishing, Trails, Cross-Country Skiing.

WATER GAP TROLLEY
Main Street (I-80, exit 53), **Delaware Water Gap** 18327

- ❑   Activity: Tours
- ❑   Telephone: (717) 476-9766
- ❑   Hours: Daily, 10:00 am - 4:00 pm (April - November)
- ❑   Admission: Adults $6.00, Children $3.50
- ❑   Tours: All weather trolleys, narrated scenic, historical tour of area. 1 hour.

Replica streetcars take a relaxed tour of the Water Gap - Shawnee area where you can learn about Indians, early settlers, and some history. The first half of tour may be boring to kids but the second half stops at Chief Taminy's face formed from rough edges in the mountain rocks (like a natural profile - Mt. Rushmore). Also stop at the Cold Air Cave (regardless of the outside temperature; the air rushing out of the entrance to the small cave is always - 38 degrees F. – your kids will say – really cool!).

BUSHKILL PARK
2100 Bushkill Park Drive, **Easton** 18040

- ❑   Activity: Amusements
- ❑   Telephone: (610) 258-6941, **www.bushkillpark.com**
- ❑   Hours: Weekends, (3rd week of May - Mid-June), Noon - 6:00 pm. (Mid-June - Labor Day) Tuesday - Sunday, Noon -6:00 pm. Friday - Saturday 'til 9:00 pm.
- ❑   Admission: Free. Individual Ride Tickets.
- ❑   Miscellaneous: Picnic. Concessions.

A 1926 Herschel Carousel with Grand Wurlitzer organ. 9 Kiddie rides and 8 large rides. Carousel Candy Factory - chocolate handmade before your eyes.

CRAYOLA FACTORY

30 Centre Square, Two Rivers Landing (Look for the giant box of crayons on top) **Easton** 18042

- ❑ Activity: Tours
- ❑ Telephone: (610) 515-8000, **www.crayola.com**
- ❑ Hours: Monday - Saturday, 9:00 am - 6:00 pm., Sunday, 11:00 am - 6:00 pm (Summer). Tuesday - Saturday, 9:30 am - 5:00 pm., Sunday, Noon - 5:00 pm (September -May)
- ❑ Admission: General $7.00 (3+), Seniors $6.50
- ❑ Miscellaneous: The Crayola Store - Colorful collection of anything using color is sold. Also area to try new products. To get the most benefit from the full admission price, be prepared to do most or all of the activities (that includes you Mom & Dad - you get to be kids...again!).

Each person is asked to learn and think "Outside the Lines". Learn Crayola history at the Hall of Fame. Do you know what celebrity molded the 100 billionth crayon? What was his favorite color? Next, do a dozen or so interactive exhibits. "Color on the Wall" - Go ahead, it's glass and is wiped clean easily. Hurry, kids, this may be your only chance to break the rules! Everyone creates "their own souvenirs to take home". Especially great is the Factory Floor exhibit where a worker mixes melted wax and colors to help you make your own souvenir crayons to take home. The most favorite color is red and our kids got to help put the wrappers on real (just manufactured) crayons. Older kids will like the Bright Ideas area where you experiment with color and light combinations. Parents, it does get crazy in here, but if you go with the flow and start creating yourself...you CAN survive and have FUN!

HUGH MOORE CANAL RIDE PARK

30 Centre Square - High Moore Park (off I-78 or off US22)
Easton 18042

- ❑ Activity: Tours
- ❑ Telephone: (610) 559-6613 **http://canals.org/hmpark.htm**
- ❑ Hours: Tuesday - Saturday, 10:30 am - 4:30 pm., Sunday, 1:30 - 4:30 pm (Memorial Day - Labor Day). Tuesday - Friday, 9:30 am - 3:30 pm, Saturday, Sunday & Holidays, 1:00 - 4:30 pm. (May - Memorial Day)
- ❑ Admission: Adults $5.00, Seniors $4.50 (65+), Children $3.00 (3-15)
- ❑ Tours: Costumed interpreter guides you on a 50-60 minute ride.
- ❑ Miscellaneous: Trails, picnic, boat rentals, gift shop.

The mule-drawn canal boat Josiah White II ride is on a restored section of the LeHigh Canal. The large boat and costumed drivers are carried by a mule or two. Visit the Loctender's House Museum - lifestyle of his family and also a great view of the dam, lock, and bridge.

NATIONAL CANAL MUSEUM

30 Centre Square (I-78, Easton exit & US22 - 3rd floor - Two Rivers Landing), **Easton** 18042

- ❑ Activity: Museums
- ❑ Telephone: (610) 515-8000 or (610) 559-6613
  http://canals.org/museum.htm
- ❑ Hours: Tuesday - Saturday, 9:30 am - 5:00 pm, Sunday Noon - 5:00 pm. (Closed Mondays except school holidays)
- ❑ Admission: Included in the purchase price of Crayola Factory tickets. (not available separately)
- ❑ Miscellaneous: Admissions are limited based on building capacity. Call ahead if you're travelling from out of town.

Visit a short time in history before railroads, highways, and airplanes. Follow the story lines of immigrants and locals who built and ran the canals. Hear the boatman tell stories and sing canal songs. Walk through the middle of a full size replica boat. Hands-on exhibits help kids understand this mode of transport. Actually operate a lock model and pilot your play boat through it. Then dress up as socialites travelling the canal in luxury with Mr. Tiffany (of Tiffany glass in 1886). The Molly Polly Chunker was a luxury liner canal boat decorated in Victorian fashion. This is the best interactive way to truly understand canals and this brief era of time.

KNOEBEL'S AMUSEMENT RESORT

PO Box 317 (SR 487), Elysburg 17824

- ❑ Activity: Amusements
- ❑ Telephone: (800) ITS-4-FUN, **www.knoebels.com**
- ❑ Hours: Daily, 11:00 am - 10:00 pm, Summers. Weekends only, May & September
- ❑ Admission. Free. $.40 - $1.50 per ride or all-day ride passes.
- ❑ Miscellaneous: Restaurants. Gift shops. Games. Mini-golf.

41 rides including the "Phoenix" - rated one of America's 10 best roller coasters. Pool and water slides. Games, entertainment. An extremely family friendly attraction!

LEHIGH VALLEY VELODROME

Emmaus - 217 Main Street (Routes 100 and 222), 18049. *Activity: Sports.* (610) 967-7587. **www.lvvelo.org**. Friday evenings (June - August). *Tickets:* $3-6.00. Cheer on cyclists from around the world as they compete in pro bike racing.

LOST RIVER CAVERNS

726 Durham Street (I-78, Exit 21, Rt. 412 South)
Hellertown 18055

- ❑ Activity: Outdoors
- ❑ Telephone: (610) 838-8767, **www.lostcave.com**

❏   Hours: Year-round. 9:00 am - 6:00 pm (Memorial Day - Labor Day), Rest of year closes at 5:00 pm. Closed, Thanksgiving, Christmas, and New Year's Day.

❏   Admission: $4.00 - $8.00

Guided walking tours through beautiful crystal formations. Limestone cavern with five chambers and underground stream. Indoor tropical garden, rock museum.

JIM THORPE RIVER ADVENTURE

Jim Thorpe - 1 Adventure Lane, 18229. *Activity: Outdoors.* (800) 424-RAFT or (570) 325-2570 **www.jtraft.com**

POCONO WHITEWATER ADVENTURES

Jim Thorpe - 18229. *Activity: Outdoors.* (800) 944-8392, **www.whitewaterrafting.com**

YESTERDAY'S TRAIN TODAY RAIL TOUR

Jim Thorpe - P.O. Box 285 (I-476 exit 34 South- US209 -Depot) 18229. *Activity: Tours.* (888) 546-8467 or (570) 325-4606. *Hours:* Weekends & Holidays, 12:00, 1:00, & 2:00 pm (Mid-May - Weekend after Labor Day). *Admission:* Adults $5.00, Children $3.00 (2-11). *Tours:* 40 minutes long (just the right amount of time for kids). A similar ride to local passenger trains years ago during the glorious rail excursion era.

SPLIT ROCK RESORT SKI AREA

Lake Harmony - P.O. Box 567, 18624. *Activity: Outdoors.* (717) 722-9111. (800) 255-ROCK (Lodge). Snow Report: (717) 722-9111, **www.splitrockresort.com.** Longest Run: 1700 ft.; 7 Slopes & Trails.

POCONO MUSEUM UNLIMITED

517 Ashtown Road (SR443 West), **Lehighton** 18235

- ❏ Activity: Museums
- ❏ Telephone: (570) 386-3117
- ❏ Hours: Wednesday - Monday, 10:00 am - 5:00 pm (Summer).
  Wednesday - Monday, Noon - 5:00 pm (September – December),
  Friday - Sunday, 10:00 am - 5:00 pm (Rest of Year).
- ❏ Admission: Adults $4.00, Seniors $3.00 (60+), Children $2.00
  (5-12)

This is a large "O" scale model railroad display with 16 operating rail lines, a highway with moving vehicles, waterfalls, amusement park and drive-in theatre. Animals and nature are represented in a rain storm (complete with thunder and lightning), a large lake full of live fish and a zoo.

BELTZVILLE STATE PARK

Leighton - 2950 Pohopoco Drive, 18235. *Activity: Outdoors.* (215) 377-0045. **http://parec.com/state_parks/beltstpk.htm**. Beach, Pool, Boat Rentals, Fishing, Trails, Cross-Country Skiing.

DOE MOUNTAIN SKI AREA

Macungie - 101 Doe Mountain Lane, 18062. *Activity: Outdoors.* (610) 682-7100. **www.doemountain.com.** Snow Report: (800) I-SKI - DOE, Long Run: 1.5 miles; 15 Slopes & Trails.

POCONO SNAKE AND ANIMAL FARM

Marshalls Creek - US 209 (I-80 to US 209 Northeast), 18335. *Activity: Animals & Farms.* (570) 223-8653. *Hours:* Monday - Friday, Noon - 5:00 pm., Weekends, 11:00 am - 6:00 pm. *Admission:* Adults $5.00, Children $4.00 (2-12). Over 100 reptiles, birds and animals. Petting and feeding areas.

CHAMBERLAIN CANOES

Minisink Hills - Minisink Acres (Delaware Water Gap), 18341. *Activity: Outdoors.* (800) 422-6631 or (570) 421-0180.

MOUNT AIRY LODGE SKI AREA

Mt. Pocono - Route 611, 18344. *Activity: Outdoors.* (717) 839-8811. (800) 441-4410 (Lodge). Snow Report: (717) 839-8811 **www.mountairylodge.com**. Longest Run: 2300 ft.; 7 Slopes & Trails.

MARTIN GUITAR COMPANY

510 Sycamore Street (I-80 to SR33 South to SR191 South to North Broad to Beil St - Follow Signs), **Nazareth** 18064

- ❏ Activity: Tours
- ❏ Telephone: (610) 759-2837, **www.mguitar.com**
- ❏ Hours: Monday - Friday, 8:30 am - 4:30 pm. Closed Holidays and week of Christmas.
- ❏ Admission: Free
- ❏ Tours: Monday - Friday, 1:15 pm.
- ❏ Miscellaneous: 1833 shop memorabilia, strings, books and accessories.

Founded in 1833, Martin guitars are know as "America's guitar". Used by many legendary performers, you'll start your tour in the museum shop of vintage guitars. Children are encouraged to "gently play" several guitars in the waiting area. If any of your children play the guitar, they will be especially interested in all the posters of famous performers who use Martins. The tour shows step-by-step production and is very educational. See the types of wood (cured for 4 months prior to production) used - from the usual to the exotic. Watch how each piece is computer routed or bent in special jigs. Martin even makes their own strings to insure that "one of a kind" Martin sound. They've even produced a $50,000 custom order guitar with diamonds in the guitar neck! Sometimes famous performers (or their band members) stop by the Martin plant...maybe even on your tour!

NAZARETH SPEEDWAY

Nazareth - Highway 191, 18064. *Activity: Sports.* (888) 629-RACE. (April - July). "America's Finest and Fastest Mile." NASCAR Championship, Grand National and Truck Series.

WHITEWATER RAFTING ADVENTURES

Nesquehoning - 101 Adventure Trail Road, 18240. *Activity: Outdoors.* www.adventurerafting.com. (570) 722-0285 or (800) 876-0285.

BLUE MOUNTAIN SKI AREA

Palmerton - 1600 Blue Mountain Drive, 18071. *Activity: Outdoors.* (610) 826-7700. Snow report: (800) 235-2226, www.skibluemt.com. Longest Run: 6400 ft.; 20 Slopes & Trails.

BIG DIAMOND RACEWAY

Pottsville - (Near Forestville, off Rt. 901), 17901. *Activity: Sports.* (570) 544-6434. www.bigdiamondraceway.com. Fridays at 8:00 pm. (April - Labor Day). Nascar - Winston Series Stock Car Racing.

POTTSVILLE MINI-GRAND PRIX

Pottsville - Downtown, 17901. *Activity: Sports.* (570) 628-4647. (August). One-third scale Indy 500 racing Club.

SCHUYLKILL COUNTY MUSEUM

Pottsville - 14 North Third Street, 17901. *Activity: Pennsylvania History.* (570) 622-7540. *Hours:* Tuesday - Saturday, 10:00 am - Noon, 1:00 - 4:00 pm. Historical wealth of fossils and fuel beneath surface. Native Americans, German settlers, Anthracite Industry.

MRS. T'S PIEROGIES

600 East Center Street (off SR61, turn right on Center Street -
SR924 North), **Shanandoah** 17976

- ❑ Activity: Tours
- ❑ Telephone: (570) 462-2745, **www.pierogy.com**
- ❑ Admission: Free
- ❑ Tours: (approx. 40 minutes) - By appointment only with 30 days
  notice. Ages 3rd grade+ (5-6 minimum - 15 maximum)

As you adorn hair nets and lab coats, you begin your tour
seeing first the raw materials (mostly eggs, flour, and potato
flakes) as they arrive and are prepared for cooking. You'll see
hundreds of pierogies floating in boiling water, after they have
been secretly prepared. The Secret Room (called the Black Box)
has a special pierogy making machine. No one (except a few
workers sworn to secrecy) ever enters this room. The 9,500,000
unique pasta pockets made here weekly are flash frozen and
packaged immediately. Every kid's favorite part of this tour has to
be the complimentary warm pierogies offered at the end of the
tour. We sampled the cheddar and potato variety and drank soft
drinks from Mrs. T's souvenir mugs. The tour and personnel are
wonderful. Ask for unique recipes - great new ways to use a classic
ethnic food. Their snack line of "Rogies" are cute, bite sized pasta
pockets (just right for kids!).

SHAWNEE MOUNTAIN SKI AREA

Shawnee-on-Delaware – P.O. Box 339 (Exit 52, Off I-80), 18356.
Activity: Outdoors. (570) 421-7231. (800) VILLA-4-U. (Lodge).
Snow Report: (800) 233-4218, **www.shawneemt.com**. Longest
Run: 5100 ft.; 23 Slopes & Trails.

QUIET VALLEY LIVING HISTORICAL FARM

1000 Turkey Road (US209 SW - Business Route to Hickory Valley
Road South - follow signs), **Stroudsburg** 18360

- ❑ Activity: Animals & Farms
- ❑ Telephone: (570) 992-6161, **www.pastconnect.com/quietValley**

- ❏ Hours: Tuesday - Saturday, 10:00 am - 5:00 pm., Sunday, 1:00 - 5:30 pm. (June 20 - Labor Day)
- ❏ Admission: Adults $7.00, Children $4.00 (3-12)
- ❏ Tours: 90 minute, costumed guided. Last tour leaves at 4:00 pm.

M eet a Pennsylvania Dutch family as they go about their numerous daily chores – pretend the time is the early 1800's. Daily activities include spinning, weaving, smoking and drying meats, vegetables and fruits; cooking, gardening, and tending to animals. Kids can touch barnyard animals and jump in a giant haystack! Usually one craft is highlighted weekly - ex. quilting, butter churning, candle dips, basket making, natural wool dying (how do they get color naturally?) and blacksmithing. Actual aunts, uncles, cousins, and siblings escort you around the farm and treat you like visiting relatives.

DELAWARE STATE FOREST

Swiftwater - HC 1, Box 95A, 18370. *Activity: Outdoors.* (717) 895-4000. **http://parec.com/forests/delaware.htm**. Horse Trails, ATV Trails (35 miles), Fishing, Cross-Country Skiing.

CAMEL BACK SKI AREA

Tannersville - (Exit 45 on I-80), 18372. *Activity: Outdoors.* (717) 629-1661. **http://www.skicamelback.com**. Snow Report: (800) 233-8100. Longest Run: 1 mile; 33 Slopes & Trails.

ECKLEY MINERS' VILLAGE

Route #2, Box 236 (I-80 West to Exit 40 - SR940 West - then follow signs), **Weatherly** 18255

- ❏ Activity: Museums
- ❏ Telephone: (570) 636-2070

  www.state.pa.us/PA_Exec/Historical_Museum/BHSM/toh/ec kley/eckley.htm
- ❏ Hours: Daily, 9:00 am - 5:00 pm, Closed Monday. (April - October)

- ❑   Admission: Adults $3.50, Children $1.50 (6-12), Family $8.50
- ❑   Miscellaneous: Great supplement to a tour of a coal mine. The
      Company Store is a museum gift shop.

W hat is a Patch Town? A patch was a cluster of a few dozen company houses along a crooked, unpaved street built within the shadow of black silt ponds and strip mining pits. See an actual town (only slightly restored) just as it appeared in a movie (in the 1970's). Retired miners, miner's widows, and children still live here. Watch a 15 minute video at the Visitor's Center first, then walk by audio displays of a typical miner's day or week (including church on Sunday). School-aged kids will want to take the tour which includes going inside a house (1870's - 1890's - notice all of the updates!), a company store, and a doctor's office. Just imagine having to be a young boy then, usually helping support the family by being a "breaker boy" in the smoky, dangerous mill!

HICKORY RUN STATE PARK

White Haven - R.D. 1, Box 81 (PA Route 534), 18661. *Activity: Outdoors.* **http://parec.com/state_parks/hickstpk.htm.** (717) 443-0400, Pool, Visitor Center, Sledding, Campsites. LeHigh Gorge and mountain biking.

LEHIGH RAFTING

Whitehaven - P.O. Box 296, 18661. *Activity: Outdoors.* (800) 291-RAFT or (570) 443-4441. **www.lehighrafting.com**

JACOBSBURG STATE PARK

Wind Gap - 835 Jacobsburg Road, 18091. *Activity: Outdoors.* (610) 746-2801, **http://parec.com/state_parks/jacbstpk.htm.** Historical Center, Year-round Education & Interpretation Center, Horseback Riding, Mountain Biking.

FRANCES SLOCUM STATE PARK

Wyoming - 565 Mt. Olivet Road, 18644. *Activity: Outdoors.* (717) 696-3525.   **http://parec.com/state_parks/fslostpk.htm**. Pool, Visitor Center, Campsites, Boat Rentals, Sledding.

AREA "CW"

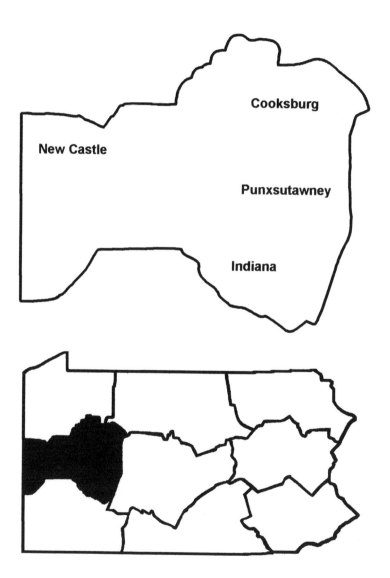

Our Favorites...

1) Cook Forest State Park
2) DeBence Antique Music Museum
3) Log Cabin Inn
4) Raccoon State Park
5) Punxsutawney Groundhog Zoo

BUTLER COUNTY MUSEUMS

Butler - 106 South Main Street, 16001. *Activity: Pennsylvania History.* (724) 283-8116. *Hours:* Call for current hours. (May - September). Country life at 4 different sites: Cooper Cabin (1810), Shaw House (1828), Little Red Schoolhouse (1838), and the Heritage Center (industry in the area including tin shop, Bantam Jeep, and Franklin glassworks).

COOK FOREST STATE PARK

Cooksburg - River Road - P.O. Box 120 (I-80 Exit 13, Route 36 South), 16217. *Activity: Outdoors.* **www.cookforest.com**. (814) 744-8407. Virgin white pine and hemlock timber stands nick-named the "Black Forest". Highlights are the Forest Cathedral, Log Cabin Inn Visitor Center, Sawmill Craft Center and Theater, the Fire Tower and Seneca Point Overlook. Near the entrance on Route 36 is Double Diamond Deer Ranch, (814) 752-6334 where deer are raised from birth. Children can bottle-feed fawns June - August. Pool, Horseback Riding, Campsites, Rustic Cabins, Boating, Fishing, Skiing, Snowmobiling.

DOUBLE DIAMOND DEER RANCH

Cooksburg - (SR36, South of Cook Forest), 16217. *Activity: Animals & Farms.* (814) 752-6334. *Hours:* Daily, 10:00 am - Dusk (May-November), Weekends Only, (December - April). *Admission:* Adults $3.50, Children $2.50 (5-12). Photograph or watch white tail deer in natural habitats. Covered walkways, scenic trails, and a gift shop.

PALE WHITE CANOE LIVERY

Cooksburg - P.O. Box 109, 16217. *Activity: Outdoors.* (800) 680-0160 or (814) 744-8300.

DARLINGTON POLO

Darlington - (Darlington Polo Field), 16115. *Activity: Sports.* (412) 325-8127. Fridays, 8:00 p.m. (May - August). Sundays at 2:00 pm (Powers Field) (September - October). Admission $3.00 (16+).

DEBENCE ANTIQUE MUSIC MUSEUM
1261 Liberty Street (Downtown, off I-80 to exit 3), **Franklin** 16323

- ❑   Activity: Museums
- ❑   Telephone: (814) 432-5668 or (888) 547-2377
     www.franklin-pa.org/html/debence.htm
- ❑   Hours: Tuesday - Saturday, 10:00 am - 5:00 pm., Sunday, 12:30 - 5:00 pm
- ❑   Admission: Adults $6.00, Seniors $5.00, Children $4.00 (6+)

"To See and Hear Museum". 100+ antique, automated music machines from the gay 90's - roaring 20's. See and hear demonstrations of nickelodeons, Swiss & German music boxes, waltzes and polkas, merry-go-round band organs, calliopes, player pianos, and a variety of antique organs. We were most fascinated by the nickelodeons that had a glass panel inserts showing the musical instrument "guts". This was the first time we have ever seen a violin or accordion playing as accompaniment. Be sure grandparents are along for this visit.

LOG CABIN INN

Harmony - 430 Perry Highway (US19 - 2 miles north of Zelienople), 16037. *Activity: Theme Restaurants.* (724) 452-4155. *Hours:* Daily, Lunch & Dinner. Rural and rustic 160 year old log cabin. The original dining room area floor is tilted and the logs are huge. All American fare with children's menu complete with coloring and crayons.

RACCOON STATE PARK

Hookstown - R.D. 1, Box 900 (3000 SR 18), 15050. *Activity: Outdoors.* **http://parec.com/state_parks/racnstpk.htm**. (412) 899-2200. *Hours:* 8:00 am – Sunset. Wild Flower Reserve (Route 30.) A 315 acre tract of land with over 500 species of wildflowers and wildlife. Frankfurt Mineral Springs - explore the reported "medicinal" properties of the water. Beach, Visitor Center, Boat Rentals, Horseback Riding, Sledding, Campsites, Modern Cabins.

JIMMY STEWART MUSEUM

9th & Philadelphia Streets (Indiana Public Library - 3rd Floor)
Indiana 15701

- ❑ Activity: Museums
- ❑ (800) 83-JIMMY, **www.jimmy.org**
- ❑ Hours: Monday - Saturday, 10:00 am - 5:00 pm., Sunday & Holidays, Noon - 5:00 pm.
- ❑ Admission: Adults $5.00, Seniors $4.00, Children $3.00 (7-17)

A legendary actor (every Christmas we still all watch "It's a Wonderful Life") who had accomplishments in film, radio and television plus civic and family roles. Displays of his great grandfather's uniform, baby photographs, furniture from the family hardware store, original movie posters, props and costumes. Watch films that are shown in a small 1930's vintage movie theatre.

ARMSTRONG COUNTY MUSEUM

Kittanning - 300 North McKean Street, 16201. *Activity: Pennsylvania History.* (724) 548-5707. McCain House (1842) features a drawing room, Indian room, and changing exhibit room.

HARLANSBURG STATION'S MUSEUM OF TRANSPORTATION

New Castle - West Pittsburgh Road (US19 & SR108), 16101. *Activity: Museums.* (724) 652-9002. *Hours:* Tuesday - Saturday, 10:00 am - 5:00 pm., Sunday, Noon - 5:00 pm (May – October).

Weekends Only (March, April, November, December). *Admission:* Adults $3.00, Children $2.00 (under 12). Olde time railroad station with display of real Pennsylvania railroad cars outside and memorabilia displayed inside the cars. Meet the mascot conductor and see lots of railroad uniforms. In the station are trains, cars, planes, trucks, and trolleys.

LIVING TREASURES ANIMAL PARK
US422, **New Castle** 16101

- ❑ Activity: Animals & Farms
- ❑ Telephone: (724) 924-9571
- ❑ Hours: Daily, 10:00 am - 8:00 pm (Summer), Weekends Only, 10:00 am - 6:00 pm (May, September, October)
- ❑ Admission: Adults $5.50, Seniors $5.00, Children $4.50

Watch kangaroos, tigers and wolves and ride the miniature horses. Kids love the petting area (babies, reindeer, and camels) and feeding areas (bears, otters, monkeys, goats, sheep, and llamas).

NEW CASTLE PLAYHOUSE

New Castle - 202 Long Avenue (The Old State Theatre), 16101. *Activity: The Arts.* (412) 654-3437. Six main productions plus classes and workshops for youth.

PAROU BALLET COMPANY

New Castle - 1807 Moravia Avenue, 16101. *Activity: The Arts.* (412) 652-1762. Composed of approximately 30 youths performing classics like "The Nutcracker" and "Showcase". Ages 6+.

YELLOW CREEK STATE PARK

Penn Run - R.D. 1, Box 145-D (US Route 422), 15765. *Activity: Outdoors.* **http://parec.com/state_parks/yelcstpk.htm**. (412) 357-7913, Beach, Visitor Center, Boat Rentals, Sledding, Fishing, Trails.

MORAINE STATE PARK

Portersville - 225 Pleasant Valley Road, 16051. *Activity: Outdoors.* **http://parec.com/state_parks/morastpk.htm.** (412) 368-8811, Beach, Visitor Center, Horseback Riding, Mountain Biking, Modern Cabins, Fishing, Trails, Winter Sports.

MCCONNELL'S MILL STATE PARK

Porterville -R.D. 2, Box 16, 16051. *Activity: Outdoors.* (412) 368-8091. **http://parec.chttp://parec.com/state_parks/mccnstpk.htm** A 400 ft. deep gorge with giant boulders and unique eco-system. Slippery Rock Creek flows through the gorge. Historical Center, sledding, boating, fishing, swimming, biking, camping, skiing, snowmobiling.

PUNXSUTAWNEY GROUNDHOG ZOO

East Mahoning Street, Civic Center Complex (I-80 to exit 17, US119), **Punxsutawney** 15767

- ❑ Activity: Animals & Farms
- ❑ Telephone: (800) 752-PHIL, **www.groundhog.org**
- ❑ Hours: Museum: Tuesday, Wednesday, Friday, 1:00 - 4:00 pm. Thursday, 10:00 am - 4:00 pm., Saturday, 1:00 - 4:00 pm., Sunday, 2:00 - 4:00 pm. Zoo: (Dawn to Dusk)
- ❑ Admission: Free
- ❑ Miscellaneous: At 401 West Mahoning Street, (814) 938-2555 is the Punxutawney Museum devoted to groundhog history and legend.

On Groundhog Day (February 2) the world looks for "Punxsutawney Phil" each year to peek out of his burrow on Gobbler's Knob and see if his shadow appears. His prediction indicates how much of the winter season is left. The legend was brought to this country by German immigrants. Phil and his descendants have been popping out every year since February 2, 1887. He and his family reside at this zoo. We might suggest you watch the movie "Groundhog Day" starring Bill Murray prior to your visit to get into the spirit of things! By the way, Phil gets almost as much mail as Santa Claus and on Groundhog Day up to 35,000 people come to see him each year! (they have pictures to prove it). It's worth a trip anytime of the year to meet a live groundhog up close ... your family may be surprised how they can change shape to fit the landscape.

CLEAR CREEK STATE PARK

Sigel - R.R. 1, Box 82 (1-80 to exits 12 or 13), 15860. *Activity: Outdoors.* **http://parec.com/state_parks/clrcstpk.htm**. (814) 752-2368, Beach, Visitor Center, Historical Center, Boat Rentals, Sledding, Campsites, Rustic Cabins, Fishing, Winter Sports, Trails.

JENNINGS STATE PARK

Slippery Rock - 2951 Prospect Road, 16057. *Activity: Outdoors.* (412) 794-6011, **http://parec.com/state_parks/jennstpk.htm**. Visitors Center, Year-round Education & Entertainment Center.

AREA "NC"

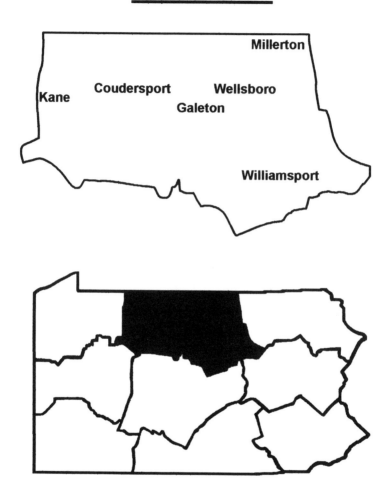

Our Favorites...

1) **Pennsylvania Lumber Museum**

2) **Holgate Toy Factory**

3) **Draper's Super Bees Apiary**

4) **Leonard Harrison State Park –
   Grand Canyon of Pennsylvania**

5) **Children's Discovery Workshop**

SINNEMAHONING STATE PARK

Austin - R.D. 1, Box 172, 16720. *Activity: Outdoors.* (814) 647-8401, **http://parec.com/state_parks/sinnstpk.htm**. Campsites, Modern Cabins.

PENNSYLVANIA LUMBER MUSEUM
US 6, Coudersport 16915

❑   Activity: Museums

❑   Telephone: (814) 435-2652, **www.lumbermuseum.org**

❑   Hours: Daily, 9:00 am - 5:00 pm. (April - October)

❑   Admission: Adults $3.50, Seniors $3.00 (61+), Children $1.50 (6-12)

Pennsylvania once had a prosperous lumber heritage with it's wealth of white pine and hemlock trees. Now on display are 3000+ objects including old-fashioned logging tools and a logging locomotive. The best part of the visit is the short walk to the preserved remains of, a once very busy, logging camp. See the huge sawmill (buzzing logs that have floated down river), mess hall, dormitories, rails, and engines used for transport. The well kept operational facility is extremely interesting and educational.

SKI DENTON

Coudersport - P.O. Box 367, 16915. *Activity: Outdoors.* (814) 435-2115. **www.skidenton.com**. Longest Run: 1 mile; 20 Slopes & Trails.

SUSQUEHANNOCK STATE FOREST

Coudersport - P.O. Box 673, 16915. *Activity: Outdoors.* (814) 274-8474. **http://parec.com/forests/susque.htm**. 261,784 acres of Fishing, Trails, Winter Sports, ATV Trails.

OLE BULL STATE PARK

Cross Fork - Box 9 (PA Route 144), 17729. *Activity: Outdoors.*
http://parec.com/state_parks/olebstpk.htm.   (814)   435-5000,
Beach, Campsites, Modern Cabins, Fishing, Trails, Cross-Country
Skiing.

BUCKTAIL STATE PARK

Emporium - R.D. 1, Box 1-A (Route 120), 15834. *Activity:*
Outdoors. **http://parec.com/state_parks/buckstpk.htm**.   (814)
486-3365, Scenic Drive (State Forest National Area), Boating
permitted, Fishing, Trails.

ELK STATE FOREST

Emporium - R.R. 1, Route 155, Box 327, 15834. *Activity:*
Outdoors. (814) 486-3353.   **http://parec.com/forests/elk.htm**.
Quehanna Wild Area Trail System. Fish Habitat Project on Hick's
Run. Known for high quality fishing.

SIZERVILLE STATE PARK

Emporium - R.D. 1, Box 238-A (PA Route 155), 15834. *Activity:*
Outdoors. **http://parec.com/state_parks/sizrstpk.htm**. (814) 486-
5605, Pool, Visitor Center, Campsites, Butterfly Area, Garden.

SKI LIBERTY

Fairfield - 78 Country Club Trail, 17320. *Activity: Outdoors.*
(717) 642-8282. (717) 642-8288 (Hotel). Snow Report: (717) 642-
9000,   **http://www.skiliberty.com**. Longest Run: 5300 ft.; 16
Slopes & Trails.

CHERRY SPRINGS STATE PARK

Galeton - R.D. 1, Box 136 (PA Route 44 - Potter County), 16922.
Activity: Outdoors. **http://parec.com/state_parks/chspstpk.htm**.
(814) 435-5010.

LYMAN RUN STATE PARK

Galeton - 545 Lyman Run Road, 16922. *Activity: Outdoors.* (814) 435-5010. **http://parec.com/state_parks/lymrstpk.htm**. Beach, Campsites, Fishing, Trails.

PATTERSON STATE PARK

Galeton - R.D. #1, Box 136 c/o Lyman Run, 16922. *Activity: Outdoors.* **http://parec.com/state_parks/pattstpk.htm**. (814) 435-5010.

PROUTY PLACE STATE PARK

Galeton - R.D. #1, Box 136 c/o Lyman Run, 16922. *Activity: Outdoors.* **http://parec.com/state_parks/proustpk.htm**. (814) 435-5010.

DENTON HILL STATE PARK

Galeton (Coudersport) - RD #1, Box 136, 16922. *Activity: Outdoors.* **http://parec.com/state_parks/dentstpk.htm**. (814) 435-2115, Downhill skiing, Modern Cabins, Concessions, Fishing.

CRYSTAL LAKE SKI CENTER

Hughesville - R.R. #1, Box 308, 17737. *Activity: Outdoors.* (717) 584-2698. Snow Report: (717) 584-4209. Longest Run: 1300 ft.; 4 Slopes & Trails.

HYNER RUN STATE PARK

Hyner - Box 46 (Hyner Run Road), 17738. *Activity: Outdoors.* (717) 923-6000, **http://parec.com/state_parks/hynrstpk.htm**. Pool, Campsites, Fishing, Winter Sports, Trails.

BENDIGO STATE PARK

Johnsonburg - Glen Hazel Rd (Route 24201), 15845. *Activity: Outdoors.* **http://parec.com/state_parks/bendstpk.htm**. (814) 965-2646, Pool, Sledding. Kinzua Bridge - very high railroad bridge.

HOLGATE TOY FACTORY

One Holgate Drive (US6 to Kane, follow signs - west of downtown),
Kane 16735

- ❏ Activity: Tours
- ❏ Telephone: (800) 499-1929 or (814) 837-7600
  www.holgatetoy.com
- ❏ Hours: Monday - Friday, 9:00 am - 5:00 pm., Saturday, 10:00 am - 4:00 pm, Sunday, Noon - 4:00 pm (April - December)
- ❏ Miscellaneous: Toy Store with discount seconds at great prices! Bring your infant to pre-K kid's gift list.

This is where they make "Mr. Roger's Neighborhood" trolleys! What a fun, cute place to visit and learn! The colorful shop draws kids and parents in to explore. Grandparents will love the old pull toys in the museum. All the toys are made from wood - no plastic to break or batteries to replace - We like that! While the young kids may gravitate to the play areas with toys galore (try before you buy), the older kids and adults will want to watch the operations. During weekdays, you can see actual operators make the different pieces of a toy. The giant computerized routers are the most fun to watch. Other times, the factory is silent, but you can watch a 25 minute video of the manufacturing process. Our favorite was watching the wood shapes "dance" for the paint sprayers. Although old-fashioned toys are their namesake, they are still progressive. Their new toy, the G-Yo is a geometric wood Yo Yo shaped very differently. We thought the one shaped like Mr. Roger's trolley was the coolest - and it really works!

DRAPER'S SUPER BEE APIARIES

RR #1, Box 96 (SR15 & SR238. Follow signs), **Millerton** 16936

- ❏ Activity: Tours
- ❏ Telephone: (570) 537-2381 or (800) 233-4273,
- ❏ Hours: Monday - Saturday, 8:00 am - 5:00 pm
- ❏ Admission: Free
- ❏ Tours: Vary per day
- ❏ Miscellaneous: Gift shop with honey products galore and bee keeping equipment for sale. They even sell "bee" theme "knick knacks" which the owner said is also found in her house.

Every visit warrants a view of the observation hive (don't worry, it's enclosed in safety glass). On tour, you'll learn about different products produced from bee hives. Hopefully, you'll be able to get to a bee site, help extract some honey, and then take a taste test. If you call ahead, Mrs. Draper might make some baked goods and beverages (Kool-Aid with honey) for you to sample. TIDBITS YOU MIGHT LEARN - The White House Presidents use Draper Honey; Wildflower honey has the most nutrients (why? - Find out!); the Queen Bee lays 2000 eggs per day (the larva are what bears really love!). Speaking of bears, can you guess how they keep the "locals" away from their outdoor hives? Learn why honey is liquefied in a "hot room" and not boiled. Learn how to identify the difference between worker bees, male drones, and the Queen. This is an extremely family oriented, educational, and helpful (health-wise) tour given by people who care deeply about what they do. Well worth the trip into the "Endless Mountains".

SKI SAWMILL MOUNTAIN RESORT

Morris - P.O. Box 5, 19963. *Activity: Outdoors.* (717) 353-7521. Snow Report: (800) 532-SNOW, **www.skisawmill.com**. Longest Run: 3250 ft.; 10 Slopes & Trails.

KETTLE CREEK STATE PARK

Renovo - Box 96 (SR 4001), 17764. *Activity: Outdoors.* (717) 923-6004. **http://parec.com/state_parks/kttlstpk.htm**. Beach, Horseback Riding, Sledding, Campsites, Fishing, Trails, Winter Sports.

TIADAGHTON STATE FOREST

South Williamsport - 423 E. Central Avenue, 17701. *Activity: Outdoors.* (717) 327-3450. **http://parec.com/forests/tiadagh.htm** Fishing, Camping, Trails, ATV Trails, Winter Sports.

LITTLE PINE STATE PARK

Waterville - Box 100. 17776. *Activity: Outdoors.* (717) 753-6000, **http://parec.com/state_parks/ltpnstpk.htm**. Beach, Boat Rentals, Sledding, Campsites, Fishing, Trails, Winter Sports.

HILLS CREEK STATE PARK

Wellsboro - R.D. 2, Box 328 (US Route 6 or PA Route 287), 16901. *Activity: Outdoors.* (717) 724-4246, Beach, Visitor Center, Boat Rentals, Campsites, Modern Cabins. **http://parec.com/state_parks/hcrkstpk.htm**.

LEONARD HARRISON STATE PARK

Wellsboro - R.R. 6, Box 199, 16901. *Activity: Outdoors.* (717) 724-3061, **http://parec.com/state_parks/lnrdstpk.htm**. Visitor Center, Grand Canyon of Pennsylvania. Well worth the drive off the beaten path for the scenic views. If your children are able, we suggest hiking one of the trails up or down the gorge. Bring along quarters (for viewers) or binoculars to get detailed views. Canoe, raft liveries threaded throughout the park system. Also in the area is Colton Point State Park.

TIOGA STATE FOREST

Wellsboro - Box 94, Route 287 South, 16901. *Activity: Outdoors.* (717) 724-2868. **http://parec.com/forests/tioga.htm**. Fishing, Camping, Trails, Winter Sports.

CHILDREN'S DISCOVERY WORKSHOP

434 West 4th Street (Runs parallel to I-180. In YMCA building - Downtown), **Williamsport** 17701

- ❑   Activity: Museums
- ❑   Telephone: (717) 322-KIDS
- ❑   Hours: (Summer) Tuesday - Saturday, 10:00 am - 4:00 pm., Sunday, 1:00 - 4:00 pm. (September - May) Tuesday - Friday & Sunday, 1:00 - 5:00 pm., Saturday, 11:00 am - 5:00 pm.
- ❑   Admission: Adults $3.50 (over age 2)
- ❑   Miscellaneous: Educational Gift Shop

This hands-on children's museum is designed for kids ages 3-11. There are many rooms of exhibits but our favorite, most unique areas were the Kids' Clinic, Human Habitrail, Ice Cream Parlor, and Funnel. The Kids' Clinic was full of actual size equipment that got the kids into the act by pretending to be nurses, doctors, or x-ray technicians (with real x-rays to review - a real hospital bed too!). The Ice Cream Parlor featured life size equipment that taught children how to be "soda jerks". The Human Habitrail and Funnel are giant-sized environments where you would usually find small animals - but now they're re-sized for human kids! The habitrail is like the one that your hamster might play in, and the FUN-nel is like a pipe a rodent might wander through underground. Both teach adaptation to a new environment and encourage strengthening large motor skills. Well done!

HIAWATHA RIVERBOAT TOURS

Susquehanna State Park (Docked at Arch Street - US220 to Reach
Road Exit - Follow signs), **Williamsport** 17701

- ❑   Activity: Tours
- ❑   Telephone: (800) 358-9900 or (570) 326-1221
     www.citybus.org/hiawatha
- ❑   Hours: Tuesday - Sunday, 1:00, 2:30, and 4:00 pm. (Summer).
     Weekends Only in May, September & October
- ❑   Admission: Adults $7.00, Seniors $6.50 (60+), Children $3.00
     (3-12)
- ❑   Tours: 1 hour

An old-fashioned paddlewheel boat cruises along the river as
your narrator tells tales of the river when "lumber was king".
Snacks and gifts are available on board. Tuesday night is "Family
Night" during the summer (reduced family rates).

LITTLE LEAGUE WORLD SERIES BASEBALL

Williamsport - 1700 West 4th Street (Bowman Field), 17701.
Activity: Sports. (570) 326-1921. **www.littleleague.org**. The
birthplace of Little League is host to the world championship.
Nationally televised. (Last weekend in August) Also, visit the
Peter J. McGovern Little League Museum - learn about the
legends, swing the bat or test your arms. (Admission for museum).

LYCOMING COUNTY MUSEUM

Williamsport - 858 West 4th Street, 17701. *Activity: Pennsylvania
History.* **www.lycoming.org/lchsmuseum**.   (570)   326-3326.
Hours: Tuesday - Friday, 9:30 am - 4:00 pm., Saturday, 1:00 - 4:00
pm., Sunday, 1:00 - 4:00 pm (May - October). *Admission:* Adults
$3.50, Children $1.50. Over 12,000 square feet of exhibits include
the history of lumbering, The LaRue Shempp model train exhibit,
an American Indian gallery, and period rooms. See a one room
schoolhouse and a working gristmill.

SUSQUEHANNA STATE PARK

Williamsport - 454 Pine Street, 17701. *Activity: Outdoors.* (717) 326-1971. **http://parec.com/state_parks/susqstpk.htm**. 20 Acres. Picnicking, Playfield.

WILLIAMSPORT CUBS BASEBALL

Williamsport - 1700 West 4th Street - P.O. Box 3173 (Bowman Field), 17701. *Activity: Sports.* (717) 326-3389. *Admission: $3-$5.00.* Minor League Class Affiliate of Chicago Cubs.

WILLIAMSPORT SYMPHONY ORCHESTRA

Williamsport - 220 West Fourth Street (Community Arts Center), 17701. *Activity: The Arts.* **www.williamsportsymphony.org.** (570) 322-0227, Concerts feature international guest artists performing classical and contemporary.

WILLIAMSPORT TROLLEYS

100 Pine Street (Trolley Gazebo @ Sheraton Inn - Downtown), **Williamsport 17701**

- ❑ Activity: Tours
- ❑ Telephone: (800) CITY-BUS or (570) 326-2500,
- ❑ Hours: Tuesday, Thursday, Saturday, 10:45 am & 12:15 pm. (Summer). Call ahead to confirm times - (Only 10:45 am on Saturday)
- ❑ Admission: General $2.00
- ❑ Tours: Taped narration in replica streetcars - lasts about 70 minutes.

Millionaires Row (impressive mansions built by lumber barons) is the focus of this tour. Kids enjoy Memorial Park (the site of the first Little League Baseball game). For fidgety children, there are several on and off stops throughout the trip.

AREA "NE"

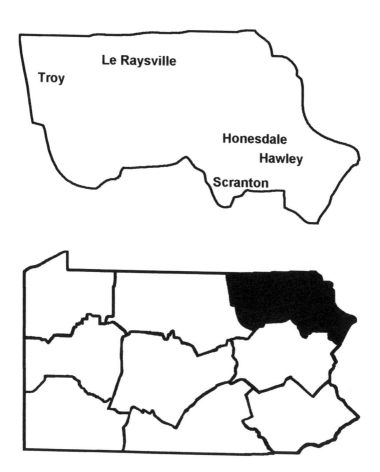

Le Raysville

Troy

Honesdale

Hawley

Scranton

Our Favorites...

1) Bushkill Falls

2) Delaware Water Gap Recreation Area

3) "Claws N Paws"

4) Steamtown National Historic Site

5) Bradford Basket Company

NORTHEASTERN PENNSYLVANIA PHILHARMONIC

Avoca - 957 Broadcast Center, 18641. *Activity: The Arts.* (570) 457-8301. **www.nepaphil.com**. Performing classical and pops in Scranton and Wilkes-Barre.

CAROUSEL WATER AND FUN PARK

Beach Lake - Box 134 (Route 652), 18405. *Activity: Amusements.* (717) 729-7532. *Hours:* Daily, 11:00 am - 10 pm (Summers) Weekends, 11:00 am - 6:00 pm (Spring and Fall). *Admission:* Pay one price ticket or pay per activity. Water slides, go-carts, bumper boats, Kiddie cars, wading pool, mini-golf, batting range, arcade, snack bar.

WYOMING STATE FOREST

Bloomsburg – R.D. 2, Box 47, 17815. *Activity: Outdoors.* (717) 387-4255. Almost 43,000 acres of Fishing, Trails, Winter Sports, Horse Trails, Camping. **http://parec.com/forests/wyoming.htm**.

BUSHKILL FALLS

Bushkill Falls Road (I-80 to Exit 52 - SR209 North), **Bushkill** 18324

- ❑ Activity: Outdoors
- ❑ Telephone Number: (888) 628-7454 or (570) 588-6682
  www.visitbushkillfalls.com
- ❑ Hours: 9:00 am - Dusk (April - November)
- ❑ Admission: Adults $8.00, Seniors $7.00, Children $2.00 (4-10)
- ❑ Miscellaneous: Wildlife exhibit, gift shops, fishing, concessions, miniature golf, paddleboats.

Experience the Lenni Lanape Native Americans longhouse exhibit where kids can walk into an Indian home with "beds" - pretty neat! The main falls include Upper Canyon (craggy glen), Bridle Veil Falls (long, misty), Laurel Glen (mountain laurel wildflowers), Pennell Falls and Main Falls (over 100 foot cliff). Trails and bridges lace the area. Call ahead for seasonal conditions.

DELAWARE WATER GAP NATIONAL RECREATION AREA

(US209), **Bushkill** 18324

❑   Activity: Outdoors
❑   Telephone: (570) 828-7802 or (570) 588-2451
    www.nps.gov/dewa
❑   Admission: Only for guarded beaches.

Stretching over 37 miles along the Delaware River, you'll find extremely scenic roads and trails to wander along. Great canoeing & rafting (some short - kid friendly), fishing, skiing, and snowmobiling. (For updated brochures or information call 1-800-POCONOS or www.poconos.org).

- **DINGMAN'S FALLS VISITOR'S CENTER** - audiovisual program, nature exhibits, followed by a mapped walk. 9:00 am - 5:00 pm (May - October). Overnight accommodations.
- **BUSHKILL VISITOR'S CENTER** - Monday - Friday, 8:00 - 4:30 pm.

Both Visitor's Centers offer "ranger picked must sees" during each season. They also have a Junior Ranger program which includes a kid's self-guided exploring booklet.

POCONO INDIAN MUSEUM

Bushkill - P.O. Box 261 (SR209 North off I-80), 18324. *Activity: Museums.* (570) 588-9338. **www.pocoindianmuseum.com**. *Hours:* Daily, 9:30 am - 5:30 pm. *Admission:* Adults $3.50, Seniors $2.50, Children $2.00 (6-16). The museum recreates the life of the Delaware Indians from B.C. to the contact period with Europeans to post American Revolution. See their lifestyle through homes (some made of bark - and you thought they only lived in tee-pees!), weapons, and kitchen pottery. Most of these items were unearthed in the Delaware Water Gap. Boys like the 150 year old scalp and buying an authentic "peace pipe".

FERNWOOD SKI AREA

Bushkill - Route 209 North, 18371. *Activity: Outdoors.* (717) 588-9500. **www.usskiing.com/stats.cfm/pa11.htm**. Snow Report: (800) 233-8103. Longest Run: 1500 ft.; 2 Slopes & Trails.

LACKAWANNA STATE PARK

Dalton - R.D. 1, Box 230, Lackawanna County, 18414. *Activity: Outdoors.* **http://parec.com/state_parks/lackstpk.htm**. (717) 945-3239. Includes Salt Spring - a 36 acre natural area with old-growth hemlocks, streams and 3 waterfalls. Also Archbold Pothole - world's largest geological pothole - 38 ft. deep, 42 ft. wide. Boating, fishing, swimming, picnicking, biking, camping, skiing, snowmobiling.

KITTATINNY CANOES

Dingman's Ferry - HC 67 Box 360, 18328. *Activity: Outdoors.* (800) FLOAT-KC or (570) 828-2338. **www.kittatinny.com**

PECH'S POND RENTALS

Dingman's Ferry – 18328. *Activity: Outdoors.* (570) 775-7237.

WORLD'S END STATE PARK

Forksville - P.O. Box 62, 18616. *Activity: Outdoors.* (717) 924-3287. **http://parec.com/state_parks/wrldstpk.htm**. Beach, Rustic Cabins, Horseback Riding, Visitor's Center, Fishing, Boating, Hiking, Horse Trails, Winter Sports.

PROMISED LAND STATE PARK

Greentown - R.D. 1, Box 96 (PA Route 390), 18426. *Activity: Outdoors.* **http://parec.com/state_parks/promstpk.htm**. (717) 676-3428, Beach, Historical Center, Boat Rentals, Rustic Cabins, Fishing, Boating, Hiking, Winter Sports.

CLAWS AND PAWS ANIMAL PARK

(SR590 East - then follow signs), **Hamlin** 18427

❑   Activity: Animals & Farms
❑   Telephone: (570) 698-6154, **www.clawsnpaws.com**
❑   Hours: Daily, 10:00 am - 6:00 pm (May - October)
❑   Admission: Adults $8.95, Seniors $7.95, Children $5.95 (2-11)
❑   Miscellaneous: Snack bar. Gift shop. Picnic Area. Large walk-in petting zoo.

"Get Close to the Animals" is their theme...and you will! Many cages have glass front enclosures - so animals can walk right up to your face and you're still protected. During posted times you can feed giraffes using a long stick or hand feed fruits and vegetables to Lory Parrots (colorful small tame parrots). The animals are comfortable with visitors and they're not bashful about getting close to get a good nibble from your snack- filled hands. During the summer months they have unique Performing Parrot shows and Wildlife Encounter shows. When was the last time you saw a parrot ride a bike or you got to pet an alligator?

LAKE WALLENPAUPACK

Hawley - US 6, 18428. *Activity: Outdoors.* Created as a project of the Pennsylvania Power and Light for hydroelectrics (see Visitor's Center on US6 - South of Hawley). While at the center, ask about Shuman Point, Ledgedale, and Beech House Creek natural and wildlife areas, all maintained for public use by PP & L. Notable attractions include:

• CLUB NAUTICO - SR507. (570) 226-0580. Powerboats and waverunners for rent.
• SPIRIT OF PAUPAK - US6 & SR507. (570) 226-6266. (June - October). Daily scenic tours for one hour. 9:00 am - 5:00 pm. Admission.

- TRIPLE "W" RIDING STABLE RANCH - Beechmont Drive - off Owego Turnpike. (570) 226-2670. Horse ranch and western riding trips from one hour to overnight camping ($25 - 100+). Overnight accommodations at Double "W" Bed and Breakfast. Year round except hunting season.

SCOTTY'S WHITE WATER RAFTING

Hawley – R.R. 1 Box 646, 18428. *Activity: Outdoors.* (570) 226-3551. **www.myfreeoffice.com/rafting/index.html.** Scotty's White Water Rafting.

STOURBRIDGE RAIL EXCURSION GREAT TRAIN ROBBERY RUN

Honesdale - (I-84, exit 5 - SR191 north - to Main Street), 18431. *Activity: Tours.* **www.waynecountycc.com/trhome.htm.** (800) 433-9008. *Hours:* Sundays @ 1:30 pm (Sunday before July 4th - Sunday before Labor Day), *Admission:* Adults $12.00. See masked men from the "Triple W Ranch" ambush the train on a 3 hour round trip (includes a one-hour stop for sightseeing).

WAYNE COUNTY HISTORICAL MUSEUM

Honesdale - 810 Main Street, 18431. *Activity: Pennsylvania History.* (570) 253-3240. *Hours:* Year round - Call for seasonal hours. *Admission:* Adults $2.00, Children $1.00 (12-18). Life-size replica of the first U.S. locomotive, canals, glass, America Indians. Housed in 1860 in the former office of canal company.

HOLLY ROSS POTTERY

LaAnna - R.R.2, Box 1016 (SR191), 18326. *Activity: Tours.* (570) 676-3248. **www.holleyross.com.** Free admission. *Tours:* Monday - Friday at 11:00 am & 3:30 pm (demonstrations). Picnic wooded park. Factory outlet.

SKI BIG BEAR

Lackawaxen - HC #1 - 1A 353 Karl Hope Blvd., 18435. *Activity: Outdoors.* (570) 685-1400. Snow Report: (570) 685-1400. Longest Run: 6300 ft.; 10 Slopes & Trails.

WILD AND SCENIC RIVER TOURS

Lackawaxen – 18435. *Activity: Outdoors.* (800) 836-0366.

MOUNT TONE SKI AREA

Lake Como - Wallerville Road (Off Route 247), 18437. *Activity: Outdoors.* (570) 798-2707. (570) 842-2544. Snow Report: (570) 798-2300. **www.mttone.com**. Longest Run: 2500 ft.; 11 Slopes & Trails.

LERAYSVILLE CHEESE FACTORY

Leraysville - R.R. 2 Box 71A (Off SR467 - turn on dirt road 1/2 mile from town), 18829. *Activity: Tours.* (800) 859-5196 or (570) 744-2554. *Hours:* Daily, 9:00 am - 5:00 pm. (March - December). Free admission. *Tours:* Twice per week they make cheese in 6000 pound vats. Specialize in traditional cheddar cheese. Store.

POCONO RACEWAY

Long Pond - 184 Sterling Road, 18344. *Activity: Sports.* **www.poconoraceway.com**. (800) RACEWAY, NASCAR 2.5 Mile super speedway - NASCAR Winston Cup racing, 3rd weekend in June, 4th weekend in July.

PIKE COUNTY MUSEUM

Milford - 608 Broad Street, 18337. *Activity: Pennsylvania History and Government.* (570) 296-8126. *Hours:* Vary, call first. County artifacts, home of the Lincoln Flag.

UPPER MILL WATERWHEEL CAFÉ

Milford - (150 Water Street on Sawkill Creek), 18337. *Activity: Theme Restaurants.* (717) 296-2383. *Hours:* Daily, 10:00 am - 5:00 pm (May - October). An early 1800's water powered 3 story gristmill still operates and you can watch the giant water wheel turn which drives a series of shafts, gears, and pulleys. Through the glass walls of the café you can see the stones and grain milling equipment at work. Sit down and enjoy whole grain pancakes, muffins, and scones or multi-grain bread sandwiches.

LACKAWANNA COAL MINE

McDade Park (I-81, Exit 57B or 51 – follow signs), **Scranton** 18503

- ❑   Activity: Tours
- ❑   Telephone: (570) 963-MINE or (800) 238-7245
- ❑   Hours: Daily, 10:00 am – 4:30 pm (April – November)
- ❑   Admission: Adults $6.00, Children $4.00 (3-12)
- ❑   Miscellaneous: Company Store – souvenir coal jewelry and such. Food service. Constant 55 degrees F. below so bring along a jacket. McDade Park has excellent areas for picnics and play.

"Go down in history" where you descend (by railcar) 300 feet below the ground to see how men "hand harvested" coal. Actual miners are your guides as they share personal stories about the hard life, the work, and the dangers of digging for "black diamonds". A walking tour of three veins of mine floor.

LACKAWANNA STATE FOREST

Scranton - 401 Samters Building, 101 Penn Avenue, 18503. *Activity: Outdoors.* **http://parec.com/forests/lackawan.htm**. (717) 963-4561. Fishing, Camping, Trails, Winter Sports.

STEAMTOWN NATIONAL HISTORICAL SITE

150 South Washington Avenue (I-81, Exit 57B or Exit 53 - toward
downtown), **Scranton** 18503

- ❑   Activity: Museums
- ❑   Telephone: (888) 693-9391 or (570) 340-5200
  www.nps.gov/stea
- ❑   Hours: Daily, 9:00 am - 6:00 pm (July - Labor Day weekend).
  Daily, 9:00 am - 5:00 pm (Rest of Year). Closed New Years Day,
  Thanksgiving Day, and Christmas Day
- ❑   Admission: Adults $7.00, Seniors $6.00 (62+), Children $2.00
  (6-12)
- ❑   Tours: On Train ($5.00 - $10.00 per person). 2 hours long.
  Reservations recommended - mostly Friday - Sunday (Late May -
  October)

"This is just like Thomas the Train" squealed our kids as we
all saw the roundhouse come to life! This fully restored
roundhouse and turntable are incredible to watch. As the Baldwin
#26 enters the yard it stops on the turntable and advances to the
correct numbered house where it will "sleep" or receive
maintenance. While you are out walking around the roundhouse,
talk with the crew as they share stories about their jobs and the
engines. The conductors love to wave and are good photograph
opportunities. The Visitor's Center (mostly oriented for older kids)
has both a Technology Center and History Museum of American
Steam Railroading. When the train rides aren't running (Monday -
Wednesday), yard shuttles operate several times daily. This is a
short excursion best for younger children who can't endure a 2
hour train ride. Yard shuttles are seasonal (April - December).

PENNSYLVANIA ANTHRACITE HERITAGE MUSEUM

RD #1 - Bald Mountain Road (I-81 - Exit 57B or Exit 51 - Follow
signs to McDade Park), **Scranton** 18504

- ❑   Activity: Museums

❑   Telephone: (570) 963-4804 or 4845
    www.state.pa.us/PA_Exec/Historical_Museum/BHSM/toh/ant
    hheritage/anthraciteheritage.htm
❑   Hours: Monday - Saturday, 9:00 am - 5:00 pm, Sunday, Noon -
    5:00 pm (Closed holidays - except summer holidays)
❑   Admission: Adults $3.50, Seniors $3.00 (60+), Children $2.00
    (6-11)

E xplore the culture created by life and work in the coal towns.
Their collections include highlights of the mines, canals,
railroads, mills, and factories. This was really hard work! To see a
close-up of the mills producing iron "T" rails for America's
railroads, stop over to the park setting of Scranton Iron Furnaces.

PENNSYLVANIA SUMMER THEATRE

Scranton - McDade Park, Bald Mountain Road (Scranton Public
Theatre), 18504. *Activity: The Arts.* (570) 344-3656. Professional
theatre company performs musicals, comedies and children's
theatre.

MONTAGE SKI AREA

Scranton - 1000 Montage Mountain Road, 18505. *Activity:
Outdoors.* (570) 969-7669. Snow Report: (800) GOT-SNOW.
www.skimontage.com. Longest Run: 1+ miles; 21 Slopes &
Trails.

SCRANTON/WILKES-BARRE RED BARONS
BASEBALL

Scranton - 225 Montage Mountain Road (Lackawanna County
Stadium), 18507. *Activity: Sports.* **www.redbarons.com**. (570)
969-BALL. *Admission:* $4-$7.00. AAA Class affiliate of the
Philadelphia Phillies.

HOUDINI TOUR AND SHOW MUSEUM

1433 North Main Avenue (I-81 to exit 56), **Scranton** 18508

❑   Activity: Museums

❑   Telephone: (570) 342-8527 or 5555.
    www.microserve.net/~magicusa/houdini.html

❑   Hours: 11:00 am - 6:00 pm (Memorial Day Weekend), 1:00 -
    5:00 pm (May 27 - June 13), 11:00 am - 6:00 pm (June 14 -
    September 14)

❑   Admission: Adults $10.00, Children $8.00 (under 10)

❑   Miscellaneous: Gift/Magic Shop. Admission includes video
    presentation and live magic shows. Very enthusiastic magicians
    answer questions and perform illusions before your eyes.

The world's only exhibit devoted entirely to Houdini. Houdini
and his brother Hardeen toured through this area often. Now,
nationally known magicians re-create these shows daily. Wander
around and see Houdini's favorite trick props and photographs.
How did he do it?

EVERHART MUSEUM

Scranton - 1901 Mulberry Street (Mulberry and Arthur Avenue),
18510. *Activity: Arts.* www.everhart-museum.org. (570) 346-
7186. *Hours:* Daily, Noon - 5:00 pm. Closed Monday and Tuesday
(Mid-October - March). *Admission:* Adults $3.00, Students $2.00,
Children $1.00 (6+). Housing exhibits of American Folk, Native
American, Oriental and primitive art. They also have fun exhibits
for kids in dinosaur hall and the bird collection. Children's store.

LACKAWANNA COUNTY MUSEUM (CATLIN HOUSE)

Scranton - 232 Monroe Avenue (I-81 to exit 53, Monroe Avenue -
next to University of Scranton), 18510. *Activity: Pennsylvania
History.* www.visitnepa.org/members/hist_ society. html. (570)
344-3841. *Hours:* Tuesday-Friday 10 am to 5 pm. Saturdays Noon
to 3 pm. *Guided Tours:* Tuesday - Saturday, 1:00 - 3:00 pm.
English Tudor style home with artifacts, photographs and archives
relating to local history, Victorian culture and the area's industry.

SHAWNEE PLACE CHILDREN'S PLAY AND WATER PARK

P.O. Box 339 (I-80, Exit 52, US 209 North, Follow signs)
Shawnee on Delaware 18356

- ❑ Activity: Amusements
- ❑ Telephone: (570) 421-7231. **www.shawneemt.com**
- ❑ Hours: Weekends (beginning May 23 - Mid -June). Daily, 10:00 am - 5:00 pm (Mid-June - Labor Day)
- ❑ Admission: Participants $10.00, Spectators $5.00

Ball pits, cable glide, cargo nets, water slides, wading pools, magic shows, arcade, snack bar. Children, ages 2 - 12.

TANGLWOOD SKI AREA

Tafton - P.O. Box 165 (Lake Wallenpaupack - on Route 390), 18464. *Activity: Outdoors.* (570) 226-SNOW. Snow Report: (888) 226-SNOW. **www.tanglwood.com**. Longest Run: 1.25 miles; 10 Slopes & Trails.

CAMEL BEACH WATER PARK

PO Box 168 (I -80, Exit 45), **Tannersville** 18372

- ❑ Activity: Amusements
- ❑ Telephone: (570) 629-1661, **www.camelbeach.com**
- ❑ Hours: Daily, opens 11:00 am (Summer). Weekends (Fall/Spring)
- ❑ Admission: Combo ticket $20.00, Average, $5.00 per area.

4 water slides, Lazy River Ride, Family Play Pool, 3200 foot long Alpine Slide, bumper boats, go-carts, mini-golf, chairlift rides, Cameltop Restaurant (lunch only).

TOBYHANNA STATE PARK

Tobyhanna - P.O. Box 387, 18466. *Activity: Outdoors.* (717) 894-8336. **http://parec.com/state_parks/tobystpk.htm**. Beach, Boat Rentals, Campsites. Also in this location are Big Pocono and Gouldsboro State Parks. Trails, Winter Sports.

FRENCH ASYLUM

RD #2, Box 266 (off SR187 - follow signs), **Towanda** 18848

❏　Activity: Museums

❏　Telephone: (570)265-3376, **www.bradford-pa.com/sites/azilum**

❏　Hours: Wednesday - Sunday, 11:00 am - 4:00 pm. (June - August). Weekends, 11:00 am - 4:30 (May, September, October)

❏　Admission: Adults $4.50, Seniors $4.00, Children $3.00 (6-18)

❏　Miscellaneous: Picnic pavilion. Nature trails.

Few sites in Pennsylvania address another country's historic events like this one does. Founded in 1793, 50 log cabins were created as a refuge for French nobility fleeing the Revolution. After Napoleon's pardon, most left the area. There are still a few log cabins standing and an 1836 Laporte House containing period furnishings.

BRADFORD COUNTY MUSEUM

Troy - Alparon Park (SR14 North - rear US6), *Activity: Pennsylvania History.* (570) 297-3410. *Hours:* Friday - Sunday & Holidays, 10:00 am - 4:00 pm. (April - October). *Admission:* Adults $2.50, Seniors $2.00, Children $1.00 (6+). A re-created barn of local resident and dairy farmer Wildner Wilcox houses rooms of farm antiques that tell the story of rural farm life. Features a bedroom, kitchen, craftsmen area, doctor's office, and country store. **www.bradford-pa.com/sites/museum.phtml#brad**

BRADFORD BASKET COMPANY

P.O. Box 157 (SR14 North - Go 1.1 miles off US 6) **Troy** 16947

❏　Activity: Tours

❏　Telephone: (800) 231-9972 or (570) 297-1020
　　www.bradfordbaskets.com

❏　Hours: Monday - Saturday, 9:00 am - 4:00 pm

❏　Tours: 1/2 hour. Monday - Friday, 9:30 am - 1:30 pm (reservations suggested)

❏ Miscellaneous: Don't look for factory seconds or discounts. They only allow a first quality product to leave their facility.

See an old world craft brought back to modern day usefulness. Bradford and Bradford Wee baskets (so-o-o cute) are hand-woven maple baskets in 23 styles and trimmed in 7 colors. First watch the weavers as they form different shapes of baskets using hard maple veneer strips (2 at a time for strength). You'll see many of the different forms they use - some are really unusual shapes – like, the Millennium, the peanut, or the cloverleaf basket. It takes 6-16 weeks of training (on 3rd shift) to be good enough to be a weaver. You'll also see ladies dye strips of wood, shape and attach handles. They "hand dip" each basket individually. All baskets are personally hand signed by the master weaver.

MT. PISGAH STATE PARK

Troy - R.D. 3, Box 362 (2 miles north of US Route 6), 16947. *Activity: Outdoors.* **http://parec.com/state_parks/mtpsstpk.htm.** (717) 297-2734. Pool, Visitor Center, Fishing, Boating, Trails, Winter Sports.

ELK MOUNTAIN SKI AREA

Union Dale - R.R. 2, Box 3328, 18470. *Activity: Outdoors.* (570) 679-4400. Snow Report: (800) 233-4131. **www.elkskier.com.** Longest Run: 1.75 miles; 27 Slopes & Trails.

WILKES-BARRE DIAMONDS BASKETBALL

Wilkes-Barre - 80 North Washington Avenue (Coughlin High School), 18701. *Activity: Sports.* (570) 823-3320. *Admission:* $4-$6.00. Eastern Basketball Alliance.

AREA "NW"

Our Favorites...

1) Presque Isle State Park & Erie Maritime Area
2) Wendell August Forge
3) Daffins Candies
4) Drake Well Museum
5) Quaker Steak & Lube

MOUNTAIN VIEW SKI AREA

Cambridge Springs - 14510 Mount Pleasant Road, 16403. *Activity: Outdoors.* (814) 734-1641. Longest Run: 2500 ft.; 9 Slopes & Trails. **www.skiresortsguide.com/stats.cfm/pa16.htm**.

CHAPMAN STATE PARK

Clarendon - R.D. 2 Box 1610 (off US Route 6), 16829. *Activity: Outdoors.* **http://parec.com/state_parks/chapstpk.htm**. (814) 723-0250, Beach, Boat Rentals, Campsites, Fishing, Trails, Winter Sports.

CLEAR CREEK STATE FOREST

Clarion - 158 South Second Avenue, 16214. *Activity: Outdoors.* (814) 226-1901. **http://parec.com/forests/clrcreek.htm**

KITTANNING STATE FOREST

Clarion - 158 South Second Avenue, 16214. *Activity: Outdoors.* (814) 226-1901. 13,000 acres of Fishing, Camping, Trails, Winter Sports.

TARA – "A COUNTRY INN"

2844 Lake Road (I-80, Exit 1 to SR18 North to SR258), **Clark** 16113

- ❑ Activity: Theme Restaurants
- ❑ Telephone: (800) 782-2803 or (724) 962-3535
  www.innbook.com/tara.html
- ❑ Hours: Breakfast, Lunch, Dinner - Generally higher priced
- ❑ Tours: On the hour daily, 10:00 am - 3:00 pm. Guides wear Civil War era costumes. $5.00
- ❑ Miscellaneous: Food is available in Ashley's (probably too gourmet for kids). Old South Restaurant (family style meals) or Stonewall's (colonial style with pewter goblets and hearty meats)

See a country inn with a "Gone With the Wind" theme. Southern atmosphere with long verandas, white wicker furniture in a mid-1800's Greek Revival mansion. Each room is named after a character from "Tara" and is decorated to that person's taste. Wander around after your meal to view any unoccupied rooms open - ready for a peek (the rooms are roped off but you can still use your eyes to see all of the splendor). Which room would you like to spend the night in?

CONNEAUT LAKE PARK

Conneaut Lake - P.O. Box 646 I-79, Exit 36B to Route 322, 16316. *Activity: Amusements.* **www.conneautlake.com**. (814) 382-5115. *Hours:* Daily, (May - October). *Admission:* Free - Pay for each ride. Old-fashioned 100 year old park with rides, water attractions, kiddie land and beach/boardwalk. One coaster dates back to 1938.

STERNWHEELER "BARBARA J."

Conneaut Lake - (SR618 to Conneaut Lake Park entrance - follow signs), 16316. *Activity: Tours.* (888) 802-3301. *Hours:* Daily, Noon & 8:00 pm. (Summers). *Admission:* Adults $6.50, Children $3.50. *Tours:* 45 minutes narrated tours. Leave on the hour.

OTTO CUPLER TORPEDO COMPANY & NITROGLYCERIN MUSEUM

Dotyville Road (I-79, exit 36A, SR6/19/322 East to Route 27)
East Titusville, 16354

- ❏ Activity: Museums
- ❏ Telephone: (814) 827-2921
- ❏ Hours: Monday - Thursday, 9:30 am, 11:00 am, 12:30 pm, 2:00 pm, 3:30 pm.
- ❏ Tours: Special Effects Friday - Sunday at 12:30 pm and 2:30 pm. Wednesday at Noon.
- ❏ Miscellaneous: Additional fee for show. Movie available of oil well shootings in Oil Creek Valley recently.

NITROGLYCERIN SPECIAL EFFECTS SHOW- Demonstrates the role nitroglycerin played in oil fields in the late 1800's. The living history re-enactment includes real wells shot in a burst of huge flames. The only oil well shooting organization still in operation. Torpedoes were used to clean out oil wells that had clogged with paraffin or they were used to establish the initial "boom" to get the oil flowing. What were "torpedo wars" and dangerous "moonlighters"? Why should you run when a shooter yells, "Fire in the hole"?

WOODEN NICKEL BUFFALO FARM

Edinboro - 5970 Koman Road (I-79 to exit 38 - go east - follow signs), 16412. *Activity: Animals & Farms.* (814) 734-BUFF, **www.woodennickelbuffalo.com**. *Hours:* Daily, 11:00 - 5:00. *Admission:* Adults $1.00, Children $0.50 ($5.00 per tour, minimum charge). The owners loved the meat when they first tried it and decided to breed and sell buffalo products. American Indian folklore. Feel a real buffalo hide!

ERIE / PRESQUE ISLE BOATS

Erie - *Activity: Tours.* PRESQUE ISLE EXPRESS - 36 passenger water taxi departs Dobbins Landing. (800) 988-5780. VICTORIAN PRINCESS - 149 passenger paddlewheel dinner cruises. PRESQUE ISLE STATE PARK SCENIC BOAT TOURS - M/V Lady Kate. 49 passenger, 90 minute narrated cruises. (800) 988-5780. $9.00-13.00 (ages 5+).

BICENTENNIAL OBSERVATION TOWER

Erie - Dobbins Landing, 16501. *Activity: Tours.* (814) 455-6055, **www.erie.net/~chamber/tower.html**. *Hours:* Open at 10:00 - closing varies seasonally (April - October). *Admission:* Adults $2.00, Children $1.00 (6-12) Free admission on Tuesdays. 185 foot tower with a view of Lake Erie, downtown, and Presque Isle. 210 stairs to the observation deck (or, yes, there is an elevator!). If you climb the stairs, follow the 16 stations that highlight various landmarks.

ERIE ART MUSEUM

Erie - 411 State Street, 16501. *Activity: The Arts.* (814) 459-5477, **www.erie.net/~erieartm**. *Hours:* Tuesday - Saturday, 11:00 am - 5:00 pm. Sunday, 1-5:00 pm. *Admission:* Adults $2.00, Seniors & Students $1.00, Children $0.50 (under 12). Art exhibits, concerts, tours and children's programs. Western and Asia; famous "The Avalon Restaurant" is a mini-sculpture of town diner and local residents.

ERIE COUNTY MUSEUM

Erie - 417 - 422 State Street (I-79 to Bayfront Parkway), 16501. *Activity: Pennsylvania History.* (814) 454-1813. *Hours:* Tuesday - Saturday, 9:00 am - 5:00 pm. *Admission:* Donations. Local history, architecture and industry. Cashiers House - life in Erie during the antebellum period.

ERIE OTTERS HOCKEY

Erie - 809 French Street (office) (Louis J. Tullio Civic Center), 16501. *Activity: Sports.* (814) 452-4857 (Box Office) or 455-7779 (office), **www.ottershockey.com**. *Admission:* $6 - $10.00. Ontario Hockey League.

ERIE SEA WOLVES BASEBALL

Erie - 110 East 10th Street (office) (Jerry Uht Ballpark), 16501. *Activity: Sports.*   **www.seawolves.com**.   (814)   456-1300. *Admission:* $3-$6.00. AA Class affiliate of the Pittsburgh Pirates.

YOUTHEATE

Erie -13 West 10th Street Erie Playhouse, 16501. *Activity: The Arts.* (814) 454-2852. **www.erieplayhouse.com**.

PRESQUE ISLE STATE PARK

Erie - P.O. Box 8510 - Lake Erie, 16505. *Activity: Outdoors.* (814) 833-7424.   **http://parec.com/state_parks/presstpk.htm**.   Seven miles of sandy beaches (Top 100 swimming holes). Canoe and Boat Livery. 321 species of birds. Lighthouses. Visitor Center, Year-round Education & Interpretation. Boating, Fishing, Swimming, Picnicking, Biking, Camping, Skiing, Snowmobiling.

WALDAMEER PARK AND WATER WORLD

220 Peninsula Drive (Close to entrance of Presque Isle State Park), **Erie** 16505

- ❑ Activity: Amusements
- ❑ Telephone: (814) 838-3591, **www.waldameer.com**
- ❑ Hours: Tuesday - Sunday, (Mid-May - Labor Day)
- ❑ Admission: Per ride prices and General Admission ranging from $8.00 - 15.00.
- ❑ Miscellaneous: Restaurants. Tubes and life jackets are free.

Beautiful parks. 11 water slides for adults, 5 for children. 16 major rides, 7 for kids. Thunder River log flume ride. Puppet shows and concerts. Heated pool and "tad pool" areas.

ERIE MARITIME MUSEUM / U.S. BRIG NIAGARA

150 East Front Street (I-79 North to Bayfront Parkway),**Erie** 16507

- ❑ Activity: Museums
- ❑ Telephone: (814) 871-4596 or (814) 452-BRIG
  www.erie.net/~chamber/niagara.html
- ❑ Hours: Monday - Saturday, 9:00 am - 5:00 pm., Sunday, Noon - 5:00 pm.
- ❑ Admission: Adults $6.00, Seniors $5.00, Children $3.00 (6-12), Family $15.00
- ❑ Miscellaneous: Shipwright gift shop

New, artistic exhibits about the ship "Niagara" (video), Lake Erie ecology, the bow of the Wolverine, bilge pumps in action, cannon fire, knots and sails. Tour the flagship "Niagara" (when in port) built to fight in the War of 1812 - the Battle of Lake Erie - Commodore Perry. Once aboard, see over 200 oars, steered with a tiller instead of a wheel, sleeping quarters, and rows of cannons. Do you know the difference between a Brig (2 sails) and a ship (3 sails)? How do you preserve a ship? - Sink it in freshwater! (it's the air & salt that causes deterioration) Why can't cannons fire all at once on one side of the ship?

EXPERIENCE CHILDREN'S MUSEUM

420 French Street (Discovery Square) (I-79 North to Bay Front Highway), **Erie** 16507

- ❑ Activity: Museums
- ❑ Telephone: (814) 453-3743
- ❑ Hours: Tuesday - Saturday, 10:00 am - 4:00 pm., Sunday, 1:00 - 4:00 pm. Closed Tuesday during school year.
- ❑ Admission: Adults $3.50 (ages 2+)
- ❑ Miscellaneous: Aimed at 2-12 year old children. The Much More Store gift shop.

The first floor is full of science - from giant bubble creations to energy, light, and motion. Check out Radar Rooster weather, a Bedrock Cave, or the New Circles and Cycles (pollution - unregulated and innumerable, and, its effects on the Lake Erie watershed). Children are challenged to create a safe community. The second floor is the "Gallery of the Human Experience" and has career dress up areas, Rookie Reporter newsroom, the Corner Store, Senses, Safety, Construction, and your heartbeat.

FIREFIGHTER'S HISTORICAL MUSEUM

428 Chestnut Street (I-79 to Route 5), **Erie** 16507

- ❑ Activity: Museums
- ❑ Telephone: (814) 456-5969
- ❑ Hours: Saturday, 10:00 am - 5:00 pm., Sunday, 1:00 - 5:00 pm. (May - August). Saturday - Sunday, 1:00 - 5:00 pm. (September, October)
- ❑ Admission: Adults $2.00, Seniors $1.50, Children $1.00 (8-12)

The #4 Erie Firehouse has 1300+ items on display. Items include antique equipment, uniforms, badges, helmets, masks, fire extinguishers, hand pumps and horse drawn carts. They have the only display of an 1889 horse drawn fire engine and an understandable demonstration of the relay system in fire call boxes.

ERIE ZOO

423 West 38th Street (I-90 to exit 7), **Erie** 16508

- ❑ Activity: Animals & Farms
- ❑ Telephone: (814) 864-4091
    www.erie.net/~chamber/rec3.html#ZOO
- ❑ Hours: Daily, 10:00 am - 5:00 pm. Children's Zoo is open May - September
- ❑ Admission: Adults $4.75, Seniors $4.25 (62+), Children $2.75 (3-11)
- ❑ Miscellaneous: Train rides ($1.00 extra)

See over 300 animals (100 species). Children's Zoo - feed and pet babies - "Critter Encounters". Monkey and otter's habitats are especially fun to watch.

VENANGO COUNTY MUSEUM

Franklin - 301 South Park Street, 16323. *Activity: Pennsylvania History.* (814) 437-2275. *Hours:* Tuesday - Thursday, Saturday 10:00 am - 2:00 pm. (May - December). Saturdays Only (January - April). Located in the historic Hoge-Osmer House. Displays include: Indian artifacts, clothing, household furniture and tableware.

CANAL MUSEUM

Greenville - 60 Alan Avenue (Lock 22 - Alan Avenue), 16125. *Activity: Museums.* (724) 588-7540. *Hours:* (Summers) Tuesday - Sunday, 1:00 - 5:00 pm. (May, September, October)Weekends, 1:00 - 5:00 pm. *Admission:* Adults $1.50, Children $1.00 (6-18).

History of Erie Extension Canal - artifacts like tools and photographs. See a full size replica of an 1840's canal boat - Rufus Reed, and view a working model of a canal lock.

GREENVILLE RAILROAD PARK AND MUSEUM

Greenville - 314 Main Street - Route 358, 16125. *Activity: Museums.* (724) 588-4009. *Hours:* Daily, Noon - 5:00 pm (Summer). Friday - Sunday, Noon - 5:00 pm (May, September, October). Free Admission. Climb aboard the largest switch engine - #604 - used in the steel industry. Plenty of railroad cars - hopper cars, cabooses, and a 1914 Empire auto touring car. World's first parachute invented by local Stefan Banie in 1914. Stationmasters quarters, dispatch office and displays of railroad uniforms.

BISON HAVEN RANCH

Grove City - 316 Elliott Road (I-80 exit 3A to SR173 North), 16127. *Activity: Animals & Farms.* (724) 458-9199. *Hours:* Monday - Saturday, 9:00 am - 6:00 pm., Sunday, 1:00 - 6:00 pm. *Admission:* Adults $2.00, Children $1.00 (pre-arranged tour). View farm raised bison that produce a low fat, nutritional meat used for food, clothing, shelter, and the focus of many folklores. 36+ bison are in an average herd.

WENDELL AUGUST FORGE

620 North Madison Avenue (I-79, exit 31 or I-80, exit 3A - follow signs), **Grove City** 16127

- ❏ Activity: Tours
- ❏ Telephone: (800) WAF-GIFT or (724) 458-8360
  www.wendellaugust.com
- ❏ Hours: Monday - Thursday, Saturday, 9:00 am - 6:00 pm., Friday, 9:00 am - 8:00 pm., Sunday, 11:00 am - 5:00 pm.
- ❏ Admission: Free
- ❏ Tours: Monday - Friday, 8:00 am - Noon, and 12:30 - 4:00 pm.

❑   Miscellaneous: Country's oldest and largest forge producing aluminum, pewter, sterling silver, and bronze items by hand. Old time Nickelodeon, W.A. Parrot (who talks and does impressions), LGB train (on a surrounding track up above) and a 225 gallon ocean reef tank. These keep the kids amused while adults gift shop.

A self-guided tour of the production workshop is fascinating to watch as metal is taken through an eleven step process. The gift metal is hammered over a pre-designed template with random hand, or machine operated hammer motions. At one point, you'll get a chance to pick up a hammer that is used - they weigh up to 3 pounds. You'll understand why a craftsman thought to automate the hammering process - tired, tired hands! Once the impression is set, the item is forged (put in a log fire) to produce smoke marks that bring out the detail of the design. The item is cooled and cleaned and finished by thinning the edges. Each piece is marked with a sign particular to the craftsman. This is a wonderful place to show children the balance between old world craft and new, automated craftsmanship.

AVENUE OF FLAGS

Hermitage - 2619 State Street (Hillcrest Memorial Park), 16148. *Activity: Pennsylvania History.* (724) 346-3818. *Hours:* Anytime. Free admission. Walk or drive the Avenue of Flags lined with 444 American flags - making it the world's largest display. One flag is for each day that 53 American hostages were held captive in Iran. Also see the monument, eternal flame, and American Freedom Museum (photographs & video).

PHILADELPHIA CANDIES

1546 East State Street (off SR18 North), **Hermitage** 16148

❑   Activity: Tours
❑   Telephone: (724) 981-6341, **www.philadelphia-candies.com**
❑   Hours: Daily, 9:00 am - 4:00 pm (lunch between 12 - 1:00 pm)

- ❏ Admission: Free
- ❏ Tours: Pre-arranged, 15-20 minutes around floor.

Have you ever tried chocolate covered potato chips? We have - and this is where we saw them being made! Here are some "fun" numbers for you: 30,000 square foot facility, 80 year old family business, 7000 pounds of chocolate are melted at one time, sugar comes in 50 pounds bags, and corn syrup is delivered in 55 gallon drums!

PYMATUNING DEER PARK
Route 58 (SR58, off US 322), Jamestown 16134

- ❏ Activity: Animals & Farms
- ❏ Telephone: (724) 932-3200
- ❏ Hours: Monday - Friday, 10:00 am - 5:00 pm., Saturday, Sunday, Holidays, 10:00 am - 6:00 pm (Summer). Weekends only in May.
- ❏ Admission: Adults $4.00, Seniors $3.50 (65+), Children $3.00
- ❏ Miscellaneous: Train and pony rides.

Petting zoo plus other animals like lions, tigers, bears, camels, and kangaroos (and farm animals).

PYMATUNING STATE PARK

Jamestown - Box 425, 16134. *Activity: Outdoors.* (724) 932-3141.**http://parec.com/state_parks/pymastpk.htm**. Flood control reservoir along the Ohio border. The largest body of water in the state. Wildlife Museum - state's largest colony of nesting eagles. Beach, Boat Rentals, Sledding, Campsites, Modern Cabins, Fishing, Trails.

KNOX, KANE, & KINZUA RAILROAD
South Forest Street (SR66), Marienville 16239

- ❏ Activity: Tours
- ❏ Telephone: (814) 927-6621
  www.parec.com/state_parks/kinzstpk.htm

- ❑ Hours: Daily, (May - October). Closed Mondays in July & August. Weekends only - Rest of year.
- ❑ Admission: Adults $20.00, Children $13.00 (3-12)
- ❑ Tours: 96 miles (8 hours) from Marienville. 33 miles from Kane (4 hours - reduced rates).
- ❑ Miscellaneous: Box lunches. Snack bar on train.

Cross over the Kinzua Bridge - the 2nd highest railroad viaduct in the United States (2053 feet long and 301 feet high). The rail line was originally used to carry coal, timber, and oil to market. Legend has it that there is a bank robber's treasure of gold hidden within sight of the viaduct!

CRAWFORD COUNTY MUSEUM

Meadville - 848 North Main Street (off French Creek Parkway), 16335. *Activity: Pennsylvania History.* (814) 724-6080, **http://ccfls.org/historical**. *Hours:* Wednesday - Sunday, 1:00 - 5:00 pm. (Summer). *Admission:* Adults $3.00, Children $1.50 (under 16). Baldwin-Reynolds Home - esp. nursery and toys, Native American artifacts, songbird carvings, Dr. Mosier's office with pharmacy, David Mead log cabin.

MERCER COUNTY MUSEUM COMPLEX

Mercer - 119 South Pitt Street (I-79 to I-80 west - exit 2 to SR19 north), 16137. *Activity: Pennsylvania History.* (800) 841-0824. *Hours:* Tuesday - Saturday, 1:00 - 4:30 pm. (Summers open at 10:00 am). Free admission. Maguffin House - Doctor's home, pioneer and Indian artifacts. Helen Black chapel. McClain print shop.

CORNPLANTER STATE FOREST

North Warren - 323 N. State Street, 16365. *Activity: Outdoors.* (814) 723-0262. **http://parec.com/forests/cornplnt.htm**. 1,256 acres named for Chief Cornplanter, a famous Indian Chief of the Seneca tribe. Highlights include Hunter Run Demonstration Area and Lasure Trail. Winter Sports, ATV Trails.

OIL CREEK STATE PARK

Oil City - R.D. 1, Box 207, 16301. *Activity: Outdoors.* (814) 676-5915. **http://parec.com/state_parks/oilcstpk.htm**. Petroleum Centre - displays and programs on oil history. Wildcat Hollow - outdoor classroom and 4 theme trails. Boat Rentals, Sledding, Fishing, Hiking Trails, Cross-Country Skiing.

VENANGO MUSEUM OF ART, SCIENCE, & INDUSTRY

Oil City - 270 Seneca Street, 16301. *Activity: Museums.* (814) 676-2007. **www.ibp.com/pit/venango**. *Hours:* Tuesday- Saturday, 10:00 am - 4:00 pm, Sunday, 1:00 - 4:00 pm. *Admission:* Adults $2.00, Children $0.75 (12 and under). Oil history exhibits. "Scientific" hands-on elementary physics.

OIL CREEK & TITUSVILLE RAILROAD

7 Elm Street & 409 South Perry Street (Route 8)
Oil City & Titusville 16301

❑   Activity: Tours
❑   Telephone: (814) 676-1733, **http://octrr.clarion.edu**
❑   Hours: Mid-June - October, Daily departures at 2:00 pm.,
     Wednesday - Sunday (Fall)
❑   Admission: Adults $10.00, Seniors $9.00, Children $6.00 (3-17)
❑   Tours: 2 1/2 hour narrated trip by guide and audio recording.
❑   Miscellaneous: Railroad memorabilia displays, souvenir area, and
     snack shop.

See the first oil fields in the world tell a story of the oil rush boom days in the valley (similar to the gold rush). Stop by Rynd Farm and Drake Well Park. Ride in restored 1930's passenger cars. One car is the only working railway Post Office car - have your postcard to grandma hand stamp cancelled as you watch.

BRUCKER GREAT BLUE HERON SANCTUARY

Reynolds - (SR18 - Thiel College), *Activity: Animals & Farms.*
(724) 589-2117. Free admission. 400 Blue Herons nest here - the
largest colony in Pennsylvania (over 200 nests). Most are over 4
feet tall with a 7 foot wingspan - and they can fly up to 35 MPH!
Nesting (March - May). Fly ins (June - August). Fall migrations.

MAURICE K. GODDARD STATE PARK

Sandy Lake - 684 Lake Wilhelm Road, 16145. *Activity: Outdoors.*
http://parec.com/state_parks/mkgdstpk.htm. (412) 253-4833.
Boat Rentals, Sledding, Fishing, Trails, Winter Sports.

QUAKER STEAK & LUBE

East State Street (Downtown - SR60 exit 1), **Sharon**

- ❑   Activity: Theme Restaurants
- ❑   Telephone: (724) 981-WING, **www.bestwingsusa.com**
- ❑   Hours: Lunch & Dinner
- ❑   Miscellaneous: Multiple locations including Pittsburgh (412)
      494-3344, Hermitage (724) 983-8646, Cranberry

Former Quaker State & Lube gas stations with fun classic cars
(some from famous movies) in front or <u>on top</u> of the stores!
Pickup trucks hang above as the roof over the drive through
windows. Best Wings, USA. Cute food item names like Bucket of
Bolts, O-Rings, Wrench Fries, Stick Shifters, French Dip Stick,
and Engine coolants (soft drinks).

<u>DAFFIN'S CANDIES</u>

496 East State Street (Factory - SR60), **Sharon** 16146

- ❑   Activity: Tours
- ❑   Telephone: (724) 342-2892, **www.daffins.com**
- ❑   Hours: Monday - Saturday, 9:00 am - 9:00 pm, Sunday, 11:00 am
      - 5:00 pm.
- ❑   Admission: Free

❑ Tours: Monday - Friday, 9:00 am - 3:00 pm (lunch Noon - 1:00 pm). By reservations. 10+ people. 45 minutes long.

❑ Miscellaneous: Tours in the fall and winter are best - more activity preparing for Christmas and Easter Holidays. The Chocolate Kingdom is available to view whenever the store is open.

Start in the Chocolate Kingdom. The display is filled with giant rabbits, elephants, turtles and castles made of chocolate. Click a picture or pick up free postcard pictures of these unique creatures. Each giant figurine can require up to 700 lbs. of chocolate! As the tour continues you'll learn how cocoa beans are removed from pods, mashed into paste, and finally processed into the chocolate forms we all know and love.

FOREST COUNTY MUSEUM

Tionesta - 206 Elm Street, 16353. *Activity: Pennsylvania History.* (814) 755-4422. *Hours:* Daily, 10:00 am - 4:00 pm (May - October). Housed in an 1875 pre-Victorian Eastlake style home. Artifacts from Native Americans and early settlers, trade tools. Products produced in the county.

DRAKE WELL MUSEUM

East Bloss Street (I-80 to exit 3, off SR8 North), **Titusville** 16354

❑ Activity: Museums

❑ Telephone: (814) 827-2797 **www.usachoice.net/drakewell**

❑ Hours: Monday - Saturday, 9:00 am - 5:00 pm., Sunday, Noon - 5:00 pm (May - October). Closed Mondays - Rest of Year.

❑ Admission: Adults $5.00, Children $2.00, Family Rate $10.00

❑ Miscellaneous: Head over to Pithole City (off SR227 between Pleasantville and Plummer) Visitor's Center. Summer only. Summer Sundays have living history performed by 6th graders.

The birthplace of the petroleum industry. Edward Drake drilled the first oil well in 1859 through layers of rock. Start your visit with a video of Drake's success, failures, and initial disbelief.

Because of Drake's and "Uncle Billy Smith's" ingenuity, others built wells nearby and put Drake's company out of business. The museum's indoor and outdoor exhibits explain the progress of the oil industry. Operating oil equipment and models demonstrate primitive and modern drilling processes. Many exhibits have "push buttons" and "cutaways" of the machinery in action (the kids will really like pushing the small button to make all the working parts move). Be sure to purchase a vial of real crude Pennsylvania oil in the gift shop as a souvenir. Play games to determine what products are petroleum based. Some will surprise you (ex. Tape, aspirin, eggs).

MOLLY'S MILL & CASEY'S CABOOSE STOP

Titusville - 221 South Monroe Street, 16354. *Activity: Theme Restaurants.* (814) 827-6597. *Hours:* Lunch & Dinner. A real restaurant featuring country style favorites like "choo-choo" chicken. Meals are served in an old grain mill. Stay the night in a real caboose on the grounds next to the working railroad.

WORLD OF MAZES

Townville - 16902 Mercer Road (Off Route 77), 16360. *Activity: Amusements.* (814) 967-3307. *Hours:* Tuesday - Sunday, 10:00 am - 10:00 pm. NW PA's only walk-thru maze. Rides. Golf. Games.

ALLEGHENY NATIONAL FOREST

Warren – P.O. Box 847, 222 Liberty Street, 16365. *Activity: Outdoors.* **http://parec.com/forests/alleghny.htm** (814) 723-5150.. 600 miles of trails. Hundreds of Mountain Laurel in June. 1/2 million acres of land. Twin Lakes and Loleta Recreation Areas. Black Cherry and Tracy Ridge trails. Longhouse Byway and Old Powerhouse. Rimrock Overlook, Jake's Rock, Buzzard Swamp and Owl's Nest.

BIG BEND VISITOR'S CENTER / KINZUA DAM

Warren - 1205 Kinzua Road - Route 59 (I-79 to Route 6 east to Route 59 east), 16365. *Activity: Outdoors.* (814) 726-0661. *Hours:* Daily, 10:00 am - 4:00 pm. (Summer). Weekends, 10:00 am - 4:00 pm (September, October). Free admission. A flood control dam has created a vast waterway known as the Allegheny Reservoir. Center features exhibits, displays, and slide programs which explain the purpose of the dam and power plant.

WARREN COUNTY MUSEUM

Warren - 210 4th Avenue, 16365. *Activity: Pennsylvania History.* (814) 723-1795. *Hours:* Monday - Friday, 8:30 am - 4:30 pm., Saturday, 9:00 am - Noon. *Admission:* General $1.00 (over 18). Second Empire-style home features several period exhibit rooms. Industries like lumber and oil. General store.

AREA "SC"

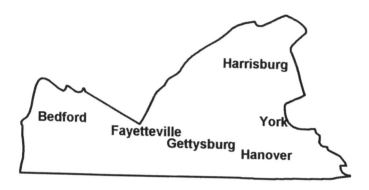

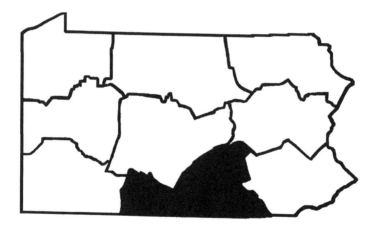

Our Favorites...

1) National Apple Museum
2) Gettysburg National Park
3) Lincoln Train Museum
4) National Civil War Wax Museum
5) Land of Little Horses
6) Snack Food Tours (Utz, Snyder's)
7) State Museum & Capitol
8) Hershey's Chocolate World & Park
9) Harley-Davidson Tour
10) Wolfgang Candy Company Tour

INDIAN STEPS MUSEUM

Airville - 205 Indian Steps Road (4 1/2 miles Northeast on
SR425), 17302. *Activity: Museums.* (717) 993-3392.
www.fieldtrip.com/pa/77553777.htm. *Hours:* Thursday, Friday,
10:00 am - 4:00 pm., Saturday, Sunday, Holidays, 10:00 am - 5:00
pm. (Mid-April - Mid-October). *Admission:* Donations. Nature
Center Arboretum. See Indian artifacts from 10,000 BC -
Susquehanna Indians through Colonial times that are imbedded in
rock. A 350 year old holly tree on the property has a unique story.
Each year a twig is broken off and presented to the Pennsylvania
Power and Light Company as payment for rent of the land behind
the museum.

FORT BEDFORD MUSEUM

Fort Bedford Drive (I-76, exit 11, SR320 - Pitt Street - Downtown),
Bedford 15522

❑ Activity: Pennsylvania History
❑ Telephone: (814) 623-8891 or (800) 259-4284
   www.bedfordcounty.net/attract/fort
❑ Hours: Daily, (except Tuesday in Summer) 10:00 am - 5:00 pm.
   (May - October)
❑ Admission: Adults $3.00, Seniors $2.50 (60+), Children $1.50
   (6-18), Family $7.00

The French and Indian War fort site - "The Fort in the Forest".
A blockhouse structure that houses the large scale model of
the original fort along with Native American household artifacts.
From flint rock rifles to hand tools to clothing – each help you
explore pioneer and frontier days in western Pennsylvania. The fort
controlled the river gap and served a British stockade against the
French for years.

OLD BEDFORD VILLAGE

220 Sawblade Road (1/2 mile south of PA Turnpike, exit 11- Route 220), **Bedford** 15522

- ❑ Activity: Pennsylvania History
- ❑ Telephone: (814) 623-1156 or (800) 238-4347
  www.bedford.net/village
- ❑ Hours: Daily (except Wednesday), 9:00 am - 5:00 pm. (1st Saturday in May - Last Sunday in October)
- ❑ Admission: Adults $6.95, Seniors $5.95 (60+), Children $2.00
- ❑ Tours: Self-guided. Guide tours are available with advance notice.
- ❑ Miscellaneous: Dress for walking on the natural roadways. Pendergrass Tavern. Village craft shop (items made in village).

Craftsmen are in action as you relive the past walking through 40 log homes and shops (see them making brooms, baskets, bread, pottery). There are seasonal productions such as "Welcome to Early America" - a recreated world of the 1790's Pioneer America. In 1794, President George Washington led federal troops with his battle headquarters here in Bedford. After the troops left, the colonial industry flourished with blacksmiths, attorneys, a doctor, distillers, innkeepers, soldiers, millers, and farmers setting up shop in the village.

NATIONAL APPLE MUSEUM

154 West Hanover Street (SR234 & SR394 - Look for big red barn), **Biglerville** 17307

- ❑ Activity: Museums
- ❑ Telephone: (717) 677-4556
- ❑ Hours: Weekends (May - October). Call for special group arrangement during other times.
- ❑ Admission: Adults $2.00, Seniors $1.75, Children $1.00 (6-12)
- ❑ Tours: Guided
- ❑ Miscellaneous: Picnic area. Gift shop - guess what…everything in there has apples on it! Antique equipment displays upstairs. The bug displays really appeal to the kids.

What a treat this place is! America's favorite fruit (red delicious, the most popular) is highlighted here. Kids can get involved right from the beginning (they eat a snack of apple juice and cookies). As you sip on your juice, they show a film about apple varieties, picking, and production (bet you didn't know the apple is part of the rose family!). This film is very entertaining (not boring at all) and the kids are thrilled seeing thousands of apples in every scene. Because many apple production facilities don't give tours, you'll get a great video look at how they "produce" apples for applesauce. They even clean them up just to go to your local market. Learn how lots of water and CA (controlled air - 29 degrees F. and only 2% oxygen) keep apples unbruised and ripe all year long. Do you know why orchards love bees, ladybug beetles, and dwarf trees?

CUMBERLAND COUNTY MUSEUM

Carlisle - 211 North Pitt Street, 17013. *Activity: Museums.* (717) 249-7610. *Hours:* Tuesday - Friday, 10:00 am - 4:00 pm., Saturday, 10:00 am - 1:00 pm. *Admission:* Donations. One of the oldest American printing presses, see early mechanical banks, Carlisle Indian school, and country products that are made here.

KINGS GAP STATE PARK

Carlisle - 500 Kings Gap Road, 17013. *Activity: Outdoors.* (717) 486-5031. **http://parec.com/state_parks/knggstpk.htm**. Year-round Education & Interpretation Center.

CALEDONIA STATE PARK

Fayetteville - 40 Rocky Mountain Rd (US Route 30), 17222. *Activity: Outdoors.* **http://parec.com/state_parks/caldstpk.htm**. (717) 352-2161. Pool, Visitor Center, Campsites, Modern Cabins, Fishing, Trails, Cross-Country Skiing.

MICHAUX STATE FOREST

Fayetteville -10099 Lincoln Way East, 17222. *Activity: Outdoors.* (717) 352-2211. **http://parec.com/forests/michaux.htm**. ATV Trails, (33 miles), Fishing, Camping, Trails, Winter Sports.

TOTEM POLE PLAYHOUSE

Fayetteville - 9555 Golf Road (PO Box 603) (Junction of US 30 & PA233), 17222. *Activity: The Arts.* (717) 352-2164, (June – August). **www.totempoleplayhouse.org**. *Admission:* Varies by performance, $18.00 - $27.00 (Children under 5 not admitted). Professional theatre featuring comedies and musicals.

COWAN'S GAP STATE PARK

Fort Loudon - 17224. *Activity: Outdoors.* (717) 485-3948. **http://parec.com/state_parks/cownstpk.htm**. Beach, Visitor Center, Boat Rentals, Campsites, Rustic Cabins. Buchanan's Birthplace State Historical Park nearby.

PINE GROVE FURNACE STATE PARK

Gardners - 1100 Pine Grove Road (PA Route 233), 17324. *Activity: Outdoors.* **http://parec.com/state_parks/pinestpk.htm**. (717) 486-7174. Beach, Visitor Center, Boat Rentals, Campsites, Kite-flying Area. Fishing, Trails, Cross-Country Skiing.

BATTLEFIELD BUS TOURS

Gettysburg - 778 Baltimore Street, 17325. *Activity: Tours.* (717) 334-6296, **http://gettysburgaddress.com/HTMLS/gtour.html**. *Hours:* Daily, 9:00 am - 9:00 pm. (Summer), Monday - Saturday, 9:00 am - 7:00 pm (Spring & Fall), 9:00 am - 5:00 pm (rest of year). *Admission:* Adults $5 - 6.00. Tours: 23 mile tour of "The Battle of Gettysburg". 2 hour narration audio tape by professional actors. Double decker bus - choose enclosed or panoramic open air seats. (Might be too long of a tour for pre-schoolers).

FARNSWORTH HOUSE INN

Gettysburg - 401 Baltimore Street, 17325. *Activity: Theme Restaurants.* (717) 334-8838. Lunch/Dinner - Moderate lunch prices, fine dining dinner. A historic building with 100 bullet holes from the battle. Gettysburg's only Civil War dining. Tours are available. We recommend a lunch (indoor/outdoor) because the menu at lunch is kid friendly and casual.

GETTYSBURG BATTLE THEATRE

571 Steinwehr Avenue, **Gettysburg** 17325

- ❑ Activity: Arts
- ❑ Telephone: (717) 334-6100
- ❑ Hours: Daily, 9:00 am - 9:00 pm (Summer), Daily, 9:00 am - 7:00 pm (April, May, September, October), 9:00 am - 5:00 pm (March, November)
- ❑ Admission: Adults $5.25, Children $3.25 (6-11)

B egin with a viewing of a movie featuring a multi-media battle re-enactment. To further visualize the battlement during the Civil War, take a close look at the electronic map.

GETTYSBURG NATIONAL MILITARY PARK

97 Taneytown Road (SR134 or Steinwehr Avenue)
Gettysburg 17325

- ❑ Activity: Pennsylvania History
- ❑ Telephone: (717) 334-1124, **www.nps.gov/gett**
- ❑ Hours: Daily, 8:00 am - 5:00 pm.
- ❑ Admission: Adults $2.50, Seniors $2.00 (61+), Children $1.00 (6 - 15)
- ❑ Tours: Park - Self guided tours, 6:00 am - 10:00 pm.
- ❑ Miscellaneous: Visitor Center - Free. Adults may want to take the shuttle bus out to the Eisenhower Historic Site Summer Home also (additional fee).

Here is the site of the major Civil War battle and Abraham Lincoln's Gettysburg Address:

- **BATTLEFIELD** - The most important major blow to the Confederate Army and the most casualties (51,000) on the first few days of early July 1863. See key places, Cemetery Hill and Ridge, Culp's Hill, Little Round Top, and Observation Tower. (We suggest the audio tape tour for kids under 8-10 years old).
- **NOVEMBER 19, 1863** - President Lincoln dedicated the National Cemetery on the battlefield and delivered famous speech "The Gettysburg Address".
- **CYCLORAMA** - A 30 minute description while standing in the middle of a 356 X 36 floor circular painting of the battlefield (a sight and sound experience). 9:00 am - 4:30 pm (every 1/2 hour)
- **ELECTRIC MAP** - A 30 minute show with highlights of strategic moves of battle. 8:15 am - 4:15 pm (every 45 minutes)
- **MUSEUM OF THE CIVIL WAR** - The largest collection of Civil War artifacts anywhere.

GETTYSBURG SCENIC RAIL TOURS

Gettysburg - 106 North Washington Street (Near Lincoln Square - Downtown), 17325. *Activity: Tours.* **www.gettysburgrail.com.** (717) 334-6932. *Admission:* Adults $10.00+, Seniors $9.00+, Children $6.00+. Tours: 16 and 50 mile trips - at least 90 minutes long. Theme trains that pass by the Gettysburg Battlefield and through the countryside.

HALL OF PRESIDENTS AND FIRST LADIES

789 Baltimore Street, **Gettysburg** 17325

- ❑ Activity: Museums
- ❑ Telephone: (717) 334-5717

- ❑ Hours: Daily, 9:00 am - 5:00 pm (also evening hours during April - August)
- ❑ Admission: Adults $5.25, Students $3.25 (6-11)
- ❑ Miscellaneous: Gift shops

W atch life-sized reproductions tell the "Story of America" through taped messages. First ladies appear in the type of gown they wore at the inauguration of their husbands. They've also added a heartwarming Eisenhower at Gettysburg exhibit. If your children are studying Presidential history, this is the best way to learn or re-learn important facts about each man.

JENNIE WADE HOUSE & OLDE TOWN

547 Baltimore Street (Adjacent to Olde Town),**Gettysburg** 17325

- ❑ Activity: Pennsylvania History
- ❑ Telephone: (717) 334-4100
- ❑ Hours: Daily, 9:00 am - 9:00 pm (Summer), Daily, 9:00 am - 5:00 pm (rest of year)
- ❑ Admission: Adults $5.75, Children $3.50 (6-11)
- ❑ Miscellaneous: Caution: Due to the dramatic nature and story of this tour - parents with children younger than 1st or 2nd grade should probably arrange to be part of a school tour. They only give brief descriptions of the events and not explicit details.

J ennie Wade was the only civilian killed during the battle of Gettysburg and the situations that led to her death were quite dramatic. While baking bread for the soldiers in her kitchen, a stray bullet hit and killed young 20 year old Jennie. (a realistic hologram of Jennie is seen in the kitchen - and you see the actual bullet hole). A soldier tells you all the details including the fact that her fiancé was killed just days later in battle, but never knew of Jennie's fate!

LAND OF LITTLE HORSES

125 Glenwood Drive (3 miles West on US30, then follow signs),
Gettysburg 17325

- ❑ Activity: Animals & Farms
- ❑ Telephone: (717) 334-7259, **www.landoflittlehorses.com**
- ❑ Hours: Monday - Saturday, 10:00 am - 5:00 pm., Sunday, Noon-
  5:00 pm. (Summers). Weekends Only (Spring & Fall)
- ❑ Admission: Adults $7.00, Children $5.00 (2 - 12)
- ❑ Miscellaneous: Air-conditioned arena. The Gift Horse Shop.
  Carousel, train tram, petting farm. Put on a "feed bag" at the
  Hobby Horse Café.

A s you enter, you'll be greeted by those adorable small horses
(most only a few feet tall) that seem to be just the right size
for kids to enjoy. Many are in separate pens throughout the park,
some are in the barn, others are getting ready for the show in the
arena. We took in the Barn Show first and loved the chance to see
the horses prance around and be gently petted. Especially cute are
the mothers with their young. The highlight of this farm is the
Performing Animals Show. They get the kids involved by "kissing
a pig" (there's a trick involved - 2 kids volunteered and did it!), or
helping with the "Horse With the Human Brain" Show. This horse
can really add, subtract, multiply, divide, and recognize currency
values of $1, 2, 5, 10 and 20.00 bills. See for yourself...it did over
10 problems with complete accuracy. They also have cart races,
saddle kids, and host the "Bacon Downs" pig races - so cute, pick
your favorite pig and cheer it on! A great attraction for children of
all ages.

LINCOLN ROOM MUSEUM

Gettysburg - Lincoln Square (US15 - Business Route and US30 -
Wills House), 17325. *Activity: Museums.* (717) 334-8188. *Hours:*
Daily, 9:00 am - 7:00 pm (Summer). Home of the friend Lincoln
stayed with in 1863 and where he completed his Gettysburg
Address. Original furnishings. He gave a brief speech from the
front door of this home the night before the cemetery dedication.

His words were brief because he feared that he might say something foolish!

LINCOLN TRAIN MUSEUM

425 Steinwehr Avenue, **Gettysburg** 17325

- ❑ Activity: Museums
- ❑ Telephone: (717) 334-5678
- ❑ Hours: Daily, 9:00 am - 9:00 pm (Summer), Daily, 9:00 am - 5:00 pm (Spring & Fall)
- ❑ Admission: Adults $5.25, Children $3.25 (6-11)
- ❑ Miscellaneous: Events (in the diorama display) that led up to this historic train ride. Large train collection layout that reproduces the Civil War Era.

A simulated 1836 train ride with Lincoln and statesmen on a 12 minute trip. See Civil War grounds and overhear conversations that might have occurred on that trip. They project actual footage of a steam train ride as your seat and floorboards move to the straights, curves, and rumbles of the track. Statesmen speak of this time, in the still present war, Mr. President's ill son, and thoughts of re-election. We suggest this stop for young kids (all ages for that matter) because it easily and uniquely illustrates the emotion/history behind the Gettysburg Address.

NATIONAL CIVIL WAR WAX MUSEUM

297 Steinwehr Avenue (US15-Business Route), **Gettysburg** 17325

- ❑ Activity: Museums
- ❑ Telephone: (717) 334-6245
  www.gettysburggiftcenter.com/wax.htm
- ❑ Hours: Daily, 9:00 am - 9:00 pm (Summer), Daily, 9:00 am - 7:00 pm (mid-April - mid-June), Daily, 9:00 am - 5:00 pm (September - December, March - Mid-April), Weekends Only (Winter)
- ❑ Admission: Adults $4.50, Students $2.50 (13-17), Children $1.75 (6-12)

More than 200 life-size wax figures in 30 different scenes re-create crucial moments but also describe the cause and effects of the conflict. The last scene is of an animated wax figure of Lincoln making his speech the night before his famous address. At the end of the tour, you'll enter the Battleroom Auditorium where the battle is re-enacted (with wax figures and lighting). It's the easiest explanation of those three days (not too technical for kids). Lincoln arrives and gives his address at the end.

NATIONAL GETTYSBURG BATTLEFIELD TOWER

999 Baltimore Pike (1/2 mile south on US97 or SR134)
Gettysburg 17325

❑   Activity: Pennsylvania History
❑   Telephone: (717) 334-6754, **www.gettysburgtower.com**
❑   Hours: Daily, 9:00 am - 6:30 pm (Summer), Daily, 9:00 am - 5:00 pm (Spring/Fall), Weekends only, 10:00 am - 4:00 pm (November)
❑   Admission: Adults $5.00, Seniors $4.50 (62+), Children $3.00 (6-12)
❑   Miscellaneous: Gift shop. Picnic area.

See the historic battlefield from the 307 foot tower complete with a sights and sounds program (don't worry, you can choose to view from open or enclosed decks). High speed elevators take you to a 360 degree view - you might want to use their high powered telescopes for more detail and really "scope things out".

SOLDIER'S NATIONAL MUSEUM

777 Baltimore Street, **Gettysburg** 17325

❑   Activity: Museums
❑   Telephone: (717) 334-4890
❑   Hours: Daily, 9:00 am - 9:00 pm (Summer), 9:00 am - 7:00 pm (Spring), 9:00 am - 5:00 pm (Fall)
❑   Admission: Adults $5.25, Children $3.25 (6-11)

10 dioramas depict battles of the Civil War. There's also a life-sized, narrated confederate encampment. The building was once General Howard's headquarters and later the Soldier's National Orphanage.

THE CONFLICT

Gettysburg - 213 Steinwehr Avenue, 17325. *Activity: Arts.* (800) 847-0911 or (717) 334-8003, *Hours:* Daily, 9:00 am - 9:00 pm (Summer), Monday - Saturday, 10:00 am - 7:00 pm (Spring & Fall). **www.gettysburgaddress.com/HTMLS/cteatro.html.** *Admission:* Adults $5-6.00, Seniors $4-5.00, Children $4-5.00 (6-12). Theatre features "Adventure at Gettysburg" which explains the battle to ages 8-14. "Mr. Lincoln Returns to Gettysburg" is a live one man performance that traces Abraham Lincoln's life from boyhood to presidency with emphasis on Gettysburg (only performed summers at 8:00 pm, Monday - Friday and various times on weekends).

LAKE TOBIAS WILDLIFE PARK

760 Tobias Drive, **Halifax** 17032

- ❑ Activity: Animals & Farms
- ❑ Telephone: (717) 362-9126
- ❑ Hours: Monday - Friday, 10:00 am - 6:00 pm., Saturday, Sunday, 11:00 am -7:00 pm (Summer), Weekends only, (May, September, October)
- ❑ Admission: Adults $1-4.00 per activity, Children $1-3.00 per activity (2-12)

Hundreds of wild and exotic animals - alligators, buffalo, llamas, monkeys and reptile animal shows. Safari tours of 200 acre park, petting zoo and fishing ponds.

CODORUS STATE PARK

Hanover - 1066 Blooming Grove Road (PA Route 216), 17331. *Activity: Outdoors.* **http://parec.com/state_parks/codostpk.htm.** (717) 637-2816. Pool, Visitor Center, Boat Rentals, Horseback Riding, Sledding, Campsites, Fishing, Trails, Winter Sports.

HANOVER SHOE FARMS

Hanover - Route 194 South, 17331. *Activity: Animals & Farms.* (717) 637-8931. *Hours:* Monday - Saturday, 8:00 am - 3:30 pm. Free Admission. One of the largest Standard bred horse breeders in the world. 1800 horses roam the 4000 acre grounds - many horses are record-breaking pacers and trotters. The self-guided brochure tour lets your family wander at you leisure.

UTZ POTATO CHIPS

900 High Street (SR94 North and Clearview Streets)
Hanover 17331

- ❑   Activity: Tours
- ❑   Telephone: (717) 637-6644, **www.utzsnacks.com**
- ❑   Hours: Monday - Thursday, 8:00 am - 4:00 pm
- ❑   Admission: Free
- ❑   Tours: Self-guided. (20 minutes)
- ❑   Miscellaneous: Outlet store just down the road. Lots of sampling and buying goes on there.

Walk along an elevated, glass enclosed observation gallery to observe potato chips in production. View close up TV monitors and listen to the descriptions of each step of the process. This is a modern and very clean facility. We probably got the closest to large conveyors of fried chips here (behind glass of course!). A new experience was watching home-cooked kettle chips being made. A lounge with family history photographs and a free bags of chips for everyone is available. We especially liked the "platform bridges" that they had throughout the tour so the "little ones" could see too!

SNYDERS OF HANOVER

1350 York Street, **Hanover** 17731

❑   Activity: Tours

❑   Telephone: (717) 632-4477 or (800) 233-7125
    www.snyders-han.com

❑   Admission: Free

❑   Tours: Tuesday, Wednesday, Thursday at 10:00, 11:00 am &
    1:00 pm. (24 hour notice is needed - approximately 35 minutes)

M eet at the factory storefront (where you'll no doubt be nibbling on samples before touring). It's no wonder that Pennsylvania is the "snack food" capital of the US. Watch a short video covering the company history starting with potato chips made at home in the early 1920's to the 1970's when they established sourdough hard pretzels. The differences you'll notice on this snack food tour are the numerous and extra large baking ovens and highly automated packaging systems. Machines build boxes while another machine fills the bags and yet another machine boxes the bags and then seals the cases shut. Kids love all the automation!

RIVERBOAT "PRIDE OF THE SUSQUEHANNA"

Harrisburg - (Docked at City Island). *Activity: Tours.* (717) 234-6500. *Hours:* Tuesday - Sunday, Noon - 3:00 pm. (May - October). *Admission:* Adults $4.95, Children $3.00 (3-12). Wednesday has reduced fares. *Tours:* Indoor and outdoor seating. 40 minute narrated cruise leaves on the hour. Pass under 6 bridges and by the grave of the city's founder, John Harrison on an authentic paddlewheel boat.

ART ASSOCIATION OF HARRISBURG

Harrisburg - 21 North Front Street, 17101. *Activity: The Arts.* (717) 236-1432. **www.visithhc.com/artassn.html**. Regional and national art. Art classes.

STATE CAPITOL BUILDING

Third & State Streets, **Harrisburg** 17101

- ❑ Activity: Pennsylvania History
- ❑ Telephone: (800) TOUR-N-PA, **www.pasen.gov**
- ❑ Hours: Monday - Friday, 8:30 am - 4:30 pm., Saturday & Sunday, 9:00 am - 4:00 pm
- ❑ Admission: Free
- ❑ Tours: Guided - every 1/2 hour to 1 hour (except lunch - Noon-1:00 pm)
- ❑ Miscellaneous: Stop at the Information Center first for a brochure on the self-guided tour.

The 272-foot dome will stun everyone as you stand underneath it and look up. Your neck could get sore because you'll be staring a good while. As you pass though bronze and ornately carved wooden doors, you can climb the stairs to the second and fourth floors to view the elegant and handsome Senate and House chambers. The favorite (and most educational) area is the Welcome Center. From the Ben Franklin video in miniature, to Hello History (take a telephone call from famous Pennsylvania leaders and athletes) to the glass window case full of colored balls (representing the number of bills that a state legislator considers in a year - there's a lot!). Other exhibits that encourage learning about laws (for kids and adults) are interactive displays of a "Day in Life of a Legislator (try to get your birthday as a holiday), voting (actually sit in a voting desk) and the making of a law (presented through a colorful display - like the game "Mousetrap" full of tracks, pulleys, and chains that follow a funny course). What a wonderful way to teach government!

CITY ISLAND

Harrisburg - Walnut & Market Street Bridges (Susquehanna River), 17104. *Activity: Outdoors. Hours:* Dawn – Dusk. Enjoy 63 acres of parkland developed as a recreational center. Current facilities include Riverside Stadium, Skyline Sports Complex, Harbourtown, Riverpool, Riverboat, Harbour Ferries, marinas,

Riverside Village Park, Walnut Station train depot with steam driven mini-train, water golf, beach house, trading post, historic carriage house, stables, concessions, trails, and picnic areas. What a treat for locals and a nice appeal to visitors!

STATE MUSEUM OF PENNSYLVANIA

3rd & North Streets - PO Box 1026 (Downtown),**Harrisburg** 17108

❑ Activity: Pennsylvania History
❑ Telephone: (717) 787-4978, **www.statemuseumpa.org**
❑ Hours: Tuesday - Saturday, 9:00 am - 5:00 pm., Sunday Noon-
5:00 pm. (Closed holidays except Memorial Day and Labor Day)
❑ Admission: Free
❑ Miscellaneous: Planetarium (additional charge) shows. Gift shop
- we bought some neat Dinosaur DNA dust (cherry or grape
flavor) to commemorate our Dino Lab experience.

The Official Museum of the Commonwealth features 4 floors of historical exhibits: Geology, Archeology (pretend to dig like the professionals), Military (Gettysburg, etc.), Industry, The Arts, Technology. Our favorite was the Dino Lab - a real paleontology lab tech at work carving skeleton from a fossil rock. It is a fascinating experience that you'll never get to see elsewhere - and you can even ask questions while they work! The original charter granted to William Penn by King Charles II in 1861 is also on display. CURIOSITY CORNER - It's Interactive Computer and dress up. Kids will want to check out activities that correspond to the displays in the museum. There is a small charge per child for this area.

HARRISBURG HEAT SOCCER

Harrisburg - Cameron Street & Maclay Street (PA State Farm Show Arena), 17110. *Activity: Sports.* (717) 652-HEAT. (May - September). Admission $7 - $12.00. National Pro Soccer League.

HARRISBURG HORIZON BASKETBALL

Harrisburg - Union Center @ Penn State, 17111. *Activity: Sports.* (717) 986-0499. *Admission:* $4-$8.00. Eastern Basketball Alliance.

HARRISBURG SENATORS BASEBALL

Harrisburg (City Island) - P.O. Box 15757, 17105. *Activity: Sports.* (717) 231-4444. **www.senatorsbaseball.com**. *Admission:* $3-$8.00. AA Class affiliate of the Montreal Expos.

HERSHEY BEARS HOCKEY

Hershey - 100 West Hershey Park Drive (Hershey Arena), 17033. *Activity: Sports.* (717) 534-3911. **www.hersheybears.com**. *Admission:* $10-$16.00. AHL, Colorado Avalanche affiliate.

HERSHEY GARDENS

Hershey - 170 Hotel Road, 17033. *Activity: Outdoors.* (717) 534-3493. **http://mgfx.com/butterfly/hershey**. Daily, 9:00 am - 5:00 pm. (Mid-April - October). *Admission:* Adults $5.00, Children $2.50 (ages 3-15).

HERSHEY MUSEUM

Hershey - 170 West Hersheypark Drive (next to arena), 17033. *Activity: Museums.* (717) 534-3439 or (800) HERSHEY, **www.hersheys.com**. *Hours:* Daily, 9:00 am - 5:00 pm (Summer), 10:00 am - 5:00 pm (Winter). *Admission:* $2.50 - $5.00. The Children's area has a Hands-on Discovery Room - life in the 1800's. Learn how Mr. Hershey failed as a candy maker in Philadelphia and New York but became a millionaire manufacturing caramels in Lancaster, PA. He sold that business to start a chocolate factory in his birthplace farmland. See how it developed as Hershey, PA. Also exhibits on Pennsylvania German and Native American clothing, tools, art.

HERSHEY THEATRE

Hershey - 15 East Caracas Avenue, 17033. *Activity: The Arts.* (717) 534-3405. **www.hersheytheatre.com**. Broadway shows and concerts.

HERSHEY TROLLEY WORKS

Hershey - (Departs at entrance to Hershey's Chocolate World), 17033. *Activity: Tours.* (717) 533-3000. **www.hersheys.com**. *Hours:* Rain or Shine. Same hours as the park. Last tour is 1 hour before closing. *Admission:* Adults $6.75, Children $5.00 (3-12).Family adventure through America's sweetest town. Old time songs and visits throughout from famous "characters".

HERSHEY WILDCATS SOCCER

Hershey - (Hershey Park Stadium), 17033. *Activity: Sports.* (717) 534-3911. **www.hersheywildcats.com**. (May - September). *Admission:* $5 - $10.00. A - League Soccer.

HERSHEY'S CHOCOLATE WORLD
VISITORS CENTER

800 Park Blvd, **Hershey** 17033

- ❑ Activity: Tours
- ❑ Telephone: (717) 534-4900 or (800) HERSHEY
  www.hersheys.com
- ❑ Hours: Daily, 9:00 am - 5:00 pm (every day except Christmas). - Extended hours for special events.
- ❑ Admission: Free
- ❑ Miscellaneous: Free sample. 8 unique gift shops. Food court. Chocolate Town Café.

Pseudo factory tour of an automated tram into the simulated world of chocolate production! Start at the cocoa bean plantation (rainforests and tropic) to dairy farms to making chocolate through the years at Hershey. Actual video footage of a real factory and the wonderful scent of chocolate pervades. It even gets warmer as you pass through the "roaster oven" part of the ride. Souvenir photographs are taken of the passengers in each car (you can purchase them for $10.00) at the end of the tour. Learn why different chocolate manufacturers have different flavors (the secret is where the cocoa beans came from).

HERSHEYPARK

100 W. Hersheypark Drive (Off SR 743 & US 422), **Hershey** 17033

- ❑ Activity: Amusements
- ❑ Telephone: (800) HERSHEY OR (717) 534-3090 **www.800hershey.com**
- ❑ Hours: Daily, opens at 10:30 am (June - August). Weekends only, (May, September)
- ❑ Admission: Range $16-$30.00. (Ages 3+)

110 acre theme park with 50 rides and attractions including:

- • Great Bear - inverted looping roller coaster
- • German Area, English Area, Penn Dutch Area
- • Whitewater rapids - Tidal Force, 21 kiddie rides and live entertainment at Music Box Theater.

INDIAN ECHO CAVERNS

Box 745 (Off I-283 and US 322 at Hummelstown / Middletown Exits), **Hershey** 17033

- ❑ Activity: Outdoors
- ❑ Telephone: (717) 566-8131 **www.indianechocaverns.com**
- ❑ Hours: Daily 9:00 am - 6:00 pm (Summer). 10:00 am - 4:00 pm (Spring/Fall). Call for times (Winter)
- ❑ Admission: $4.00 - $8.00
- ❑ Tours: 45 minutes, guided
- ❑ Miscellaneous: Gift shop - Southwestern, Rocks. Pan for gems at Gem Mill Junction. Wagon ride to the Petting Barnyard. Playground with Indian Teepee and Conestoga Wagon.
  - • <u>RAINBOW ROOM</u> - "Mystery Box".

- WILSON ROOM - Story of William Wilson who lived in the caverns for 19 years - "Pennsylvania Hermit".
- INDIAN BALLROOM - largest.
- DIAMOND FAIRYLAND - Wedding room (lots of white)
- 3 lakes and variety of stalactites, stalagmites, flowstone.

ZOO AMERICA NORTH AMERICAN WILDLIFE PARK

Hershey - Park Avenue (opposite Hershey Park), 17033. *Activity: Animals & Farms.* **www.800hershey.com/attractions/zooamerica** (717) 534-3860. *Hours:* 10:00 am - 5:00 pm. (Open until 8:00 pm in the summer). *Admission:* Adults $5.25, Seniors $4.75, Children $4.00 (3-12). An eleven acre North American attraction that hosts wildlife from 5 regions (200+ species). "Desert of Night" area is unique and wonderful. "Visit" with creatures of the night like owls, snakes and bats.

BLUE KNOB STATE PARK

Imler - R.R. 1, Box 449, 16655. *Activity: Outdoors.* (814) 276-3576. **http://parec.com/state_parks/blukstpk.htm**. Pool, Horseback Riding, Down-hill Skiing, Campsites, Fishing, Winter Sports.

GIFFORD PINCHOT STATE PARK

Lewisberry - 2200 Rosstown Road (Route 177), 17339. *Activity: Outdoors.* **http://parec.com/state_parks/gifpstpk.htm.** (717) 432-5011. Beach, Visitor Center, Boat Rentals, Horseback Riding, Sledding, Campsites, Modern Cabins, Fishing, Trails, Cross-Country Skiing.

SKI ROUNDTOP

Lewisberry - 925 Roundtop Road, 17339. *Activity: Outdoors.* **www.skiroundtop.com**. (717) 432-9631. Snow Report: (717) 432-7000, Longest Run: 4100 ft.; 15 Slopes & Trails.

BUCHANAN STATE FOREST

McConnellsburg – R.R. 2, Box 3, 17233. *Activity: Outdoors.* (717) 485-3148. **http://parec.com/forests/buchanan.htm**. ATV Trails, (26 miles), Fishing, Camping, Trails, Winter Sports.

WHITETAIL SKI RESORT AND MOUNTAIN BIKING CENTER

Mercersburg - 13805 Blairs Valley Road, 17236. *Activity: Outdoors.* (717) 328-9400. **www.skiwhitetail.com**. Longest Run: 4900 ft.; 17 Slopes & Trails.

MIDDLETOWN AND HUMMELSTOWN RAILROAD

136 Brown Street (SR283 to Middletown exit - Race Street Station), **Middletown** 17057

- ❑ Activity: Tours
- ❑ Telephone: (717) 944-4435
- ❑ Hours: Memorial Day Weekends - Labor Day Weekends. July & August - Tuesday and Thursday also.
- ❑ Admission: Adults $7-15.00, Children $3.50-7.50 (3-11)
- ❑ Tours: Departs at 11:00 am, 1:00, 2:30, & 4:00 pm
- ❑ Miscellaneous: Special event trains (see seasonal chapter). More expensive tours include Indian Echo Cavern stop. Reservations suggested.

The yard has several rail cars on display. Cross the Swatara Creek Bridge, Horse Thief Cave, and sections of the Union Canal. Enjoy live entertainment (sing alongs) on board. Can you still "Chicken Dance"?

LITTLE BUFFALO STATE PARK

Newport - R.D. 2, Box 256A (PA Route 34), 17074. *Activity: Outdoors.* **http://parec.com/state_parks/ltbfstpk.htm.** (717) 567-9255, Pool, Visitor Center, Year-round Education & Interpretation Center, Boat Rentals, Sledding, Historic Grist Mill, Fishing, Trails.

COLONEL DENNING STATE PARK

Newville - 1599 Doubling Gap Road (PA Route 233), 17241. *Activity: Outdoors.* **http://parec.com/state_parks/coldstpk.htm.** (717) 776-5272, Beach, Visitor Center, Campsites, Fishing, Trails, Cross-Country Skiing.

SHAWNEE STATE PARK

Schellsburg - Box 67 (US Route 30), 15559. *Activity: Outdoors.* (814) 733-4218. **http://parec.com/state_parks/shawstpk.htm** Beach, Boat Rentals, Mountain Biking, Sledding, Campsites, Modern Cabins, Fishing, Trails, Winter Sports.

HISTORIC STEWARTSTOWN RAILROAD

Stewartstown - Pennsylvania Avenue, 17363. *Activity: Tours.* (717) 993-2936. *Hours:* Sundays, (May - early Fall). Call for current schedules. *Admission:* Adults $7.00, Children $4.00 (3-11). Vintage equipment travels through rural scenic areas.

YORK COUNTY COLONIAL COURTHOUSE

York - 205 West Market Street, 17401. *Activity: Pennsylvania History.* (717) 846-1977. *Hours:* Monday - Saturday, 10:00 am - 4:00 pm., Sunday, 1:00 - 4:00 pm. *Admission:* Very small. View authentic documents from '77 and '78 revolutionary history, personalities, and education. Reconstruction of the courthouse in which the Continental Congress voted to adopt the Articles of Confederation. Sound and light show.

HARLEY-DAVIDSON MOTORCYCLE MUSEUM TOUR

1425 Eden Road (off US30 or Exit 9 East of I-83), **York** 17402

- ❑ Activity: Museums
- ❑ Telephone: (717) 848-1177 Ext. 2900, **www.harleydavidson.com**
- ❑ Admission: Free

❑   Tours: Monday - Friday, 9:30 am., 10:30 am., 12:30 pm., 1:30
     pm. (Plant tour is for ages 12+, however there are no age
     restrictions on the museum tour)
❑   Miscellaneous: Tours are wheelchair accessible. Souvenir Shop.

What little traveler hasn't seen (*or better yet - heard*) a
Harley-Davidson motorcycle pass by? Founded in 1903,
Harley-Davidson has become a passion of the American
dream...selling over 150,000 cycles per year with most customers
waiting nearly 2 years for their bike to be delivered once it is
ordered. See over 20 vintage and famous Harleys (Malcolm
Forbes' custom bike) on the museum tour that is available for all
ages. You will see photographs and videos of the 24 step
manufacturing process that produces a completed motorcycle
every 6 minutes! They are so confident in their quality and
reliability that the first time an engine is started (*it contains over
400 parts!*) is when the bike is completely finished. An associate
takes a few spins around the 1 mile long test track (what a great
job!) to be sure that it meets all the standards and expectations of
the waiting customer. The plant tour allows visitors, first hand, to
experience all the automation (and hand crafting) that makes a
Harley so special. What does a doctor, a lawyer, machine
operator, actor, business owner, and pastor all have in common...a
Harley-Davidson motorcycle!

YORK SYMPHONY ORCHESTRA

York - 50 North George Street, 17402. *Activity: The Arts.* (717)
852-0550 / (717) 854-4587 tickets. Classic as well as Summer
Pops in July.

AGRICULTURAL & INDUSTRIAL MUSEUM
OF YORK CITY

480 East Market Street / 217 West Princess Street (US30 to
George Street exit), **York** 17403

❑   Activity: Museums
❑   Telephone: (717) 852-7007

www.fieldtrip.com/pa/78527007.htm
- ❏ Hours: Tuesday, Thursday, Saturday, 10:00 am - 4:00 pm.
- ❏ Admission: Adults $3.00, Children $2.00 (4-12). Combination tickets available.

A lot of products produced here have clothed, sheltered, transported, fed, and entertained the nation. Learn how the modern day farm evolved from the time of Native Americans. Then, go a few streets away to explore the numerous products made in York. Begin in an old gristmill (still working - you'll see), pull a factory whistle (time to go home!) or use an old rotary phone to dial up a friend next door (watch the mechanics of the operation station tapping out the numbers). The Pfaltzgraff pottery exhibit is well done with several stages of pottery being made (sometimes a potter comes in for live demonstrations). Since the Pfaltzgraff tour has age restrictions and is rather long, you may vote this exhibit more family friendly than an actual tour. Don't forget about CAT trucks (get in the cab) and York Peppermint Patties!

YORK COUNTY MUSEUM

York - 250 East Market Street, 17403. *Activity: Pennsylvania History.* (717) 848-1587. *Hours:* Monday - Saturday, 9:00 am - 5:00 pm., Sunday, 1:00 - 4:00 pm. *Admission:* Around $2.00. A reproduction of original York village square with Bonham House (beautiful home), General Gates House, and Bobb Log House.

WOLFGANG CANDY COMPANY

50 East 4th Avenue (SR30 to North George Street - south to Fourth Avenue), **York** 17405

- ❏ Activity: Tours
- ❏ Telephone: (717) 843-5536 or (800) 248-4273
  www.wolfgangcandy.com
- ❏ Hours: Monday - Friday, 8:00 am - 4:30 pm., Saturday, 9:00 am - 4:00 pm.
- ❏ Admission: Free

- ❑ Tours: Monday - Friday, 10:00 am (Summer) - 1/2 hour long. By appointment only (rest of year)
- ❑ Miscellaneous: Candy shoppe and soda fountain. (Das Sweeten Haus Center). Relax on an antique stool (and watch the girls make hand dipped raisin clusters) as you enjoy a dish of Wolfgang's ice cream and sip a coffee or hot chocolate.

When you enter the Bavarian style shop to wait for your tour, you undoubtedly first glance at the antique truck parked in the middle of the main floor. This was the original delivery truck used to sell chocolate candies door to door back in the 1920's. It is also the truck that helps "Candy Dan" in his flying video tour of the factory. If you choose not to go on the tour at all, this video is a great "birdseye view" of a tour but with a children's twist. The actual facility started in the back of the Wolfgang house and grew and grew. You'll pass retired family members' homes as you adorn a white hair net and walk up to the factory. Their corn starch machine is still used and original to the factory. Smell and taste samples as you go. The guide kept kid's attention by pointing out lessons they learn in school. The girls and guys on the line must pick partners and pay attention (sound like school?). We recommend Fall through Easter as the best time to see candy and fillings actually made on the line (it's easier to understand the tour during full production). Summertime has minimal production.

TUSCARORA STATE FOREST

Blain - R.D. 1, Box 42-A, 17006. *Activity: Outdoors.* (717) 536-3191. **http://parec.com/forests/tuscar.htm**. Horse Trails, Fishing, Camping, Trails, Winter Sports.

AREA "SE"

Our Favorites...

1) **Weavertown One Room Schoolhouse**
2) **National Watch & Clock Museum**
3) **Mercer Museum**
4) **Amish Homes & Farms**
5) **Snack Tours (Pretzels, Chocolate, Herr's)**
6) **Franklin Institute**
7) **Independence Park**
8) **Roadside America**
9) **QVC Broadcast Studios Tour**
10) **American Helicopter Museum**

MILL GROVE, THE AUDUBON WILDLIFE SANCTUARY

Audubon - Audubon & Pawlings Roads, 19407. *Activity: Museums.* **www.fieldtrip.com/pa/06665593.htm.** (610) 666-5593. *Hours:* Tuesday -Saturday, 10:00 am - 4:00 pm, Sunday, 1:00 - 4:00 pm. Free Admission. Early 1800's home of noted artist, author and nature lover, John James Audubon. The house displays Audubon's paintings of birds and a complete set of his greatest work, "The Birds of America". Kids seem to admire the stuffed bird collection and birds' eggs. Grounds with nature trails and bird sanctuary are open dawn to dusk.

NESHAMINY STATE PARK

Bensalem - 3401 State Road (State Road and Dunks Ferry Road), 19020. **http://parec.com/state_parks/neshstpk.htm.** *Activity: Outdoors.* (215) 639-4538. Pool, Fishing, Boating, Hiking, Cross-Country Skiing.

BLUE MARSH SKI AREA

Bernville - Route 183 & Robesonia Road, 19506. *Activity: Outdoors.* (610) 488-6399. Snow report: (610) 488-6396. Longest Run: 3500 ft.; 11 Slopes & Trails.

ABE'S BUGGY RIDES

Bird-In-Hand - 2596 Old Philadelphia Pike (Route 340), 17505. *Activity: Tours.* **www.800padutch.com/abes.html** (717) 392-1794. *Hours:* Daily, (except Sundays), 8:00 am – dusk. *Admission:* Adults $10.00, Children $5.00 (3-12). *Tours:* 20 minutes. Take a 2 mile tour in a Amish family carriage.

PLAIN & FANCY FARM

3121 Old Philadelphia Pike (7 miles east on SR340)
Bird-In-Hand 17505

❑   Activity: Tours

❑   Telephone: (717) 768-4400 or (800) 441-3505

   www.millers-plainandfancy.com

❑   Hours: (April - October) Monday - Saturday, 8:30 am - 5:00 pm,
   Sunday, 10:30 am - 6:00 pm. (Extended summer hours)   Monday
   - Sunday, 10:00 am - 5:00 pm (November - March)

❑   Admission: Adults $5.00+, Seniors $3.25+, Children $3.25+
   (Depending on Activity)

❑   Miscellaneous: Plain & Fancy Restaurant - all you can eat home
   style meals.

Here's what you can do (choose one or a combo):

- "THE AMISH EXPERIENCE" - Only one of three
  "experimental" F/X theatres in North America - they use
  actual props, 5 projectors, 3D imagery, dramatic stage
  lighting and "surround sound" to tell a story. The story is
  of an Amish family and their teenage son who is in a
  "runabout time" - trying to decide which world he wants to
  embrace. (85% of Amish teens stay within the church
  even after experiencing the outside world). It tells a great
  Amish story (past and present) and is very dramatic -
  probably best for ages 8 and older.
- AMISH COUNTRY TOURS – Air-conditioned farmland
  tours of Amish countryside that focus on stories of work
  and family ethics.
- AARON & JESSICA'S BUGGY RIDES - 3 mile buggy
  ride tour of Amish farmlands. Sleigh rides too (winter)!

WEAVERTOWN ONE ROOM SCHOOLHOUSE
SR340 (between Bird-In-Hand and Intercourse)
Bird-In-Hand 17505

- ❑ Activity: Museums
- ❑ Telephone: (717) 768-3976,
  www.800padutch.com/wvrtown.html
- ❑ Daily, 10:00 am - 5:00 pm (Good Friday - October)., Weekends (March & November)
- ❑ Admission: Adults $2.75, Seniors $2.25, Children $1.75 (5-11).
- ❑ Tours: 15 minute presentation

See the full-sized animated teacher and class having a typical school day in this authentic Amish schoolhouse. The bell, desk, and blackboard are original and the school building was used for nearly 100 years until it closed in 1969. The teacher asks questions and the children answer. We learned that kids brought potatoes from home that were baked on the cast iron heater (the only source of heat in back of the room) all morning until lunch. Kids also brought lunch boxes. Extra desks are left open so visitors can sit among Amish students after the presentations for great photo and video opportunities. Note: Visitors to Lancaster County aren't normally permitted to enter one-room schoolhouses while actual classes are in session. This is your only opportunity to get a glimpse of this unique school room.

DANIEL BOONE HOMESTEAD
400 Daniel Boone Road (off US422-1 mile north), **Birdsboro** 19508

- ❑ Activity: Museums
- ❑ Telephone: (610) 582-4900, **www.berksweb.com/boone.html**
- ❑ Hours: Tuesday - Saturday, 9:00 am - 5:00 pm., Sunday, Noon - 5:00 pm., Closed non-Summer holidays.
- ❑ Admission: Adults $4.00, Seniors $3.50 (59+), Children $2.00 (6-12), Family $10.00

Born here in 1734, the birthplace interprets colonial Pennsylvania rural life of Daniel Boone. A restored 10 room Boone homestead (originally a log cabin), a similar cabin, sawmill, smokehouse, spring kitchen, blacksmith, and barn are on site. Be sure to watch the video presentation (re-enacted) to get a sense of the Boone family's life here and out-of-state.

BOYERTOWN MUSEUM OF HISTORIC VEHICLES

28 Warwick Street (SR73 and 562 - South to Warwick)
Boyertown 19512

❑   Activity: Museums
❑   Telephone: (610) 367-2090
     www.berkscounty.com/museum/Boyertow.htm
❑   Hours: Daily, 9:30 am - 4:00 pm (except Monday).
❑   Admission: Adults $4.00, Seniors $3.50 (60+), Children $2.00
     (6-18)

See Pennsylvania's transportation heritage - carriages, wagons, trucks, bicycles, cars, electrics (like the "Ecostar"). Also on display are 18th and 19th century vehicles built by Pennsylvania Dutch craftsmen and the tools that were used to assemble them.

TERRY HILL WATERPARK

Breinigsville - 10000 Hamilton Road (SR222), 18031. *Activity: Amusements.* (610) 395-0222. **www.terryhill.com.** *Hours:* Daily, Noon - 6:00 pm (June), Monday - Friday, Noon - 7:00 pm, Weekends until 8:00 pm (July & August). *Admission:* $10.00 - $15.00. A family waterpark with nine different water slides, three pools, and kiddie waterplay area. Snack bars.

BRANDYWINE BATTLEFIELD PARK

Box 202 (US1, 1 mile east of SR100), **Chadds Ford** 19317

❑   Activity: Pennsylvania History
❑   Telephone: (610) 459-3342, **www.ushistory.org/brandywine**

- ❑ Hours: Tuesday - Saturday, 9:00 am - 5:00 pm., Sunday, Noon - 5:00 pm
- ❑ Admission: Free (except building - $1.50 - $3.50 / person)
- ❑ Tours: Maps for self-guided tour at Visitor's Center
- ❑ Miscellaneous: Museum shop. Plenty of picnic areas. Battle re-enactment every September.

Giant park and museum focused on actual Revolutionary War events. Watch the audiovisual introduction to the park first, then drive along a tour that includes 28 historic points taking you back to 1777. Remember, this defeat of American forces (led by George Washington) left the Philadelphia area open to attack and conquest by the British.

BRANDYWINE RIVER MUSEUM

Chadds Ford - US 1, 19317. *Activity: The Arts.* (610) 388-2700. **www.brandywinemuseum.org.** *Hours:* Daily, 9:30 am - 4:30 pm. *Admission:* Adults $5.00, Seniors, Students with I.D. and Children ages 6-12, $2.50. American art in a 19th century gristmill. Known for collections by three generations of Wyeths.

BYERS' CHOICE LTD

Chalfont - 4335 County Line Road (Just north of Rt. 309 & Rt. 202). 18914. *Activity: Tours.* **www.byerschoice.com.** (215) 822-6700. *Hours:* Monday - Friday, 10:00 am - 4:00 pm (Closed in January). Family and friends (employees) hand sculpt precious Caroler figurines. By a walk-through observation deck, you can watch them mold delicate faces and then apply makeup (paint) to add dimension and features. See all the costumes and background landscapes available to make each singing doll unique. What you don't see in production that day, you can watch by pre-taped video.

EVANSBURG STATE PARK

Collegeville - 851 May Hall Road (off US Route 422), 19426. *Activity: Outdoors.* **http://parec.com/state_parks/evanstpk.htm.** (610) 409-1150. Visitors and Historical Centers, Horseback Riding, Fishing, Hiking, Cross-Country Skiing.

NATIONAL WATCH & CLOCK MUSEUM

514 Popular Street (off US30 - follow signs), **Columbia** 17512

- ❑ Activity: Museums
- ❑ Telephone: (717) 684-8261, **www.nawcc.org**
- ❑ Hours: Tuesday - Saturday, 9:00 am - 4:00 pm (year round). Sunday, 1:00 - 4:00 pm (May - September)
- ❑ Admission: Adults $3.00, Seniors $2.50 (59+), Children $1.00 (6-17)
- ❑ Miscellaneous:"Yours, Mine, and Hours" Museum Shop. Library.

You've got the time, they've got the place! The National Association of Watch and Clock Collectors have a school (of horology), offices, and this fabulously renovated museum. One staff member described it as the "Disneyland of Clocks and Time". Start at the beginning, Stonehedge, then travel through time as you browse past displays of time-keeping history. You'll see thousands of watches (many still working), unique water and candle clocks, sundials and even an alarm clock that pinches you when it rings! Bells, chimes, music boxes, and organs sound on the hour.

WRIGHT'S FERRY MANSION

38 South 2nd Street (US30 - Columbia/Marietta Exit SR 441 South), **Columbia** 17512

- ❑ Activity: Museums
- ❑ Telephone: (717) 684-4325
- ❑ Hours: Tuesday & Wednesday, Friday & Saturday, 10:00 am - 3 pm., Closed July 4. (May- October)

❑   Admission: Adults $5.00, Children $2.50 (6-18). Group discounts
     available (Call for reservations - 30 days in advance and children
     must be ages 8+)

D iscover the fascinating and visionary life of Susanna Wright,
     a bright, creative Quaker woman whose diverse talents have
benefited many. Among some, she ran a ferry here, was an
unofficial doctor and lawyer, launched the silk industry in this
region, and shared ideas with people like Ben Franklin with whom
she corresponded regularly. The 1738 house reflects Quaker
lifestyles prior to 1750 and its collections are one of the most
complete and representative in the country. Because this is an
"open" museum (no velvet ropes separating you from the displays)
you certainly get the feeling that the occupants have just left for a
little while...and may be returning shortly! We recommend close
supervision for younger children, or better yet only bring them if
your children are age 8 or older.

CORNWALL IRON FURNACE

Rexmont Road - P.O. Box 251 (4 miles North of US76 off SR 72 on
SR419), **Cornwall** 17016

❑   Activity: Museums
❑   Telephone: (717) 272-9711
     www.state.pa.us/PA_Exec/Historical_Museum/BHSM/toh/cor
     nwall/cornwalliron.htm
❑   Hours: Tuesday - Saturday, 9:00 am - 5:00 pm., Sunday, Noon -
     5:00 pm. (Closed most holidays, except Summer holidays)
❑   Admission: Adults $3.50, Seniors $3.00 (60+), Children $1.50
     (6-12), Family Rate $8.50

A 1742 - 1833 iron making complex. The preserved facility
     once produced farm tools, kitchenware, stoves, cannons and
ammunition. You can see the original furnace stack, blast
machinery, blowing tubs, and a Great Wheel (76 feet around).
Remember this site was water powered. An ironmaster's mansion
and the Charcoal House Visitor's Center are on the premises.

KEYSTONE STATE PARK

Derry - R.D. 2, Box 101, 15627. *Activity: Outdoors.* (412) 668-2939. **http://parec.com/state_parks/kyststpk.htm.** Beach, Visitor Center, Year-round Education & Interpretation Center, Boat Rentals, Horseback Riding, Sledding, Campsites, Modern Cabins, Fishing, Trails, Winter Sports.

MARSH CREEK STATE PARK

Downington - 675 Park Road, 19335. *Activity: Outdoors.* (610) 458-5119. **http://parec.com/state_parks/mrshstpk.htm.** Pool, Boat Rentals, Sledding, Wind Surfing, Fishing, Trails.

HENRY SCHMIEDER ARBORETUM

Doylestown - 700 East Butler Avenue (Route 202) (Delaware Valley College), 18901. *Activity: Outdoors.* (215) 489-2244. 60 acres with arboretum, plants, museums. Admission for guided tours (by appointment only). Self-guided are free.

MERCER MUSEUM
84 South Pine Street (off SR202, near SR313 and SR611)
Doylestown 18901

❑   Activity: Museums
❑   Telephone: (215) 345-0210
      www.libertynet.org/bchs/MMuseum.htm
❑   Hours: Monday - Saturday, 10:00 am - 5:00 pm., Sunday, Noon - 5:00 pm. (open until 9:00 pm on Tuesdays)
❑   Admission: Adults $5.00, Seniors $4.50 (65+), Children $1.50 (6+)
❑   Miscellaneous: Museum Shop.

The receptionist promised us that the best past of the self-guided tour was the walk into the Center Court. It's amazing! Artifacts are hanging everywhere! While searching through junk in a barn, Henry Chapman Mercer found a jumble of objects made obsolete by the Industrial Revolution. His collection, housed in a "cement castle", represents more than 60 crafts and trades - pre

1850. Called "The Tools of the Nation Maker", play a game to try to find one tool from at least 50 trades. Some are easy to see, but over 40,000 pieces of "junk" are in every nook and cranny. This is the most eccentric, yet curiously fun, museum you'll ever find! By the way, the cement and leaded glass windows truly give that medieval feeling inside and out.

MORAVIAN POTTERY AND TILE WORKS & FONTHILL

130 Swamp Road (SR313), **Doylestown** 18901

❑   Activity: Tours
❑   Telephone: (215) 345-6722
     www.libertynet.org/bchs/TileWork.htm
❑   Hours: Daily, 10:00 am - 4:45 pm
❑   Admission: Adults $3.00, Seniors $2.50 (65+), Children $1.50 (6+)
❑   Tours: Self-guided - every 1/2 hour. Last tour at 4:00 pm
❑   Miscellaneous: Tile Shop.

This facility, beginning in 1912, produced tiles and mosaics for floors, walls and ceilings. Mercer's artistic floor tiles adorn the rotunda and halls of the Pennsylvania State Capitol, depicting 400 scenes in the Commonwealth's history. Today, the facility makes reproductions of Mercer's original line of tiles. Watch the clay being prepared, then stamped with designs, then fired, glazed and fired again. Kids will appreciate "Fonthill" (Mercer's mansion/castle that is next door - www.libertynet.org/bchs/Fonthill .htm) or the Mercer Museum a little more if they understand what made him rich and famous. His mosaics are probably the prettiest to look at.

FRENCH CREEK STATE PARK

Elverson - 843 Park Road, 19520. *Activity: Outdoors.* (610) 582-9680. **http://parec.com/state_parks/fcrkstpk.htm**. Pool, Boat Rentals, Horseback Riding, Mountain Biking, Campsites, Modern Cabins, Fishing, Trails, Cross-Country Skiing.

HOPEWELL FURNACE NATIONAL HISTORIC SITE

2 Mark Bird Lane (SR345), **Elverson** 19520

❑   Activity: Museums
❑   Telephone: (610) 582-8773
   www.parec.com/natnl_parks/hopenapk.htm
❑   Hours: Daily, 9:00 am - 5:00 pm. Closed most holidays.
❑   Admission: Adults $4.00 (over 17), Family $10.00
❑   Tours: Self-guided enhanced by recorded voices of workers and
   their families.
❑   Miscellaneous: Younger children would prefer summers when
   living history actors are in costume throughout the village. Older
   kids really get into the stories told on the tour.

The Visitor's Center features an audio visual program and
exhibits of the original iron castings and tools used in
Colonial cold blast charcoal furnaces. See a restored cast house,
water wheel cooling shed, tenant houses and ironmaster's mansion
(The Big House). Learn about "pig iron" (formed in troughs), and
stoves and weapons produced here - recreated by actual
blacksmiths shaping the hot slabs of iron alongside molders. This
is mostly a living history village (summers and special events) and
the "villagers" are well educated on iron casting. Call ahead to be
sure you get to see live demonstrations during your visit.

EPHRATA AREA COMMUNITY THEATRE

Ephrata - 124 East Main Street (I-76 Exit 21, Route. 222 South),
17522. *Activity: The Arts.* (717) 738-2ACT. Mornings, June –
August. "The Ephrata Story".

CHILDVENTURE MUSEUM

Fort Washington - 430 Virginia Drive (Ft. Washington office
complex), 19034. *Activity: Museums.* (215) 643-3233,
www.fieldtrip.com/pa/56433233.htm. *Hours:* Tuesday -Saturday,
10:00 am - 4:00 pm., Sunday, Noon - 4:00 pm. *Admission:* General
$4.00 (age 18 months & up). Targeted for kids 10 and under, this

hands-on playground has indoor climbing structures, mini furniture to play dress up, a Family Talk Theater, music room (international) and a play pretend Main Street.

FORT WASHINGTON STATE PARK

Fort Washington - 500 Bethlehem Pike (2 miles from PA Turnpike exit 26), 19034. *Activity: Outdoors.* (215) 646-2942. **http://parec.com/state_parks/fwasstpk.htm**. Hawks, Washington Encampment, Fishing, Trails, Winter Sports.

NEWLIN GRIST MILL PARK

Glen Mills - US 1 & Cheyney Road, 19342. *Activity: Outdoors.* (610) 459-2359. *Hours:* 8:00 am - 5:00 pm, (March - September). *Admission:* small. A 1704 restored gristmill, the miller's house, a blacksmith shop, springhouse, and log cabin are in the park. Call first to inquire about upcoming Summer Discovery Programs or Heritage Workshops. These programs explore traditional colonial skills, crafts, and games. Have you taken a "dip" lately (dipping candles in wax that is!)?4

SPRINGTON MANOR FARM

Glenmoore – R.D. #2, Box 455K (off US322 - Springton Road), 19343. *Activity: Animals & Farms.* (610) 942-2450. **www.fieldtrip.com/pa/09422450.htm**. *Hours:* Daily, 10:00 am - 4:00 pm. Free admission. Petting zoo. Picnic areas. Visit a casual demonstration farm once used to raise sheep (they're still plenty there). The giant Great Barn has an agricultural exhibit that follows the development of farm equipment from the late 1700's to the early 1900's. A catch and release pond lets kids fish for bass and blue gills.

MEMORIAL LAKE STATE PARK

Grantville - R.D. 1, Box 7045, 17028. *Activity: Outdoors.* (717) 865-6470. **http://parec.com/state_parks/memlstpk.htm**. Boat Rentals, Fishing, Cross-Country Skiing.

INTERCOURSE PRETZEL FACTORY

3614 Old Philadelphia Pike (at Cross Keys),**Intercourse** 17534

- ❑   Activity: Tours
- ❑   Telephone: (717) 768-3432
- ❑   Hours: Monday - Saturday, 9:00 am - 6:00 pm
- ❑   Admission: Free
- ❑   Tours: Tuesday - Saturday, 9:00 am - 6:00 pm
- ❑   Miscellaneous: Snack Bar

How do you like your pretzels? Soft, stuffed, or hard? Plan on visiting this factory for lunch/dessert treat. As you watch all the pretzels being made by hand and learn to twist your own pretzel...try to decide which flavors you're going to try now and which you'll take home. Their stuffed pretzels are wrapped around cheeses, meats, relishes, and jams. Soft and hard pretzels come in a variety of seasoning (doesn't brown butter topping sound warm and cozy?) and their chocolate covered varieties are smothered in Wilbur's (our favorite Pennsylvania chocolate) chocolate. Do you see why we suggest to save "tummy room" for snacking?

PEOPLE'S PLACE

3515 Old Philadelphia Pike (SR340),**Intercourse** 17534

- ❑   Activity: Museums
- ❑   Telephone: (717) 768-7171
- ❑   Hours: Daily, (except Sundays), 9:30 am - 8:00 pm (Summer), until 5:00 pm (rest of year)
- ❑   Admission: Adults $4.00 per activity, Children $2.00 (5-11) per activity

Educational center about Amish/Mennonites. "Who Are the Amish?" - a three screen documentary (30 minutes, especially delightful for kids that can sit still), slide show with music and narration. Younger, fidgety kids will prefer the pace of the "20Q" - imaginative museums with the "Feeling Box", the Barn Raising Book, the Energy Guy, and the Dress Up Room (getting dressed for school), puzzles, & an Alphabet Game (look thru view finder).

HAWK MOUNTAIN

1700 Hawk Mountain Road (I-78, exit 9B north to Route 895 east),
Kempton 19529

- ❑ Activity: Animals & Farms
- ❑ Telephone: (610) 756-6000, **www.hawkmountain.org**
- ❑ Hours: Daily, 9:00 am - 5:00 pm., 8:00 am - 5:00 pm (September - November)
- ❑ Admission: Adults $4-6.00, Seniors $3-4.00, Children $2-3.00 (6-12)

B etween mid-August and mid-December an average 18,000 hawks, eagles, and falcons fly past this site. Bookstore. Wildlife viewing windows. Exhibits. Trails. Live-raptor programs on weekends (May - November).

W.K. & S. STEAM RAILROAD

Kempton - P.O. Box 24 (SR143 or SR737 into Kempton. - follow signs), 19529. *Activity:* *Tours.* (610) 756-6469, **www.fieldtrip.com/pa/07566469.htm**. *Hours:* Sundays (May - October), Saturdays also, (July, August, October). *Admission:* Adults $4.00, Children $2.00 (2-11). Gift shop. Snack bar. Nice short ride (40 minutes) where you can get off at picnic groves throughout the countryside and get back on later.

LONGWOOD GARDENS

Route 1, P.O. Box 501, **Kennett Square** 19348

- ❑ Activity: Outdoors
- ❑ Telephone: (610) 388-1000, **www.longwoodgardens.com**
- ❑ Hours: Daily, 9:00 am - 5:00 pm (open later during peak Spring & Summer seasons)
- ❑ Admission: Adults $12.00 ($8.00 on Tuesdays), Youths $6.00 (ages 16-20), Children $2.00 (ages 6-15), Under age 6 FREE

Special children's programs like Peter Rabbit and Friends, Christmas and Mazes. 1,050 acres with 40 indoor/outdoor gardens. Conservatory and rainbow fountains. Terrace Restaurant. Special too are the water platters, Topiary garden and Idea Garden.

MIDDLE CREEK WILDLIFE MANAGEMENT AREA

Kleinfeltersville - Hopeland Road- P.O. Box 110, 17039. *Activity: Outdoors.* (717) 733-1512. **www.dep.state.pa.us/dep/deputate/enved/mcreek.htm.** *Hours:* Tuesday - Saturday, 8:00 am - 4:00 pm, Sunday, Noon - 5:00 pm (March - November). Free admission. Approximately 6300 acre habitat for migrating waterfowls and wildlife includes Visitor Center and Nature Trails.

CRYSTAL CAVE

Kutztown - Crystal Cave Road (Off US 222. Follow signs), 19530. *Activity: Outdoors.* **www.crystalcavepa.com.** (610) 683-6765, *Hours:* Daily, 9:00 am - 5:00 pm. (March - November) Summer, to 6:00 pm. Weekends to 7:00 pm. *Admission:* $5.00 - $8.00. *Tours:* 45 minutes. Food. Gift shop. Rock shop. Mini-golf. Museum and nature trails.

KUTZTOWN RAILROAD (EAST PENN RAIL EXCURSIONS)

Kutztown - Train Depot on Railroad Street (off Main Street - US222), 19530. *Activity: Tours.* (610) 683-9202. *Hours:* Weekends & Holidays (June - August). *Admission:* Adults $8.00, Seniors $7.00 (65+), Children $4.00 (2-12). *Tours:* At Noon & 2:00 pm - 1 hour. Gift shop. Snack bar. Ride in authentic open window coaches built in 1932 through a quaint Mennonite town.

RODALE INSTITUTE EXPERIMENTAL

611 Siegfriedale Road (off US222, just northeast of town)
Kutztown 19530

❑   Activity: Animals & Farms
❑   Telephone: (610) 683-1400, **www.rodaleinstitute.org**

- ❑ Hours: Monday - Saturday, 9:00 am - 5:00 pm, Sunday, 10:00 am - 3:00 pm (early May - mid-October)
- ❑ Admission: Adults $3-6.00, Children $1.50 - 3.00 (age 5+)
- ❑ Tours: Monday - Friday, 11:00 am (By appointment)
- ❑ Miscellaneous: International Café features organic light fare and beverages. Gift shop - suggest you try homemade organic apple sauce or butter.

R egenerative Organic Farming and Gardening - Do you know what that means? If you've eaten one too many frozen or fast food meals this week - start feeling healthier here! Learn the connection between healthy soil, healthy food, and healthy people, all through demonstrations and children's gardens. Themes include "From Seeds to Supper", "The Sun and the Rain" and "The Apple Trees". At the end of a specialized tour, kids get to pot (in little pots) a seed to grow organically when they get home (using the principles they've learned).

DUTCH APPLE DINNER THEATRE

Lancaster - 510 Centerville Road, 17601. *Activity: The Arts.* (717) 898-1900. **www.dutchapple.com**. Children's matinee and Sunday twilight. Dine while watching Broadway musicals.

HANDS-ON HOUSE CHILDREN'S MUSEUM

2380 Kissel Hill Road, **Lancaster** 17601

- ❑ Activity: Museums
- ❑ Telephone: (717) 569-KIDS
  http://www.800padutch.com/handson.html
- ❑ Hours: Tuesday - Saturday, Open 10 or 11:00 am 'til 4 or 5:00 pm , Saturday, 10:00 am - 5:00 pm, Sunday, Noon - 5:00 pm.
- ❑ Admission: Adults $4.00, Children $4.00
- ❑ Recommended for ages 2-10. Everything is simply explained to allow parents and kids' imagination to explore possibilities

Favorite "spaces" include:

- <u>WHAT CHA-MA-GIGGLE COMPANY</u> - put on safety goggles to work on an assembly line or sort and deliver mail at a kid-friendly factory.
- <u>SPACE VOYAGE CHECKPOINT</u> - take a spaceship ride to learn about health and wellness as earthlings get a checkup before their journey into space. Foods good for space. Environment mission control. Feelings - talk to a giant stuffed bear.
- <u>FACE TO FACE</u> - Face paintings while learning about expressions.
- <u>ONCE UPON A FOREST</u> - Storybook forest with animals pretend play and forest sounds and communication.

LANDIS VALLEY MUSEUM

2451 Kissil Hill Road (3 miles north on Oregon Pike - SR272), **Lancaster** 17601

- ❑ Activity: Pennsylvania History
- ❑ Telephone: (717) 569-0401 **www.landisvalleymuseum.org**
- ❑ Hours: Monday - Saturday, 9:00 am - 5:00 pm., Sunday, Noon - 5:00 pm. (March - December)
- ❑ Admission: Adults $7.00, Seniors $6.50 (60+), Children $5.00 (5-17), Family, $19.00
- ❑ Miscellaneous: Weathervane gift shop.

The largest Pennsylvania German museum in the U.S. (100 acres). See 20 buildings including the craft shop, schoolhouse, country store, leather crafts, farmstead, blacksmith, transportation building, hotel, pottery shop plus others. Exhibits interpret rural life prior to 1900 through artisans and demonstrations of traditional skills. Don't forget about the traditional walkways of dirt, pebble or brick.

AMISH FARM AND HOUSE

2395 Route 30 East, **Lancaster** 17602

- ❑ Activity: Tours
- ❑ Telephone: (717) 394-6185, **www.amishfarmandhouse.com**
- ❑ Hours: Daily, 8:30 am - 6:00 pm (Summer). 8:30 am - 5:00 pm (Spring & Fall), 8:30 am - 4:00 pm (Mid-November - Mid-March)
- ❑ Admission: Adults $5.75, Seniors $5.50 (60+), Children $3.25 (5-11)
- ❑ Tours: 35 minutes
- ❑ Miscellaneous: Dutch Food Pavilion (April - October). Weekend craft demonstrations (branch carvings for example)

Guided tours of Amish home (10 rooms) - learn the history, religious customs and a simple way of life. Self-guided tour of a working farm with local crops, barns, and farm animals. Most interesting is a unique Lancaster County device - a water wheel powered pump (smaller pump in meadow) operates a larger pump via wire. In the Spring House, a large water wheel powers a pump which forces cold spring water into a kitchen refrigerator. A limestone quarry on the property supplied stone to build this barn and house.

ANDERSON BAKERY COMPANY

2060 Old Philadelphia Pike (Route 340 East off US 30 Bypass), **Lancaster** 17602

- ❑ Activity: Tours
- ❑ Telephone: (717) 299-2321, **www.andersonpretzel.com**
- ❑ Hours: Monday - Friday, 8:30 am - 4:00 pm. Closed holidays and Good Friday.
- ❑ Admission: Free
- ❑ Miscellaneous: Factory Store and Soft Pretzel Shop. Free Samples.

Self-guided tour where you can see the whole pretzel baking process including the twisting machine that gives Dutch pretzels their unique shape. It also chronicles the history of Anderson family as you walk along. Can you guess what the "Baldies" or "Peanut Butter Gems" taste like? The best view is of the numerous conveyors transporting unbaked and baked pretzels by the thousands.

DISCOVER LANCASTER COUNTY HISTORY MUSEUM

2249 Route 30 East, **Lancaster** 17602

- ❑ Activity: Museums
- ❑ Telephone: (717) 393-3679
   www.800padutch.com/museum.html
- ❑ Hours: Daily, 9:00 am - 8:00 pm (Summer), 9:00 am - 6:00 pm (Spring & Fall), 9:00 am - 5:00 pm (Winter)
- ❑ Admission: Adults $5.95, Seniors $5.50 (60+), Children $3.50 (5-11)
- ❑ Miscellaneous: Gift shop.

See 32 life-like (some with audiovisuals) scenes of historic events in Pennsylvania from the 1600's to the present. Example: Indian Treaty, Ephrata Cloister, "Penn's Woods" and early settlers. Watch a 10 minute animatronics of an Amish Barn Raising - actually it takes one day in real life - a major accomplishment until you learn about their consistent, organized teamwork. Recently updated, the museum is now equipped with seven interactive areas relating to the scenes you see. For example, cut a log and see how old the tree was or look through a mirror to see yourself grown up (just like Daniel Boone).

DUTCH WONDERLAND FAMILY AMUSEMENT PARK

2249 Route 30 East, **Lancaster** 17602

- ❑ Activity: Amusements
- ❑ Telephone: (717) 291-1888, **www.dutchwonderland.com**
- ❑ Hours: Daily, 10:00 am - 7:00 pm (Memorial Day - Labor Day), Weekends only, 10:00 am - 6:00 pm (Spring & Fall)
- ❑ Admission: Range $15 -$20.00. (ages 3+)

48 acres with 25 rides, high diving shows, and botanical gardens. Rides include: Roller Coaster, Giant Slide, Double Splash Flume, Flying Trapeze, Space Shuttle, Lady Riverboat rides, Mini-Train rides, Sky ride.

HEBREW TABERNACLE REPRODUCTION / MENNONITE INFORMATION CENTER

2209 Millstream Road (Off US30), **Lancaster** 17602

- ❑ Activity: Tours
- ❑ Telephone: (717) 299-0954, **www.mennoniteinfoctr.com**
- ❑ Hours: Monday - Saturday, 8:00 am - 5:00 pm
- ❑ Admission: Free
- ❑ Tours: Guided, hourly. Adults $4.00, Seniors $3.50 (64+), Children $2.25 (7-12)
- ❑ Miscellaneous: Gift shop featuring crafts from biblical times & craft kits to recreate tabernacle.

Film and displays explaining the faith and culture of Amish and Mennonites called "Postcards From a Heritage of Faith". Shown every half hour. Included is a reproduction of a Hebrew Tabernacle with lecture tours given on the history, construction, function, and significance on the hour (every 2 hours in the Winter). Most kids leave with an understanding of the Arc of the Covenant and can answer as to why the 66 lumps in the candleholder were prophecy of the future.

LANCASTER COUNTY MUSEUM

Lancaster - Penn Square – Downtown, 17603. *Activity: Pennsylvania History.* (717) 299-6440. *Hours:* Tuesday - Saturday, 10:00 am - 5:00 pm (April - December). Free admission. Heritage focuses upon Lancaster County furniture, silver, folk art, paintings, and toys. Children's activity area (summers and weekends).

NORTH MUSEUM OF NATURAL HISTORY AND SCIENCE

Lancaster - 400 College Avenue (Franklin Marshall College), 17603. *Activity: Museums.* **www.fandm.edu/NorthMuseum**. (717) 291-3941, Wednesday - Sunday, 1:30 - 4:30 pm. (Late June - August). Weekends only (rest of the year). *Admission:* General $2.00. Natural history displays. Child's Discovery Room. Planetarium shows Saturday afternoon.

WHEATLAND

1120 Marietta Avenue - SR23, **Lancaster** 17603

- ❑ Activity: Pennsylvania History
- ❑ Telephone: (717) 392-8721, **www.wheatland.org**
- ❑ Hours: Daily, 10:00 am - 4:15 pm (April - November)
- ❑ Admission: Adults $5.50, Seniors $4.50, Students $3.50, Children $1.75 (6-11)
- ❑ Tours: Costume guides for general or pre-arranged hands-on tours.
- ❑ Miscellaneous: Gift shop. Snack bar.

The Federal Style mansion was home to the nation's 15th President (and the only President from Pennsylvania), James Buchanan. Tours begin in the carriage hours where you view a film about Mr. Buchanan and see the actual carriage his family used to travel around town. Also see the library that served as a headquarters for his Presidential campaign. Kids are invited to dress in top hats or hoop skirts and may be asked questions like, "How often did people take baths in the mid-1800's?" Guess? (Answer - An average of 2 times per year!) His response to inquiries about "Wheatland" was..."I am now residing at this place, which is an agreeable country residence...I hope you may not fail to come this way...I should be delighted with a visit..."

AMERICAN MUSIC THEATRE

Lancaster - 2425 Lincoln Highway East (US 30), 17605. *Activity: The Arts.* **www.800padutch.com/amt.html.** (800) 648-4102 or (717) 397-7700. Spring – Fall. American Sights. American sounds. American Songs. American spirit. Musicals.

WHITE CLAY CREEK STATE PARK

Landenberg - P.O. Box 172 (off Route 896), 19350. *Activity: Outdoors.* **http://parec.com/state_parks/whtcstpk.htm.** (610) 255-5415. Horseback Riding, Fishing, Trails.

SESAME PLACE

100 Sesame Road (I-95 to US 1 north to Oxford Valley exit. Next to Oxford Valley Mall), **Langhorne** 19047

- ❏ Activity: Amusements
- ❏ Telephone: (215) 752-7070, **www.sesameplace.com**
- ❏ Hours: Daily, 9:00 am - 8:00 pm (mid May - Labor Day Weekend), Weekends, (September & October) - Call for current schedule.
- ❏ Admission: $25-28.00
- ❏ Miscellaneous: Late afternoon and family discounts. Bathing suits required for water attractions.

While your kids continue to peek over their shoulders for a glimpse of a Sesame Street character like Big Bird (great photograph opportunities), they'll be pulling your hand in every direction so they won't miss anything. Catch a show like "Rock Around the Block", then jump on Ernie's Bed Bounce (that even sounds like fun to adults, doesn't it?) or scale "Cookie Mountain". A roller coaster (the only mechanical ride in the park) called "Vapor Trail" has also been added. There's also 14 refreshing water attractions. As you float , zoom or chute through Big Bird,

Ernie's and Slimey's Rides, you'll be splashed or trickled by a giant rubber ducky. Toddlers can be water trickled in Teany Tiny Tidal Waves. Bet your kids just can't wait to walk down a full-sized replica of Sesame Street and take pictures to show their friends back home!

STURGIS PRETZEL

219 East Main Street (Route 772 - off Route 501), **Lititz** 17543

- ❑ Activity: Tours
- ❑ Telephone: (717) 626-4354, **www.sturgispretzel.com**
- ❑ Hours: Monday - Saturday, 9:00 am - 5:00 pm
- ❑ Admission: General $2.00 (A pretzel is given as your admission ticket. Be careful not to eat it all before the tour starts!)
- ❑ Tours: Every half hour
- ❑ Miscellaneous: Gift shop with all sorts of fresh baked pretzels (flavorings, galore!) to purchase.

B oy, did the memories flow at this place! Over 20 years ago my family (*Michele's*) took the same tour, in the same building and I still have my "Official Pretzel Twister" certificate. *(By the way, they still do that - our daughter now has one too!).* This is the first pretzel bakery in America (1861) and they still make their original soft pretzel by hand in the original 200 year old ovens. Julius Sturgis started the pretzel industry with a recipe he learned from a hobo. Learn the history of the "pretiolla" derived from monk's gifts to nearby children if they said their prayers. As you learn to fold your own pretzel, you'll learn how each step is related to prayer or marriage or the trinity. Definite must see while in Amish country.

WILBUR CHOCOLATE

48 North Broad Street - (Route 501), **Lititz** 17543

- ❑ Activity: Tours
- ❑ Telephone: (717) 626-3249, **www.800padutch.com/wilbur.html**
- ❑ Hours: Monday - Saturday, 10:00 am - 5:00 pm
- ❑ Admission: Free

❑   Miscellaneous: Gift shop - suggest chocolate pretzels or Wilbur
     Buds (free sample).

Candy Americana Museum - antique metal molds, tin boxes,
advertisements. View Video – "The World Of Wilbur
Chocolate" - see smooth chocolate made from the start. Pass by
the Candy Kitchen where specialty candy is hand made right
before your eyes. Pick up a "lucky" cocoa bean as you walk in
(don't eat it though!). Everyone walks out with a bag full of store
bought variety chocolates. P.S. for a walk back in time, try their
hot cocoa mix that you prepare over a stove - it's worth shoveling
snow to enter the warm house full of an aroma of rich liquid
chocolate.

RIDLEY CREEK STATE PARK

Media - Sycamore Mills Road, 19063. *Activity: Outdoors.* (610)
892-3900.**http://parec.com/state_parks/ridlstpk.htm**. Horseback
Riding, 18th Century Working Farm, Fishing, Trails, Winter
Sports.

SOCIETY FOR PERFORMING ARTS OF THE MEDIA THEATRE

Media - 321 West State Street, 19063. *Activity: The Arts.* (800)
568-7771 or (610) 566-4020. **www.mediatheatre.com**. World-
class children's theatre.

TYLER ARBORETUM

Media - 515 Painter Road, 19063. *Activity: Outdoors.* (610) 566-
5431. **www.netaxs.com/~mckenzi1/abouttyl.html**. 650 acre
historic arboretum, plants, museums. Admission.

MAPLE GROVE PARK RACEWAY RACEWAYS

Mohnton - R.R. #3 Box 3420, 19540. *Activity: Sports.* (610) 856-
7200.**www.maplegroveraceway.com**.(April-October). Admission.
320 mph NHRA drag racing. Keystone Nationals in September.

PENNSBURY MANOR

400 Pennsbury Memorial Lane (on the Delaware River)
Morrisville 19067

❑   Activity: Pennsylvania History

❑   Telephone: (215) 946-0400 **www.libertynet.org/pensbury**

❑   Hours: Tuesday - Saturday, 9:00 am - 5:00 pm., Sunday, Noon -
     5:00 pm (open Summer holidays)

❑   Admission: Adults $5.00, Seniors $4.50, Children $3.00 (6-12),
     Family $13.00

❑   Tours: 90 minutes long - a little empty for pre-schoolers

❑   Miscellaneous: Best for kids to visit (April - October), Sundays
     for living history days. Picnic areas.

A quaint, Quaker, simple homestead of William Penn, the founder of Pennsylvania. See a replica of the boat Penn used to "commute" to Philly. They may be baking bread (up to 30 loaves at one time!) in the bake house or checkout the farm where sheep and geese roam. Inside the Visitor's Center try writing with the original "pen" - a quill pen. You can also learn about Colonial James writing style here.

DONEGAL MILLS PLANTATION

Mount Joy - 1190 Trout Run Road (SR772 to Musser Road - Follow signs), 17552. *Activity: Tours.* (717) 653-2168. *Hours:* Weekends, Noon - 6:00 pm (Mid-March - December). *Admission:* Adults $4.00, Children $2.00 (6-12). *Tours:* Guided. Look for special seasonal events here. Many activities during these times are family oriented.

NEW HOPE AND IVYLAND RAILROAD

P.O. Box 634 (Depot at West Bridge and Stockton Street)
New Hope 18938

❑   Activity: Tours

❑   Telephone: (215) 862-2332

❑   Hours: Daily (April - November). Weekends (January - March)

- ❑ Admission: Adults $8.50, Seniors $7.50 (62+), Children $4.50 (2-11), $1.50 Children under 2
- ❑ Tours: Departure times vary, phone for schedule. 9 miles round trip

This ride is famous for the trestle called "Pauline" upon which actress Pearl White was bound to in the 1914 silent film "The Perils of Pauline". It might be the best way to expose young kids to the silent movies era (pictures available at the depot, too).

NEW HOPE BOAT RIDES

New Hope – 18938. *Activity: Tours*

- <u>CORYELL'S FERRY HISTORIC BOAT RIDES</u>. 22 South Main Street at Gerenser's Ice Cream. (215) 862-2050 or **www.spiritof76.com** - 1/2 hour tours on path once used to commute passengers by canoe (now they use paddleboats). (April - October)
- <u>WELLS FERRY</u> - Ferry Street and River Road. (215) 862-5965. Guided tour on a 36 passenger boat highlighting history of river and canal plus famous homes and wildlife. Admission. (May - October)
- <u>MULE BARGES</u> - New Street. (800) 59-BARGE. Instead of canal boats, they used barges here to carry loads of limestone and coal. Pulled by mules and guided by historians and folksingers (to give you a real feeling of a canal passage in the mid-1800's), the ride passes old homes, some in the 25 locks, 9 aqueducts and 106 bridges on the Delaware Canal. (April - November)

TYLER STATE PARK

Newtown - 101 Swamp Road, 18940. *Activity: Outdoors.* (215) 968-2021. **http://parec.com/state_parks/tylrstpk.htm**. Boat Rentals, Horseback Riding, Fishing, Trails, Winter Sports.

ELMWOOD PARK ZOO

1661 Harding Blvd, **Norristown** 19401

- ❑ Activity: Animals & Farms
- ❑ Telephone: (610) 277-DUCK **www.libertynet.org/epzoo**
- ❑ Daily, 10:00 am - 4:00 pm
- ❑ Admission: Adults $3.50, Seniors $2.00, Children $1.50
- ❑ Miscellaneous: Pony rides add $2.00. Snack shop. Gift shop. Picnic area.

Highlights of the zoo include: Petting Barn (goats & sheep), Duck Lake, Prairie Dog exhibits, and Aviary Wetland (waterfowl, beaver, otters), The Bayou (murky home to lovely alligators, turtles, and snakes - everything that hisses or snaps!). There's also your basic natural Grasslands (bison, elk, and new "bears" area). Animal shows on Summer weekends.

HERR'S SNACKS VISITOR'S CENTER

P.O. Box 300 (US 1 and SR272 to Herr Drive), **Nottingham** 19362

- ❑ Activity: Tours
- ❑ Telephone: (800) 63-SNACK, **www.herrs.com**
- ❑ Hours: Monday - Thursday, 9:00 am - 3:00 pm., Friday, 9:00 - 11:00 am (Extended summer hours)
- ❑ Admission: Free
- ❑ Tours: Reservations recommended
- ❑ Miscellaneous: Gift shop. Chippers Café with crunch and munch lunchroom. Very reasonable snack bar prices.

"Watch a groovy-chip movie" starring "Chipper" your tour guide and mascot. Whimsical (combination guide and TV monitor) tour takes you through the simple process of snack food production. Lots of hot oil and hot air drying, moisturizing and "spritzing" going on - a salon for snacks! Try samples warm off the "beltway" - those were a favorite point of the tour. Yes, you can have more than one! Also see other snacks made like cheesepuffs (corn meal dollops filled with air), tortilla chips, popcorn (huge poppers!) and pretzels. Your kids will be amused at the sideway mixers churning out 10 pound mounds of pretzel dough. The dough takes a long trip on a conveyor and then a "dough-bot" (robot) removes them to be shaped and baked. An excellent, organized tour - voted our best pick of snack food tours.

WHARTON ESHERICK STUDIO

Paoli - P.O. Box 595 (I-76, Exit 24), 19301. *Activity: The Arts.* (610) 644-5822, **www.levins.com/esherick.html**. *Tours:* Saturday & Sunday, by appointment only. (March - December). Small admission fee. Vanguard of early 20th century American sculpture. Primarily in wood furniture, furnishings and interiors. The studio, which took Esherick 40 years to build, reflects changing styles with age. Ex. five-sided table, world-famous spiral staircase.

NATIONAL CHRISTMAS CENTER

3427 US 30 (Lincoln Highway), **Paradise** 17562

- ❏ Activity: Museums
- ❏ Telephone: (717) 442-7950
  http://welcometo/nationalchristmascenter.com
- ❏ Hours: Daily, 10:00 am - 8:00 pm. (Early May - January 2)
- ❏ Admission: Adults $7.50, Seniors $6.50 (60+), Children $4.50 (2-12)
- ❏ Miscellaneous: Santa visits November 20th - December 23rd. Gift shop.

As you enter, you're greeted by a cute 1950's Christmas morning scene as a little boy opens and tries on his new cowboy outfit. Another scene depicts "Yes Virginia, There is a Santa Claus". Can you find Santa patiently waiting for a little girl to go to bed? This scene depicts a Christmas 100 years ago. Life cast artists create theme walk-thru displays with story lines. "Tudor Towne" is of Jolly Old England, a Once-Upon-A-Time World. "Return to Christmas Past" features antiques dating back to the early 1800's . "The First Christmas" probably has the most impact as you walk down a life-size recreation of the journey of Mary and Joseph to Bethlehem. It's very touching.

PHILADELPHIA FREEDOM SOCCER

Philadelphia - (Marple Stadium). *Activity: Sports.* (215) 545-9000. (May - September). $3-$6.00. Pro League.

PHILLY TRANSPORTATION TOURS

Philadelphia - (Downtown). *Activity: Tours. Admission:* Call for rates. Pay as you board.

- AMERICAN TROLLEY TOURS - (215) 333-2119. The complete trolley tour loop is 2 hours. On/off privileges.
- BEN FRANKLIN CARRIAGE COMPANY - (215) 923-8522. Victorian carriage rides. Leave at 2nd and Lombard Streets. 20 minute daytime tours for up to four people.
- PHILADELPHIA TROLLEY WORKS - (215) 925-TOUR. Narrated tours with on/off privileges.
- PHILLY PHLASH - (215) 4-PHLASH. Purple and teal buses run in a loop around downtown.
- RIVERLINK FERRY - (215) 925-LINK. Passenger ferry across the Delaware River between Penn's Landing and the Camden waterfront sites.

PHILADELPHIA ORCHESTRA

Philadelphia - 260 South Broad Street, 16th Floor (main office), 19102. *Activity: The Arts.* (215) 893-1900. **www.philorch.org**. Sound All Around Series (ages 3-5), learn about the different families of instruments. Family Concert Series (ages 6-12) - music featuring puppets, magicians, storytellers, and young soloists. (Saturday mornings).

ACADEMY OF NATURAL SCIENCES

1900 Benjamin Franklin Parkway, **Philadelphia** 19103

- ❑ Activity: Museums
- ❑ Telephone: (215) 299-1000, **www.acnatsci.org**

❑   Hours: Monday - Friday, 10:00 am - 4:30 pm. Saturday, Sunday & Holidays, 10:00 am - 5:00 pm. Closed Thanksgiving, Christmas, and New Year's Day.
❑   Admission: Adults $8.50, Seniors $7.75 (65+), Children $7.50 (3-12)
❑   Miscellaneous: Ask for Scavenger Hunts sheets (age appropriate) when you enter. The kids stay focused this way. Films shown daily.

The oldest and best dinosaur and natural science exhibit in the world is here. Actually peer into, or walk under, dinosaurs. You're greeted by a roaring robotic dinosaur at one entrance. A giant dinosaur skeleton hangs over the information desk at the main entrance. Most families' favorite area is the Dinosaur Hall. This is hands-on paleontology including a fossil dig, fossil prep lab, and Time Machine (get your picture image appearing with dinosaurs!). You'll also meet T-Rex, plus 11 friends, and even get to climb into a dinosaur skull. The North American Hall has some stuffed large animals that are almost 200 years old. By request only (and specific times), there are live animals shows and "Outside In"... hands-on, touching mice, snakes, frogs, and huge bugs. There's also a crystals and gems exhibit that features a 57 pound amethyst.

FRANKLIN INSTITUTE SCIENCE MUSEUM
222 North 20th Street, **Philadelphia** 19103

❑   Activity: Museums
❑   Telephone: (215) 448-1200, **www.fi.edu**
❑   Hours: Daily, 9:30 am - 5:00 pm
❑   Admission: Adults $10-15.00, Seniors $9-13.00 (62+), Children $9-13.00

❑   Miscellaneous: Ben's Restaurant - Lunch, Milky Way Café,
Scoops & Slices, Museum Stores. Special exhibits change in the
Mandell Center. When we were there they had a "Whodunit?"
Exhibit: The Science of Solving Crime. Go through the Crime
Lab Stations (even a taped autopsy) with signs designating "kids
only" areas.

What began as a national memorial to Ben Franklin is now a
hands-on exhibit and demonstration complex. At the
entrance are displays of some of Franklin's personal effects and a
famous statue by James Earle Fraser. Some exhibits have been
there forever. Walk through "Human Heart" - hear a heart beating
as "blood" races through the arteries. Also, see a full-size train or
airplane cockpit! Here's a look at other areas:

- THE FUTURES CENTER - Science and Technology of
  the future, most are push button or computer based. You
  can also watch videos of different futuristic and modern
  high tech careers. Includes a Surf Bar - pull up a stool and
  order from the computer menu of fun facts.
- SCIENCE CENTER - Flight and optical illusions.
  Planetarium. Interactive Franklin…he's electric! Liquid air
  show - weather.
- OMNIVERSE THEATER - 180 degree field of view
  motion picture made for all age groups. Titles vary
  seasonally.

PLEASE TOUCH MUSEUM

210 North 21st Street (21st and Race Streets), **Philadelphia** 19103

❑   Activity: Museums
❑   Telephone: (215) 963-0667 **www.pleasetouchmuseum.org**
❑   Hours: 9:00 am - 4:30 pm. (July - Labor Day open until 6:00 pm)
❑   Admission: General $6.95 (over age 1)

❑ Miscellaneous: Sundays between 9:00 - 10:00 am, "Pay As You Wish" donation charged only. Strollers are not permitted (inside parking area for strollers is available). Education Store - take ideas from the museum home as souvenirs or projects. Special areas for kids 3 and under.

A hands-on museum for kids 8 and under with activities that are educational, fun, and safe. Here are the highlights to look forward to:

- **SENDAK** - You probably recognize the name - does "Where the Wild Things Are" book ring a bell? Maurice Sendak's (Philadelphia native) popular books come to life as Max's giant bedroom is filled with jungle life. Children use fantasy play and daydreams to respond to feelings like anger and joy.

- **MOVE IT!** - Hop in a real full-sized bus or monorail. Learn to sail a boat or fill up your tank at the service station.

- **SUPER MARKET SCIENCE** - Shop and cook in a child sized, fully stocked grocery store, kitchen, and food science lab. Use a microscope or magnifying glass to examine those foodstuffs more closely.

- **STUDIO PTM** - Be in front of or behind a camera on TV. Try making sound effects like thunder. This is the easiest hands-on TV studio we've been in.

- **ALICE IN WONDERLAND** - The tale is explained in miniature (little doors to peek through) and then full size. Try on cover ups and pretend you're the Queen of Hearts ready for a tea party with Mad Hatter & rabbit (great photo op).

A lthough the setups are classic in here, the fresh aspects of creativity through role playing are really different. It's pricier than most kid's museums we've been to in our travels, but it's uniqueness is worth it - be sure to take advantage of science park (free with admission) across the street.

SCIENCE PARK

Philadelphia - (21st Street between Winter & Race Streets), 19103. *Activity: Amusements. Hours:* During Franklin Institute hours, weather permitting - (May - October). *Admission:* Included with either "Please Touch Museum" or "Franklin Institute Museum" admission. A 38,000 square foot learning playground. Climb on and over high tech learning structures like mazes and optical illusions. Sky bike, miniature golf, radar detector and echo chambers. Its bright colors and unusual shapes entice kids.

PHILADELPHIA ZOO

3400 West Girard Avenue (I-76, exit 36), **Philadelphia** 19104

❑   Activity: Animals & Farms
❑   Telephone: (215) 243-1100, **www.phillyzoo.org**
❑   Hours: Monday - Friday, 9:30 am - 4:45 pm., Weekends, 9:30 am - 5:45 pm. (March - November). Open 10:00 am - 4:00 pm (December - February)
❑   Admission: Adults $10.50, Seniors $8.00 (65+), Children $8.00 (5-11), Pre-Schoolers $5.00 (2-4). Parking $4.00.
❑   Miscellaneous: Zoo shop. McDonald's restaurants. Victorian picnic groves. Stroller and wheelchair rentals. Camel, elephant and pony rides and "Treehouse" interactive areas have additional fees.

The first zoo in the country - now has 1600 animals on 42 acres of beautiful landscape. Favorites include the famous white lions, Jezebel and Vinkel, the first white lions ever to be exhibited in North America. Presently, there are no white lions in the wild. Carnivore Kingdom has the country's only giant otters. Bear Country allows you to interact (viewing , that is) with playful bears that love to show off. The Children's Zoo has your typically petted animals plus cow-milking and other live demonstrations in the pavilion.

UNIVERSITY OF PENNSYLVANIA MUSEUM OF ARCHAEOLOGY & ANTHROPOLOGY

33rd and Spruce Streets, **Philadelphia** 19104

- ❑ Activity: Museums
- ❑ Telephone: (215) 898-4000, **www.upenn.edu/museum**
- ❑ Hours: Tuesday - Saturday, 10:00 am - 4:30 pm., Sunday, 1:00 - 5:00 pm. (Closed Mondays, Holidays, and summer Sundays from Memorial Day to Labor Day)
- ❑ Admission: Adults $5.00, Seniors $2.50, Students $2.50
- ❑ Tours: Guided on Weekends at 1:30 pm during the school year.
- ❑ Miscellaneous: Snack café. Pyramid Gift Shop. Most fun to come during a Family Fun Day Event (215) 898-4890.

Exhibits outstanding findings from Ancient Egypt, Asia, Central America, North America, Mesopotamia, Greece, and Africa, uncovered by University staff and student expeditions. See a giant Sphinx and real mummies. The stories of the archeologists thoughts and accompanying pictures of "digs" might inspire a budding career.

ATWATER KENT MUSEUM

Philadelphia - 15 South 7th Street, 19106. *Activity: Museums.* (215) 922-3031. **www.philadelphiahistory.org**. *Hours:* Daily, 10:00 am - 4:00 pm (except Tuesday). *Admission:* Adults $3.00, Seniors $2.00, Children $1.50. Whatever history you don't catch visiting buildings in the area, you'll get a touch of here. Be sure to call ahead for family events, other wise it could be boring for children. Family Programs - toys of the past, hat making, children of the past.

BALCH INSTITUTE OF ETHNIC STUDIES

Philadelphia - 18 South Seventh Street, 19106. *Activity: Museums.* (215) 925-8090. **www.libertynet.org/balch**. *Hours:* Tuesday - Saturday, 10:00 am - 4:00 pm. Here, kids can use a computer to explore ethnic group sites around Philadelphia. Punch in your cultural heritage and receive a printout of sites related to that ethnic group. Begin at the museum here full of memorabilia then go out and discover your roots. Ethnic museums we're aware of:

- NATIONAL MUSEUM OF JEWISH HISTORY - 44 North Fourth Street. (215) 923-3811.
- CHINATOWN - Arch & Vine Streets. (215) 922-2156. Address Listing shows: 1011 Race Street
- ITALIAN MARKET - 9th Street. (215) 922-5557.
- AFRICAN-AMERICAN MUSEUM - 701 Arch Street. (215) 574-0380.
- AMERICAN SWEDISH HISTORICAL MUSEUM - 1900 Pattison Avenue in Roosevelt Park, (215) 389-1776.
- POLISH-AMERICAN CULTURAL CENTER MUSEUM - 308 Walnut Street. Near National Historic Park. (215) 922-1700.

BETSY ROSS HOUSE

Philadelphia - 239 Arch Street (Between 2nd & 3rd Streets), 19106. *Activity: Pennsylvania History.* (215) 627-5343. **www.libertynet.org/iha/betsy**. *Hours:* Tuesday - Sunday, 10:00 am - 5:00 pm. *Admission:* Donations. Tours: Self-guided. *Miscellaneous:* Ask for the "house hunt" sheet for kids. In 1777, the first American flag made by Colonial Mrs. Ross was sewn here. You can tour her modest, working class home. Did she design the flag? Each room has a description, in Betsy's words (in old English),of what led up to her sewing the flag. She and the fellas that made the Liberty Bell were just ordinary folks who had a skill needed to enhance the cause of Independence. What was considered a routine job lead to national recognition many years later!

CARPENTER'S HALL

Philadelphia - 320 Chestnut Street (Independence Park), 19106. *Activity:* *Pennsylvania* *History.* (215) 925-0167. **www.nps.gov/inde**. *Hours:* Tuesday - Sunday, 10:00 am - 4:00 pm. (Closed January & February Tuesdays). Free admission. Displays of early carpenter's chairs and tools used by the First Continental Congress in 1774. A 10 minute video chronicles the history of the carpenter's company (they still own and operate the hall).

CHRIST CHURCH
20 North American Street (2nd Street between Arch & Market Streets), **Philadelphia** 19106

- ❑ Activity: Pennsylvania History
- ❑ Telephone: (215) 922-1695
- ❑ Hours: Monday - Saturday, 9:00 am - 5:00 pm., Sunday, 1:00 - 5:00 pm. (March - December), Wednesday - Sunday (Rest of year)
- ❑ Admission: Donation
- ❑ Miscellaneous: Services (Episcopal) held on Sundays at 9:00 & 11:00 am, Wednesday at Noon.

Fifteen signers of the Declaration of Independence worshiped here including George Washington and Benjamin Franklin. A brass plaque marks each pew of famous Colonists including Betsy Ross. The church was built in 1727 and originally had dirt or wood floors. Ask a guide what those marble rectangles are in the floor. Careful - though they won't mind...you may be stepping on the memory of a notable patron of the church!

CITY TAVERN

Philadelphia - 138 South 2nd Street (and Walnut), 19106. *Activity: Theme Restaurants.* **www.citytavern.com**. (215) 413-1443. *Hours:* Daily, Lunch & Dinner. Children's menu. Casual dress. Fine dining prices. Based on a Colonial theme in a 1774 structure, the restaurant serves traditional beef and pork pie or stew plus modern favorites (mostly meat and potatoes). Paul Revere, General Washington, Benedict Arnold, and John Adams have all stopped here. Costumed wait staff serve you as you eat and drink from pewter utensils and cups.

DECLARATION (GRAFF) HOUSE

Philadelphia - 7th & Market Streets (in Independence Park), 19106. *Activity: Pennsylvania History.* (215) 597-8974. **www.nps. gov/inde.** *Hours:* Vary by season (Call ahead). Free admission. Catch the short video and then see the rooms that Continental Congress delegate, Thomas Jefferson rented in this building where he penned the actual Declaration of Independence. Like the other buildings in this national park, our history studies come alive in these authentic places where great men once walked, worked, and lived.

FIREMAN'S HALL

Philadelphia - 147 North 2nd Street (Historic district near Elfreth's Alley), 19106. *Activity: Museums.* (215) 923-1438, **www.libertynet.org/iha/tour/_fireman.html**. *Hours:* Tuesday - Saturday, 9:00 am - 5:00 pm. Free admission. An 1876 firehouse depicts the history of firefighting. See memorabilia, films, and early equipment. Did your kids know Benjamin Franklin founded the first Philadelphia Fire Department in 1736? See old-fashioned leather buckets, fire wagons and an "around the world" display of firefighter helmets. Play pretend in the re-created living quarters or steer a fireboat. Taped firemen's stories recall high level exciting moments on the job. Are your kids attracted to large shiny objects? The Spider Hose Reel (1804) has a chariot look with brass bells and shiny mirrors that reflect all the polished metal. Also be on the lookout for the fire pole and injured firemen's hats (charred and broken).

FRANKLIN COURT

3rd, 4th, Chestnut & Market Streets, **Philadelphia** 19106

- ❑ Activity: Pennsylvania History
- ❑ Telephone: (215) 597-8974, **www.nps.gov/inde**
- ❑ Hours: Usually daily, 9:00 am - 5:00 pm but can vary. Call for details. Admission: Free

Hear "voices" of historic men such as Thomas Jefferson and Mark Twain talk about Franklin and how they felt about his character. "Bump into" Mr. Franklin as you roam his court and he'll invite you to gather around to hear stories of his life. Once owned by Ben Franklin who lived in Philadelphia from 1722 - 1790, the complex of buildings includes:

- UNDERGROUND THEATER AND MUSEUM - See "Portrait of a Family" - tells of his family life.
- NEWSPAPER OFFICE - Working reproduction of 1785 printing press and bindery.
- POST OFFICE - In 1775, Ben Franklin was appointed as the first Postmaster General. The name "Free Franklin" was used as the hand cancellation signature because Mr. Franklin chose to use "Free" referring to America's struggle for freedom. See actual hand canceled letters, then, purchase a post card and send it from this working post office! (Can you imagine Grandma getting this souvenir?)!

INDEPENDENCE HALL

5th & 6th Streets on Chestnut, **Philadelphia** 19106

- ❑ Activity: Pennsylvania History
- ❑ Telephone: (215) 597-8974, **www.nps.gov/inde**
- ❑ Hours: Daily, 9:00 am - 5:00 pm.
- ❑ Admission: Free
- ❑ Tours: Guided tours only throughout the day. Long lines move pretty fast.

❑   Miscellaneous: Congress Hall (where the first US Congress met
      and inaugurations of Presidents occurred) and Old City Hall
      (Supreme Court original house) are across the street. Hours vary
      but it is a must see for kids studying the setup of the United
      States Government.

H ey...this is the place that we see in countless movies and
     pictures. You will get a patriotic chill as you enter the hall
where the Declaration of Independence was adopted and the U.S.
Constitution was written. The Assembly Room looks just as it did
in 1776 (you'll feel like you're in a movie) and you can see the
original inkwell the Declaration signers dipped quills in to sign the
famous freedom document.

INDEPENDENCE NATIONAL HISTORICAL PARK VISITOR'S CENTER

313 Walnut Street (Third & Chestnut Streets), **Philadelphia** 19106

❑   Activity: Pennsylvania History
❑   Telephone: (215) 597-8974 or (800) 76-HISTORY - Town
      Criers, **www.nps.gov/inde**
❑   Hours: Daily, 9:00 am - 5:00 pm. - Call ahead for changing hours
      during non-peak season. Extended summer hours.
❑   Admission: Free

S tart here before you explore the well-known sites. See
    "Independence", (a 30-minute award winning film directed by
John Huston) which is shown throughout the day. Ben Franklin,
George Washington, John Adams and others come back to life to
tell the Independence story (well worth the time to view for
school-aged kids). Older children will want to sign up for the
walking tour here (little ones up to grades 1 or 2 will want to
wander at their own pace and usually aren't interested enough to
stay with the group). To keep attention spans high, we noticed they
create a theme (seasonally) of historical significance. Actors called
"Town Criers" present impromptu conversations and "street stage"
presentations along with that theme. They admired our "carriage"

(known to you and me as a wagon) and our "horse" that was pulling it (Daddy!) Most events are daily in the summer and weekends the rest of the year.

INDEPENDENCE SEAPORT MUSEUM

211 South Columbus Blvd., **Philadelphia** 19106

- ❑ Activity: Museums
- ❑ Telephone: (215) 925-5439, **www.libertynet.org/seaport**
- ❑ Hours: Daily, 10:00 am - 5:00 pm.
- ❑ Admission: Adults $7.50, Seniors $6.00 (65+), Children $3.50 (4-12)
- ❑ Miscellaneous: The Museum Store

Displayed here are the Delaware River and Bay maritime artifacts and interactive exhibits. History lessons are woven between these exhibits:

- • HOMEPORT PHILADELPHIA - Chart a course or navigate a boat under bridges.
- • WORKSHOPS ON THE WATER - Actual boatbuilder crafting new boats. Numerous models and small boats on display. If your kids are older, they can be apprentices.
- • DIVERS OF THE DEEP - Diving gear and underwater archeology.
- • SHIP ZONE: USS Becona & USS Olympia - Submarine from South Pacific and flagship during the Spanish American War. This is what the kids really come for! Self-guided tour lets kids "feel" like sailors, captains, or pirates.

LIBERTY BELL

5th, 6th, Market and Chestnut Streets (across from Independence Hall), **Philadelphia** 19106

- ❑ Activity: Pennsylvania History
- ❑ Telephone: (215) 597-8974, **www.nps.gov/inde**
- ❑ Hours: Daily, 9:00 am - 5:00 pm.
- ❑ Admission: Free

❑   Tours: Given by park rangers, relates the bell's history. Long
      lines - but they move fast.
❑   Miscellaneous: Glass encased bell is viewable 24 hours a day.

Made a few blocks away by two crafters who only made pots
and pans (usually), its famous "crack" has many folklore
stories associated with it. It would be nice to believe that each
crack was the result of zealous ringing; however, it just wasn't cast
properly to withstand its large size and temperature variances.
Initially, it was just a bell ordered to be placed in the tower of the
meeting hall (now called Independence Hall). Later, abolitionists
used it as a symbol of freedom for slaves and proclaimed it the
Liberty Bell (not until 1840 though!) - and the name stuck! It'll
give you goosebumps to stand inches from it (they even let us
touch it gently...just don't try to ring it!). Be sure to take
advantage of the photo opportunity time provided by park rangers.

LIGHTS OF LIBERTY
Public Ledger Building (6th and Chestnut Streets)
Philadelphia 19106

❑   Activity: Pennsylvania History
❑   Telephone: (215) LIBERTY or (877) GO-2-1776
❑   Hours: At Dark (Late-May - October)
❑   Admission: Adults $18.00, Seniors $16.00, Children $12.00 (6-
      12)
❑   Tours: 60 minutes

A nighttime sound-and-light show that takes visitors on a walk
through five historic sites as a drama unfolds in
Independence National Historic Park. A 3-D sound system and
enormous five-story images projected on buildings immerse
visitors into events leading up to the Colonists' fight for freedom
from the British. Groups of up to 50 people each wear audio
transmitted wrap-around headsets. Although anyone can see the
giant projected images, only those wearing the high tech headsets
hear the stories. Ask for the youth show (a fictional family, the
Warren children, serve as headset hosts).

MUM PUPPET THEATRE

Philadelphia - 115 Arch Street, 19106. Activity: The Arts. (215) 925-7MUM. Hours: October – April. Fun puppet performances aimed at various age groups.

THADDEUS KOSCIUSZKO NATIONAL MEMORIAL

Philadelphia - 301 Pine Street, 19106. *Activity: Museums.* (215) 597-9618. **www.nps.gov/thko**. *Hours:* Daily, 9:00 am - 5:00 pm. (June - October), Tuesday - Saturday, 9:00 am - 5:00 pm (rest of year). Free admission. Exhibits & audiovisual displays (English & Polish language) describing the help Thaddeus gave to the American Revolution. Learn why he was loved and then kicked out of his native Poland, why he carried a crutch and how his skills helped Americans strategically beat the British. He was a genius engineer!

TODD HOUSE

Philadelphia - 4th & Walnut Streets, 19106. *Activity: Pennsylvania History.* (215) 597-8974, **www.nps.gov/inde**. *Hours:* Daily, 9:00 am - 4:30 pm. *Admission:* Adults $2.00. This was the home of Dolly Todd before her marriage to James Madison (Dolly Madison pastries will get the kids on the same page). Representing a middle-class Quaker home, she became quite a First Lady when she moved from this house and married James Madison, fourth President of the United States.

U.S. MINT
5th & Arch Streets, **Philadelphia** 19106

- ❑ Activity: Tours
- ❑ Telephone: (215) 408-0114, **www.usmint.gov**
- ❑ Hours: Daily, 9:00 am - 4:30 pm. (July & August), Monday - Saturday (May & June), Weekdays only (Rest of Year)

While in the historic district of Philadelphia, be sure to take your family to the world's largest coinage operation (seen through a glass enclosed gallery). They make a million dollars worth of coins per day! (*29 million coins!*). See them start with blanks that are cleaned and then stamped, sorted, and bagged. To see coins in large bins or spilling out of machines is mesmerizing! Even little kids eyes sparkle. A "Stamp Your Own Medal" machine (press a big red button to operate) is located in the Gift shop. Great souvenir idea.

CITY HALL OBSERVATION DECK

Philadelphia - Broad & Market Streets, 19107. *Activity: Tours.* (215) 686-2840. *Hours:* Daily, 9:30 am - 4:15 pm. *Admission:* Donation. *Tours:* Daily, 12:30 pm. Every city has one building that stands as one of the tallest in town and usually it has a lot of history behind it. Most noted is the courtroom (available to view on the tour only) where a motion picture film was made and the 548 foot tall tower that has a statue of William Penn on top. At the base of the statue is the observation deck. This building is so breathtakingly beautiful and stands in the center of downtown...believe us, you can't miss it!

PHILADELPHIA MUSEUM OF ART
26th Street and Ben Franklin Parkway, **Philadelphia** 19130

- ❑ Activity: The Arts
- ❑ Telephone: (215) 763-8100, **www.philamuseum.org**
- ❑ Hours: Tuesday - Sunday, 10:00 am - 5:00 pm. Wednesday evening until 8:45 pm
- ❑ Admission: Adults $8.00, Seniors $5.00 (62+), Children $5.00 (5-18). Free Sunday until 1:00 pm.

The 3rd largest museum in the country. 2000 years of fine and applied arts (crafts, interiors, architecture) with 200 galleries. Museum restaurant. Your kids (or parents) will love running up the numerous steps to the top like Rocky (from the movie by the same name). Pretend you hear the crowd cheer as you step onto the brass glazed imprints of Rocky's shoes!

FAIRMOUNT PARK

Philadelphia - Benjamin Franklin Parkway (Visitor's Center at Memorial Hall), 19131. *Activity: Outdoors.* (215) 685-0000. **www.libertynet.org/iha/districts/fairmountpark.**   Free admission. *Tours:* Trolley tours (215) 925-TOUR. Stops at all points of interest within the park. Small fee. Along both sides of Schuylkill River, one of the world's largest city park's features include:

- ANDORRA NATURAL AREA - (215) 685-9285. Bartram's Historic Garden - (215) 729-5281. 18th Century home of colonial botanist, John Bartram. Furnished house tours, a botanical garden, and a wildflower meadow.
- SMITH PLAYGROUND & PLAYHOUSE - (215) 765-4325. Emphasis on playhouse (3 story) for preschoolers with trains, foam blocks and comfortable reading rooms. Pick up a Cozy Car and drive along the play roads with stop signs and traffic lights. This 100 year old playground has a Giant Slide that four generations have slid down.

INSECTARIUM

Philadelphia - 8046 Frankford Avenue, 19136. *Activity: Museums.* (215) 335-9500. **www.insectarium.com.** *Hours:* Monday - Saturday, 10:00 am - 4:00 pm. *Admission:* Adults $4.00 (ages 2+). A collection of live insects (in naturalized settings), mounted specimens and learning displays help you to become "bug friendly". Check out the cockroach kitchen, glow-in-the-dark scorpion, live termite tunnel, or the 101 butterflies!

MUMMERS MUSEUM

100 South Street & Washington Avenue, 19147. *Activity: Museums.* (215) 336-3050. **www.fieldtrip.com/pa/53363050.htm**. *Hours:* Tuesday - Saturday, 9:30 am - 5:00 pm., Sunday, Noon - 5:00 pm. (September - June). Closed Sundays in July and August. *Admission:* Adults $2.50, Seniors & Children $2.00. What is a mummer? Audio and interactive displays, musical instruments, costumes, and artifacts from the traditional New Year's Day parade. See videos of past parades or watch how those colorful sparkly costumes are made.

FIRST UNION CENTER / SPECTRUM

Philadelphia – 3601 South Broad Street (South Broad Street & Patterson Avenue), 19148. *Activity: Tours.* (215) 389-9543. *Admission:* Adults $6.00, Children $5.00 (under 12). *Tours:* Monday - Friday, 10:00, 11:00 am, Noon, and 1:00 pm (provided no events are scheduled). Guided tours of the home of the Philadelphia 76ers, Flyers, and Wings. See fields, locker rooms, and learn great inside scoops on the history of favorite players and teams.

KIXX SOCCER

Philadelphia 3601 South Broad Street (Spectrum - First Union Center), 19148. *Activity: Sports.* (888) 888-KIXX. **www.kixxonline.com**. (May - September). *Admission:* $7 -$19.00. National Professional Soccer League.

PHILADELPHIA 76ERS BASKETBALL

Philadelphia - 3601 South Broad Street (Office) (First Union Center), 19148. *Activity: Sports.* (215) 339-7676. **www.nba.com/sixers**. *Admission:* $12-$54.00. National Basketball Association.

PHILADELPHIA EAGLES FOOTBALL

Philadelphia - 3501 South Broad Street (Veteran's Stadium), 19148. *Activity: Sports.* (215) 463-5500. **www.eaglesnet.com.** *Admission:* $40-$45.00. NFL Professional football team.

PHILADELPHIA FLYERS HOCKEY

Philadelphia - 3601 South Broad Street #1A (office) (First Union Center), 19148. *Activity: Sports.* (215) 465-4500. **www.philadelphiaflyers.com.** *Admission:* $22 - $68.00. National Hockey League.

PHILADELPHIA PHILLIES BASEBALL

Philadelphia - 3551 South Broad Street (Veteran Stadium), 19148. *Activity: Sports.* (215) 436-1000. **www.phillies.com.** *Admission:* $3-$16.00. National League East Division Professional.

FORT MIFFLIN
Fort Mifflin Road (I-95 to Island Avenue Exit - follow signs)
Philadelphia 19153

- ☐ Activity: Museums
- ☐ Telephone: (215) 492-3395, **www.spiritof76.com/ftmifflin**
- ☐ Hours: Wednesday - Sunday, 10:00 am - 4:00 pm. (April - November)
- ☐ Admission: Adults $4.00, Seniors $2.00 (65+), Children $2.00 (students over 2 years old)
- ☐ Miscellaneous: Sundays suggested as there are military drills and craftspeople demonstrating their skills. Check out their educational Treasure Hunts for group tours.

"What Really Happened at Fort Mifflin?", is the heading of their brochure and you'll find out that a lot happened here. Starting in 1772, it was built by the British to protect the colonies. Ironically, in 1777, it was used by Americans trying to protect the Philadelphia and Delaware River from the British (7 long, grueling weeks of siege). It also protected the city of

Philadelphia during the War of 1812 and was active as a Confederate and Union prison camp during the Civil War. Until 1954, it was still used to store ammunition for the United States military. A great place to check out and study several wars all in one spot.

HEINZ NATIONAL WILDLIFE REFUGE

Philadelphia - Lindbergh Blvd. & 86th Street, 19153. *Activity: Outdoors*. (215) 365-3118. *Hours:* Dawn to Dusk. Visitor contact station. Hiking trails to explore butterflies, muskrats, frogs, flying geese, and loads of wildflowers. Observation tower.

RAIN FOREST CAFÉ

Philadelphia - 1133 Franklin Mills Circle - #446 (Franklin Mills Mall), 19154. *Activity: Theme Restaurants*. (215) 281-9400, **www.rainforestcafe.com**. *Hours:* Breakfast, Lunch, Dinner. A theme restaurant and wildlife preserve (and gift shop) filled with live and mechanical animals; ongoing rainstorms (even with the thunder and lightning); a talking rainforest tree; a giant walk-thru aquarium (really cool); and hand sculpted "cave like" rock everywhere. The cute jungle names of foods will wet your appetite for the American food fare to follow - Ex. Gorilla Grilled Cheese, Volcano Salad, and Wild Waffle Fries. Preschoolers and younger love the fish tanks (one is even a walk "through and under" tank so you feel as if you are with the fish!) but are a little scared with the motorized large gorillas, snakes, and elephants (request sitting on the other side of the dining room). Although your food bill is above moderate, it's certainly the atmosphere that you're paying extra for. "Your adventure safari begins now!" is the call of your hostess as you are seated - and you won't be bored - believe us!

MORRIS ARBORETUM

Philadelphia (Chestnut Hill) - 100 Northwestern Avenue (University of Pennsylvania), 19118. *Activity: Outdoors*. (215) 247-5777. **www.upenn.edu/morris**. *Hours:* Daily, 10:00 am - 4:00 pm. Open until 5pm on Saturday and Sunday, (April -

October). *Admission:* Adults $6.00, Seniors $5.00, Students $4.00 (Children under 6 free). Romantic 92 acre Victorian garden with many of Philly's rarest and largest trees, a sculpture garden, a rose garden and the Fernery.

RALPH STOVER STATE PARK

Pipersville - 6011 State Park Road (State Park Road and Stump Road), 18947. *Activity: Outdoors.* (610) 982-5560. **http://parec. com/state_parks/rlphstpk.htm**. 45 Acres for Picnicking, Fishing.

VALLEY FORGE STATE FOREST

Pottstown - 1132 Ridge Road, 19464. *Activity: Outdoors.* (610) 469-6217. Hiking Trails.

NOCKAMIXON STATE PARK

Quakertown - 1542 Mountain View Drive (PA Route 563), 18951. *Activity: Outdoors.* (215) 529-7300. Pool, Visitors Center, Boat Rentals, Horseback Riding, Modern Cabins, Fishing, Trails, Winter Sports. **http://parec.com/state_parks/nockstpk.htm**.

ROBERT FULTON BIRTHPLACE

Box 33 (US222 South of Quarryville), **Quarryville** 17566

❑ Activity: Museums
❑ Telephone: (717) 548-2679
   www.fieldtrip.com/pa/75482679.htm
❑ Hours: Saturday, 11:00 am - 4:00 pm, Sunday, 1:00 - 5:00 pm, (Summer)
❑ Admission: Adults $1.00, Children FREE (12 and under)

Robert Fulton, the inventor, the artist, and the engineer was born here in 1765. On display are many of his drawings, miniature portraits, and models (located throughout the living room). Being most famous for his steamboat, "Claremont" (the first steamboat), you'll see a strong connection between his artistic ability and his engineering ideas. Because his drawings were so well done, supporters could easily visualize his inventive ideas.

BERKS COUNTY MUSEUM

Reading - 940 Centre Avenue, 19601. *Activity: Pennsylvania History.* **www.berksweb.com/histsoc/museum.html**. (610) 375-4375, *Hours:* Tuesday - Saturday, 9:00 am - 4:00 pm (Closed holiday weekends). *Admission:* Adults $2.50, Seniors $2.00, Children $1.00 (5-12). Industry, Transportation, Pennsylvania German Arts, Country liberty bell, Diffenbach organ, Conestoga wagon. Hands-on children's museum.

READING SYMPHONY ORCHESTRA

Reading - 147 North 5th Street (Rajah Theatre), 19601. *Activity: The Arts.* (610) 373-7557. **www.readingsymphony.com**. Some concerts feature Berk's children's chorus.

JIMMIE KRAMER'S PEANUT BAR & RESTAURANT

Reading - 322 Penn Street (Downtown), 19602. *Activity: Theme Restaurants.* **www.peanutbar.com**. (610) 376-8500 or (800) 515-8500. *Hours:* Monday - Saturday for Lunch, Dinner and Late Snacks. Free peanuts, and you can throw the shells on the floor! Casual dining. Children's menu (shaped like a peanut - ready to color). Ask for family seating away from the bar.

MID ATLANTIC AIR MUSEUM

Reading - 11 Museum Drive - SR183 (Reading Regional Airport), 19605. *Activity: Museums.* (610) 372-7333. **www.maam.org**. *Hours:* Daily, 9:30 am - 4:00 pm. *Admission:* Adults $5.00, Children $2.00 (6-12). *Miscellaneous:* Aviation gift shop. Airplane rides weekends in summer for additional fee. Restored, ready to fly, classic civilian and military aircraft. Of special interest are the classic commercial airliners, and the first night fighter ever built, history of aircraft manufacturers, and aviation movies and toys.

READING PHILLIES BASEBALL

Reading - 1900 Centre Avenue (Municipal Stadium), 19605. *Activity: Sports.* **www.readingphillies.com**. (610) 370-BALL or 375-8469. *Admission:* $3-7.00. Minor League AA Class affiliate of the Philadelphia Phillies.

NOLDE FOREST STATE PARK

Reading - 2910 New Holland Road, 19608. Activity: Outdoors. (610) 775-1411. **http://parec.com/state_parks/noldstpk.htm**. Year-Round Education & Interpretation Center.

READING PUBLIC MUSEUM

Reading - 500 Museum Road, 19611. *Activity: Museums.* (610) 371-5850. **www.readingpublicmuseum.org**. *Hours:* Tuesday - Saturday, 11:00 am - 5:00 pm., Sunday, Noon - 5:00 pm. Also Wednesday eve. Closed Christmas. *Admission:* Adults $4.00, Children $2.00 (4-17). Regional and international art, sculpture gardens, planetarium, and greenhouse.

MARY MERRITT DOLL MUSEUM

Reading (Douglassville) - 907 Ben Franklin Highway - US422, 19518. *Activity: Museums.* (610) 385-3809. *Hours:* Monday - Saturday, 10:00 am - 5:00 pm., Sunday, 1:00 - 5:00 pm. *Admission:* Adults $3.00, Senior $2.50 (60+), Children $1.50 (5-12). See 1500+ dolls ranging from the 7th Century Egypt to 20th century USA. 40+ miniature period rooms including a full-size replica of a Philadelphia 1850's toy shop. Special interests in Shirley Temple dolls, Paper mache dolls, circus, safari dolls, and mechanical dolls...they're all here!

READING RAGE SOCCER

Reading (Mt. Penn) - St. Lawrence Avenue (All home games played at Central Catholic Stadium), 19606. *Activity: Sports.* (610) 375-4405. **www.readingrage.com**. (May - September) *Admission:* $4-6.00. Pro League.

ROADSIDE AMERICA

Roadside Drive (I-78 / US22, exit 8), **Shartlesville** 19554

- ❑   Activity: Amusements
- ❑   Telephone: (610) 488-6241 **www.roadsideamericainc.com**
- ❑   Hours: Weekends, 9:00 am - 6:30 pm., (July - Labor Day) Weekends until 7:00 pm., Monday - Friday, 10:00 am - 5:00 pm., Saturday & Sunday, 10:00 am - 6:00 pm (September - June)
- ❑   Admission: Adults $4.00, Children $1.50 (6-11)

Our kids lost their breath as they entered the enormous and wonderful train village! It's the largest known indoor miniature train village! As a young boy, Lawrence Gieringer saw buildings far away and felt they appeared tiny and toy-sized. As his carpentry skills grew, he began whittling blocks of wood into different scaled down models of industries and buildings he saw all around him - all of them important to the development of the area. You'll see scenes of a coal breaker, a Pennsylvania Dutch farm, downtown small town USA, gristmills, and churches. Kids are enchanted by the moving trains (over bridges, through tunnels), trolleys, bubbling fountains, or aircraft swooping and diving through the air (there's even a hot air balloon). Parents relive childhood dreams playing with toy animals, people, machinery, etc. as they examine all the details. Kids favorites are the 50+ pushbuttons that make trains or figures move - it gives them the chance to feel like they're helping to operate the huge display. Don't leave until you've seen the Night Pageant! Every half hour they turn day into night and back!

SPRING MOUNTAIN SKI AREA

Spring Mount - Spring Mount Road, 19478. *Activity: Outdoors.* **www.usskiing.com/stats.cfm/pa23.htm**. (610) 287-7300. Snow Report: (610) 287-7900. Longest Run: 2220 ft.; 7 Slopes & Trails.

AMISH VILLAGE

Highway 896 - P.O. Box 115 (1 mile south of US30 & 2 miles north of Strasburg), **Strasburg** 17579

- ❑ Activity: Tours
- ❑ Telephone: (717)687-8511,**www.800padutch.com/avillage.html**
- ❑ Hours: Daily, 9:00 am - 5:00 pm (Spring/Fall)., Daily, 9:00 am - 6:00 pm (Summer), Daily until 4:00 pm (November)
- ❑ Admission: Adults $5.50, Children $2.00 (6-12)
- ❑ Tours: 20-25 minutes
- ❑ Miscellaneous: Amish Village store.

Educational tour of an 1840 old order Amish home, authentically furnished. The site includes a blacksmith, one room schoolhouse, operating smokehouse, water wheel, farm animals, spring house and windmill.

CHOO CHOO BARN

Strasburg - Route 741 East, Box 130, 17579. *Activity: Amusements.* (717) 687-7911. **www.choochoobarn.com**. *Hours:* Daily, opens at 10:00 am (April - December). *Admission:* Adults $4.00, Children: $2.00 (5-12). 17 operating toy trains. Over 130 animated figures displaying County and PA Dutch Country landmarks like the Amish Barn Raising.

ED'S BUGGY RIDES

Strasburg - SR896, 17579. *Activity: Tours.* (717) 687-0360. *Admission:* Adults $7.00, Children $3.50. 3 mile tour through Amish farmlands in an Amish buggy. Ride through scenic backroads just like the Amish do everyday.

LIVING WATERS THEATRE

Strasburg - Route 896, 17579. *Activity: The Arts.* (717) 687-7800. **www.noahonstage.com/index5.html**. Special effects theatre with live Easter and Christmas performances. Also called Sight and Sound Entertainment Center with shows like "Noah".

NATIONAL TOY TRAIN MUSEUM

300 Paradise Lane (off SR 741 East & US 30),**Strasburg** 17579

- ❑ Activity: Museums
- ❑ Telephone: (717) 687-8976
  www.traincollectors.org/toytrain.html
- ❑ Hours: Daily, 10:00 am - 5:00 pm (May - October), Weekends in April, November, and mid-December
- ❑ Admission: Adults $3.00, Seniors $2.75 (65+), Children $1.50 (5-12)
- ❑ Miscellaneous: Hands-on layouts every Friday in the summer. Video presentation.

Five operating push button layouts in panoramic viewing. Meet toy trains from the 1800's to the present in use as part of the layout. The Train Collectors Association operates it (they are often featured on national TV).

RAILROAD MUSEUM OF PENNSYLVANIA

P.O. Box 15 (300 Gap Road - SR741 East),**Strasburg** 17579

- ❑ Activity: Museums
- ❑ Telephone: (717) 687-8628, **www.rrhistorical-2.com**
- ❑ Hours: Monday - Saturday, 9:00 am - 5:00 pm., Noon - 5:00 pm., Closed Monday (Nov - April)
- ❑ Admission: Adults $6.00, Senior $5.50, Children $4.00 (6-12), Family $16.00
- ❑ Miscellaneous: Whistle Stop Shop. Outdoor yard restoration available in good weather. Hands-On-Center. Orientation video. 2nd floor observation deck.

Traces the development of railroads and rail transportation in Pennsylvania from restored locomotives to modern streamliners. Meet "Diesel", GG 1 Electric, Logging, Freight and Passenger (actually get to look in or walk in) trains! More access than most train museums. In the center of the museum is the railroad workshop where you can actually walk under a train! Great place to bring grandmas and grandpas to pass along stories to younger generations.

RED CABOOSE RESTAURANT

Strasburg - SR741, 17579. *Activity: Theme Restaurants.* (717) 687-5001. Enjoy hearty Amish style meals in real Victorian dining cars on the property of the motel where you can stay in a real caboose (you can check out a sample room next to the restaurant). The kid's menu includes a Junior Conductor or Junior Caboose. The miniature train theme gift shop and famous Strasburg Railroad Trains passing by create a true "Thomas the Train" feeling! This is a must stop for you and your little engineers. Breakfast, lunch, and dinner. Oh...by the way...there's special railroad music and simulated motion as you dine.

ROBERT FULTON STEAMBOAT RESTAURANT

Strasburg - P.O. Box 333 (US30 & SR896), 17579. *Activity: Theme Restaurants.* **www.800padutch.com/fulton.html**. (717) 299-9999. After you spend the night sleeping on a steamboat, enjoy a meal in a room full of steamboat antiques. The outside of this Inn looks just like a steamboat complete with wheels and smoke stacks. As you hear occasional seagulls sounds, select from Steamboat or Mid-Ship Specialties for breakfast, lunch or dinner.

STRASBURG RAILROAD
SR741 East – (P.O. Box 96), **Strasburg** 17579

- ❑ Activity: Tours
- ❑ Telephone: (717) 687-7522 **www.strasburgrailroad.com**
- ❑ Hours: Daily, 10:00 am - 7:00 pm (July & August), 11:00 am - 3:00 pm (April, June, September), Noon - 3:00 pm (Rest of the year)
- ❑ Admission: Adults $9-12.00, Children $4.00 (3-11)
- ❑ Tours: 45 minutes, departs on the hour.

View Amish farmland aboard a steam train with wooden coaches. This is the oldest short-line railroad. The Victorian Parlor car offers snacks and the "Lee Brenner" dining car offers meals. Be sure to check on seasonal events that your "little engineers" will love like "A Day Out With Thomas the Train!"

BRANDYWINE POLO CLUB

Toughkenamon - Polo Road (Call for field location), 19374. *Activity: Sports.* (610) 268-8692. *Hours:* Sunday afternoons, (Mid May - September). Free admission. Pack your basket of tea sandwiches, and sparkling water, along with a blanket and lawn chairs. Be prepared to participate in the "divot stomp".

DELAWARE CANAL STATE PARK

Upper Black Eddy - 11 Lodi Hill Road, 18972. *Activity: Outdoors.* **http://parec.com/state_parks/delastpk.htm**. (610) 982-5560, Historical Center, Year-round Education & Interpretation Center, Horseback Riding, Mountain Biking, Fishing, Trails, Cross-Country Skiing.

VALLEY FORGE NATIONAL HISTORICAL PARK

SR23 & N. Gulph Rd - P.O. Box 953 (I-76 to exit 24 – SR202 south to SR422 west to SR23 west), **Valley Forge** 19482

- ❑ Activity: Pennsylvania History
- ❑ Telephone: (610) 783-1077, **www.valleyforge.org**
- ❑ Hours: Daily, 9:00 am - 5:00 pm (except Christmas)
- ❑ Admission: Adults $2.00, Seniors $1.00 (60+), Children $1.00 (under 18) *Fee only if your tour buildings.
- ❑ Tours: By bus (hop on & off at leisure) or self-guided driving with audio tape.
- ❑ Miscellaneous: Expanse of outdoor park areas available. Hiking and bike trails. Stop at the Visitor's Center first.

Explore the site of the Winter of 1777-78 encampment that was a difficult time of battling elements and disease. Some of the sites that you won't want to miss are:

- • ARTILLERY PARK - long rows of cannons and forts.
- • WASHINGTON'S HEADQUARTERS - Isaac Potts' House - looks exactly as it did when General George Washington and his wife Martha were at residence. (Initially he shared the rough conditions with the soldiers in the field tents).
- • VISITOR'S CENTER - Introduction film and exhibits. See a tent headquarters actually used by General Washington.

- GRAND PARADE - learn about the other hero (Von
  Steuben) who trained tattered, confused young men into
  soldiers.
- WORLD OF SCOUTING MUSEUM - A log cabin full
  of uniforms, handbooks, and badges. Daily, 11:00 am -
  4:00 pm (Summer), Weekends (rest of the year).

Summers are the best time to visit because the Muhlenberg
Brigade is recreated in living history encampments - bringing
the drudges of winter camp to life. Remember, these "huts"
replaced tents but only offered a little more warmth. Brave a visit
in Winter to see scout troops living under similar conditions as the
soldiers did.

WASHINGTON CROSSING HISTORIC PARK

SR32 and SR532 (off I-95, exit 31),**Washington's Crossing** 18977

- ❑ Activity: Pennsylvania History
- ❑ Telephone: (215) 493-4076
- ❑ Hours: Monday – Saturday, 9:00 am – 5:00 pm, Sunday, Noon –
  5:00 pm
- ❑ Admission: Adults $4.00, Seniors $3.50 (60+), Children $3.00
  (6-12). Park charges $1.00 per vehicle at entrance.
- ❑ Miscellaneous: Every Christmas (at 1:00 pm) the park re-enacts
  Washington's crossing and special events also occur on his
  birthday. Also on the grounds is the Bowman's Hill and
  Wildflower Preserve.

It's December 25, 1776. Washington planned his attack on the
British, first crossing the Delaware River by boat. In the
Durham Boat House, you can see the boats that were actually used.
A larger than life copy (20 ft. X 12 ft.) of the painting
"Washington's Crossing" creates the best image of this historic
Christmas Day for freedom. A total of 13 historic buildings are on
site and your tour ticket includes Bowman's Hill Tower
observation point, Thompson-Neely House (where Washington ate

and slept), The Ferry Inn (where Washington dined before crossing the icy Delaware) and the Memorial Building where the giant painting stands. All of this, plus a short historical film is shown of the event. It'll give you goosebumps!

AMERICAN HELICOPTER MUSEUM

1220 American Blvd. (Brandywine Airport - Next to QVC Studios),
West Chester 19380

- ❑ Activity: Museums
- ❑ Telephone: (610) 436-9600. **www.helicoptermuseum.org**
- ❑ Hours: Wednesday - Saturday, 10:00 am - 5:00 pm, Sunday, Noon - 5:00 pm
- ❑ Admission: Adults $5.00, Seniors $4.50, Children $3.50 (2-12)
- ❑ Miscellaneous: Older kids will want more information about the engineering of the rotorcraft. Films and mechanics are available to fill in all of the details. Helicopter Rides (every 4th Saturday) - ask for adventure here! Fly-bys…wow!

This very kid-friendly museum exhibits the adventure and history of "rotary wing flight" at the country's only helicopter museum. Visitors come back here frequently because the kids can actually go on many units and work the rotors and play pretend. Helicopters from the earliest to the most modern are here, inside and outside (Coast Guard, Navy, Army, M.A.S.H.) ,plus interactive exhibits. Climb aboard and play with the controls inside the giant helicopters being restored or red, smiley faced one). It's lots of fun!

CHESTER COUNTY HISTORY CENTER

West Chester - 225 North High Street (Brandywine Valley), 19380. *Activity: Pennsylvania History.* (610) 692-4800. **www.chesco.com/~cchs**. *Hours:* Monday - Saturday, 9:30 am - 4:30 pm. *Admission:* Adults $5.00, Seniors $4.00, Children $2.50 (under 17). History Lab – hands-on family activities. Early American furniture, clothing, dolls, and ceramics.

QVC STUDIO TOUR

Studio Park (I-76 or I-95, exit US202 to Boot Road - East to Wilson Drive), **West Chester** 19380

- ☐ Activity: Tours
- ☐ Telephone: (800) 600-9900, **www.qvctours.com**
- ☐ Admission: Adults $10.00 ($7.50 if QVC Member), Children $5.00
- ☐ Tours: Daily between 10:00 am - 4:00 pm. Leaves every hour on the hour. Groups of 10 or more must make prior reservations.
- ☐ Miscellaneous: Must be at least 6 years old. Receive a $2.50 coupon towards a QVC purchase.

Imagine a shopping medium that reaches over 16 million homes instantly and can process more than 30 calls per second! Founded in 1986, this cable shopping service stands for "Quality, Value, Convenience" and has become the largest of its kind. Your tour begins as you are greeted by photographs of famous celebrities that have visited QVC to merchandise their products. You will see 34 sets and 8 studios (there is even an 8000 square foot 2-story house in the studio complete with a garage). All of the cameras are remotely controlled from one central source during taping and the complete facility uses over 1 million watts of power (or enough to power 3000 average households!) You might even have a chance to see "Murphy the Dog" the QVC mascot - he is a golden retriever that is featured on the show and we are told he gets as much e-mail as any of the other hosts! See live broadcasts being done (without cue cards - everything is ad lib!). See the prop production and design facilities - the texture display is awesome! You can even be a part of a live studio audience with advance notice.

WEST CHESTER BALLET THEATRE

West Chester - 1514 Paoli Pike, 19380. *Activity: The Arts.* (610) 431-4321. Productions like "Swan Lake" and "Nutcracker".

PETER WENTZ FARMSTEAD

Worcester - Schultz Road (SR73 and SR363), 19490. *Activity: Animals & Farms.* (610) 584-5104. *Hours:* Tuesday - Saturday, 10:00 am - 4:00 pm, Sunday, 1:00 - 4:00 pm. Free admission. *Tours:* Every 30 minutes by costumed guides. A restored, colorfully decorated, 18th century Pennsylvania German working farm and mansion. Did you know that George Washington used this home as his headquarters (from time to time) during the Revolutionary War? Best to attend Saturdays when staff demonstrates colonial crafts, (candles, weaving, paper cut art - called "scherenschnitte") or tending to the animals.

BERK'S COUNTY HERITAGE CENTER

Red Bridge Road (off Route 183), **Wyomissing** 19610

- ❑ Activity: Pennsylvania History
- ❑ Telephone: (610) 374-8839
- ❑ Hours: Tuesday - Saturday, Holidays, 10:00 am - 4:00 pm., Sunday, Noon - 5:00 pm (May - October)
- ❑ Admission: Adults $3-5.00, Seniors $2.50 - 4.00 (60+), Children $2 - 3.00 (7-18)

Gruber Wagon Works, C. Howard Hiester Canal Center. Early American industrial transportation. Red Bridge (longest covered bridge in the state).

AREA "SW"

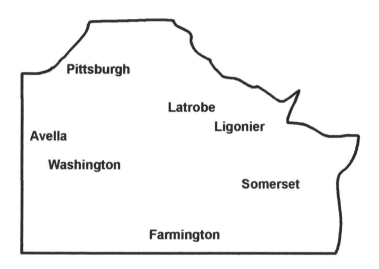

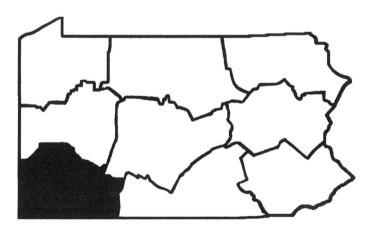

Our Favorites...

1) Idlewild Park
2) DiSalvo's Restaurant
3) L.E. Smith Glass Company
4) Pittsburgh Children's Museum
5) Pittsburgh Regional History Center
6) Westerwald Pottery Tour
7) Pennsylvania Trolley Museum
8) George Westinghouse Museum
9) Gateway Clipper Cruises
10) Pittsburgh Inclines

MEADOWCROFT MUSEUM OF RURAL LIFE

401 Meadowcroft Road (I-79 - Exit 11 Bridgeville to SR50 West),
Avella 15312

- ❑ Activity: Pennsylvania History
- ❑ Telephone: (724) 587-3412, **www.cobweb.net/~mcroft**
- ❑ Saturday, Noon- 5:00 pm, Sunday, 1:00 - 5:00 pm. (May - October)
- ❑ Admission: Adults $6.50, Senior (60+) $5.50, Children $3.50 (6-16)
- ❑ Miscellaneous: Visitors Center and Café. Best during festivals with a school or youth group for" hands on history" personalized sessions.

Re-live rugged rural life from 200 years ago as you walk the dirt and stone roads of this reconstructed village. By touring a settler log house, schoolhouse, country store, barn and blacksmith shop - you'll be introduced to inhabitants like the Native Americans, frontier settlers, farmers, lumbermen, coal miners, and conservationists who have worked the land.   Get involved by taking a real school lesson (with slate and chalk) in a 1 room schoolhouse. Shear sheep and then spin and weave wool, or, actually practice using a Native American "atlatl" (spear throwing). The grounds of this living history museum are on an archeological prehistoric dig site. See a display of artifacts they've collected.

WILLOWBROOK SKI AREA

Belle Vernon – 15012. *Activity: Outdoors.* (412) 872-7272. Longest Run: 1500 ft.; 2 Slopes & Trails.

NEMACOLIN CASTLE

Brownsville - Front Street - US 40 east, 15417. *Activity: Museums.* (412) 785-6882. *Hours:* Tuesday - Sunday, 11:00 am - 5:00 pm (Summer). Weekends, 11:00 am - 5:00 pm (April - May, September - Mid-October). *Admission:* Adults $5.00, Seniors $4.00, Children $2.00 (12 and under). *Tours:* 45 minutes. See the historic Bowman Mansion (dating 1789-1850). The Bowman family were businessmen and bank founders. It looks like a castle because of the turret towers and battlements. Tour 20 rooms of formal Victorian plus the oldest part that was the original trading post Bowman set up.

ICEOPLEX AT SOUTHPOINTE HOCKEY

Canonsburg - 114 Southpointe Blvd., 15317. *Activity: Sports.* (724) 745-6666. Official training center of the Pittsburgh Penguins.

LITTLE LAKE THEATRE COMPANY

Canonsburg - 500 Lakeside Drive - South, 15317. *Activity: The Arts.* (724) 745-6300. Plays for the entire family for 50 years.

SEVEN SPRINGS MOUNTAIN RESORT

Champion - R.R. #1 Box 110, 15622. *Activity: Outdoors.* (814) 352-7777. (800) 452-2223 (continental US). Snow Report: (800) 523-7777, **www.7springs.com**. Longest Run: 1.2 miles; 30 Slopes & Trails. Pennsylvania's largest ski and year-round resort! Be sure to get all of the latest details by calling or visiting their website. The "resort cam" shows live pictures that are updated every 5 minutes.

LIVING TREASURES ANIMAL PARK
SR 711, **Donegal** 15628

- ❑ Activity: Animals & Farms
- ❑ Telephone: (724) 593-8300
- ❑ Hours: Daily, 10:00 am - 8:00 pm (Summer). Weekends, 10:00 am - 6:00 pm (May, September, October)
- ❑ Admission: Adults $5.50, Seniors $5.00, Children $4.50

Watch kangaroos, tigers and wolves and ride the miniature horses. Kids love the petting area (babies, reindeer, camels) and feeding areas (bears, otters, monkeys, goats, sheep, & llamas).

ROUND HILL EXHIBIT FARM

Elizabeth - 651 Round Hill Road (SR51 & SR48 to Round Hill Road), 15037. *Activity: Animals & Farms.* (412) 384-8555. *Hours:* Daily, 8:00 am – DUSK. Free admission. A small scale working farm dating back to the late 1700's. A brick farmhouse with barns and fields including dairy and beef cattle, pigs, chicken, sheep, horses, and a duck pond. Be ready to watch the cows being milked daily at 8:30 am and 4:30 pm.

BOYCE PARK SKI AREA

Export – 15632. *Activity: Outdoors.* (724) 733-4656. Snow Report: (724) 733-4665. **www.usskiing.com/stats.cfm/pa06.htm**. Longest Run : 1200 ft.; 9 Slopes & Trails.

FORT NECESSITY NATIONAL BATTLEFIELD

1 Washington Parkway - US40, **Farmington** 15437

❑   Activity: Pennsylvania History
❑   Telephone: (724) 329-5512, **www.nps.gov/fone**
❑   Hours: 8:00 am - Sunset (park), Visitor's Center 9:00 am - 5:00 pm, Closed Christmas only.
❑   Admission: Adults $2.00, Children Free (16 and under)
❑   Miscellaneous: Visitor's Center with slide show, exhibits, store. Picnic areas.

Commemorates the 1754 battle - George Washington's first battle of the French and Indian War. Beginning at Jumonville Glen - the site where the first skirmish occurred with the French. Washington feared they would return with backup forces. So, he had this fort built quickly, out of "necessity". See the reconstructed fort - 53 feet in diameter, the gate is only 3.5 feet wide. Also nearby, is Mt. Washington Tavern (an 1828 famous and lively inn on the National Road used as a stagecoach stop) now housing exhibits on travel.

LAUREL CAVERNS

Farmington - 200 Caverns Park Road (Chestnut Ridge in Laurel Highlands, off US 40), 15437. *Activity: Outdoors.* (800) 515-4150 or (412) 438-3003. **www.laurelcaverns.com**. *Hours:* Daily, (May - October). *Admission:* $6.00 - $8.00. *Tours:* 2 - 3 hours. Constant temperature, 52 degrees Fahrenheit. *Miscellaneous:* Visitors center, picnic areas, indoor mini-golf.. Pennsylvania's largest cave 2.3 miles. - well-lit tours of the "Grand Canyon" or Spelunking - 3 hour tour.

NEMACOLIN WOODLANDS RESORT SKI AREA

Farmington - 1001 LaFayette Drive, 15437. *Activity: Outdoors.* **www.nemacolin.com**. (800) 422-2736. Snow Report: (724) 329-8555. Longest Run: .5 miles; 7 Slopes & Trails.

GREASE PAINT PLAYERS

Greensburg - 951 Old Salem Road (Civic Theatre), 15601. *Activity: The Arts.* (724) 836-PLAY.

WESTMORELAND MUSEUM OF ART

Greensburg - 221 North Main Street, 15601. *Activity: The Arts.* (724) 837-1500. *Hours:* Tuesday - Saturday, 10:00 am - 4:00 pm, Sunday, 1:00 - 4:00 pm. "Arty-Facts" educational programs for children. No Admission. Rural and cityscapes, toys of yesteryear, historical heroes.

WESTMORELAND YOUTH SYMPHONY

Greensburg - 21 West Otterman Street, 15601. *Activity: The Arts.* (724) 837-1850.

BUSHY RUN BATTLEFIELD

Bushy Run Road (off US22 to SR66 to SR993)
Harrison City 15636

- ❑ Activity: Pennsylvania History
- ❑ Telephone: (724) 527-5584
  www.state.pa.us/PA_Exec/Historical_Museum/BHSM/toh/bu
  shyrun/bushyrun.htm
- ❑ Hours: Wednesday - Saturday, 9:00 am - 5:00 pm., Sunday, Noon
  - 5:00 pm. (April - October)
- ❑ Admission: Adults $2.00, Seniors $1.50, Children $1.00 (under
  12)
- ❑ Tours: Guided
- ❑ Miscellaneous: Visitor Center.

The battle that opened Western Pennsylvania to settlement -
Pontiac's War in 1763. Native American forces lead by Chief
Pontiac had occupied nearby forts. The British finally stopped
advancements at Bushy Run - this reopened supply routes. Kids
will either be scared or say "cool" when they see a life-size
mannequin of an Indian Warrior dressed for battle with war paint
from head to toe. In this same area, children can take turns dressing
up like a British soldier (check out all the buttons!). Learn what
"lock, stock, and barrel" means or discover all the different ways
they used nature to provide basic needs (ex. Flour bags -
fortification and wounds, or trees for gun stock, food, and dyes).
View the electronic map of the battle then walk outside to markers
of the actual battlefield ground.

HIDDEN VALLEY SKI

Hidden Valley - One Craighead Drive, 15502. *Activity: Outdoors.*
www.hiddenvalleyresort.com. (814) 443-2600. Snow Report:
(800) 443-7544. Longest Run: 1 mile; 17 Slopes & Trails.

MOUNTAIN PLAYHOUSE

Jennerstown - Route 985 North - P.O. Box 205 (1/2 mile North of US 30), 15547. *Activity: The Arts.* (814) 629-9201, **www.mountainplayhouse.com.** (Memorial Day weekend - mid October). *Hours:* Matinees and evenings. One of the oldest summer stock theaters in the nation. Performs comedies and musicals in a converted gristmill built in 1805. Green Gables Restaurant.

DISALVO'S STATION RESTAURANT

325 McKinley Avenue (Latrobe Train Station - downtown Amtrak station), **Latrobe** 15650

- ❑ Activity: Theme Restaurants
- ❑ Telephone: (724) 539-0500
  www.westernpa.com/disalvos/home.htm
- ❑ Hours: Tuesday - Sunday, Lunch and Dinner. Early Bird specials, 4:00 - 6:00 pm ($6.95). Reservations strongly suggested. Moderate to fine dining.

An early 1900 train station that has been restored and decorated with railroad memorabilia. Ride from Pittsburgh on Amtrak to get here (adds to the railroad experience). When walking into the restaurant, you'll enter through a tunnel that trains pass over often. Feel and hear the rumble! Once through the tunnel, you may be seated in the atrium (formerly the train yard) with fountains, greenery and a full-size railroad dining car. Most families are seated in the original main concourse room with a continuously running model train above. A children's menu is offered.

PITTSBURGH STEELERS SUMMER TRAINING CAMP

Latrobe - US30 at Fraser Purchase Road (St. Vincent College), 15650. *Activity: Sports.* (724) 323-1200. **www.steelers.com.** *Hours:* Daily practice - get a schedule at the field. (Mid-July - August). Since 1967, this has been the site of the NFL - Pittsburgh Steelers pre-season training camp. Young fans can root for their favorite team member in a much smaller and more intimate setting. Children can also learn that the glamour and the glory of the NFL only comes from hard, focused work each day on the practice field.If you're lucky you might have a chance at get some autographs. Be sure to bring a pen and paper (or old program) for the players to sign!

COMPASS INN MUSEUM

P.O. Box 167 (US30 East), **Laughlintown** 15655

- ❑ Activity: Museums
- ❑ Telephone: (724) 238-4983
    www.laurelhighlands.org/compass/index.html
- ❑ Hours: Tuesday - Saturday, 11:00 am - 4:00 pm., Sunday, Noon - 4:00 pm. (May - October)
- ❑ Admission: Adults $5.00, Children $2.00 (6-17)
- ❑ Tours: Costumed tour guides

A great chance to see a restored 1799 stagecoach stop that was a typical roadside inn - complete with cramped sleeping quarters. In the reconstructed cookhouse, you'll learn what terms like "uppercrust" (the bottom of the bread was sooty from the stove - so the upper crust was much better) mean. The bottom of the bread was "caked" with soot. "Let them eat cake" had a meaning of "Let them eat dirt".

FORBES STATE FOREST

Laughlintown - PO Box 519 (Rt. 30E), 15655. Activity: Outdoors. **http://parec.com/forests/forbes.htm**. (412) 238-9533. Fishing, Camping, Trails, Winter Sports.

FORT LIGONIER

216 South Market Street (US30 & SR 711), **Ligonier** 15658

- ❑ Activity: Pennsylvania History
- ❑ Telephone: (724) 238-9701,**www.ligonier.com/fortligonier.html**
- ❑ Hours: Monday - Saturday, 10:00 am - 4:00 pm., Sunday, Noon - 4:00 pm. (May - October)
- ❑ Admission: Adults $5.00, Seniors $4.50 (62+), Children $2.25 (6-14)
- ❑ Miscellaneous: Visitor's Center film. Fort Ligonier Days in October - reenactments in summer. Quaint town shops within walking distance - some are toy stores!

B uilt by the British during the French and Indian War (1758), it was a vital link to the supply line to the West. You'll be able to view gun batteries, the very visibly and painful sharp wooden pickets of re-trenchment, the quarter master's store, a home, hospital (saws made from bone), and the commissary.

IDLEWILD PARK

Route 30 East, P.O. Box C (I-80 to I-76, exit 9, Donegal to 711, Left at Route 30), **Ligonier** 15658

- ❑ Activity: Amusements
- ❑ Telephone: (724) 238-3666 or (800) 4 FUNDAY **www.idlewild.com**
- ❑ Hours: Opens at 10:00 am (Memorial Day Weekend - Labor Day). Closed Mondays except Holidays.
- ❑ Admission: General $15.95, Seniors $11.50 (55+). (Children age 2 and under free)

I ronically, this park was the favorite for both of us as kids (*even though we never grew up together*) and each of us voted StoryBook Forest as the best spot! I guess we were meant to be together! Some featured spots include:

- • <u>MISTER ROGER'S NEIGHBORHOOD OF MAKE BELIEVE</u> - ride as a real trolley introduces you to X the Owl , King Friday the XIII and other neighbors.

- <u>STORY BOOK FOREST</u> - The Three Little Pigs, Woman Who Lived in a Shoe, etc., (over 40 nursery rhymes and tales).
- <u>JUMPIN' JUNGLE</u> - crawl, climb, swing, and bounce.
- <u>H-2-OHHH ZONE</u> - water slides, pool, Little Squirts Kiddie area.
- <u>OLDE IDLEWILD</u> - roller coasters, merry-go-round, and Raccoon Lagoon kiddie rides (largest kiddie area in the US!)

CLASSROOM RESTAURANT

McMurray - 133 Camp Lane - (off US19), 15317. *Activity: Theme Restaurants.* (724) 942-4878. *Hours:* Lunch & Dinner, Tuesday - Saturday. Dinner only on Saturday. Fine Dining. *Miscellaneous:* No children's menu. Smaller, less flavored, portions can be made by the chef. A 1904 built Thompsonville Schoolhouse (grades 1-6). Same locals remember ringing the bell (that still works). Original hardwood floors, blackboard and current kids' artwork accent this setting. The cutest mini, hand-held chalkboards that you've ever seen serve as menus.

FALLINGWATER

Route 381, P.O. Box R (I-76, exit 9, to SR31 East), **Mill Run** 15464

- ❑ Activity: Arts
- ❑ Telephone: (724) 329-8501
  www.faywest.com/fayette/fallingwater
- ❑ Hours: Tuesday - Sunday, 10:00 am - 4:00 pm. Winter weekends only. (April - Mid-November)
- ❑ Admission: Adults $8-12.00, Children $6-7.00
- ❑ Tours: 45 minutes - 1 hour
- ❑ Miscellaneous: Ages 9 and up only. (Actually get to walk around too - not roped off). Child care provided for a small fee. Falling Water restaurant. Want to see more, visit nearby Kentucky Knob, in Ohiopyle.

One of the most famous houses in America - and a memorable experience that is sure to delight all ages (Children must be at least age 9 for the inside house tour). The Edgar Kaufmann family used to vacation on this exact spot in the woods during the summer months and loved to picnic by this waterfall. They loved it so much that they commissioned Frank Lloyd Wright (the famous architect) to build a home that would allow them to live on this spot, but not take away from its natural beauty. Wright commented, "I wanted you to live with the waterfall, not just look at it." The home is built from several cantilevers (stacked like Legos) that hang over the waterfall (actually - the stream goes right through the inside of the house!). Boulders were used as flooring and windows and walls on the first floor. Closer cave-like spaces were used as bedrooms. This visit is sure to make a lasting impression!

L.E. SMITH GLASS COMPANY

1900 Liberty Street (off SR31 - follow signs), **Mt. Pleasant** 15666

- ❑ Activity: Tours
- ❑ Telephone: (724) 547-3544, **www.lesmithglass.com**
- ❑ Tours: Monday - Friday, 9:30 - 3:00 pm., Gift shop until 5:00 pm. Ages 6+ only.
- ❑ Admission: Free

The oldest industry in America - making glassware by hand, started in the early 1600's. This company makes glass pictures, goblets, plates, figurines, and even exclusives patterns for Martha Stewart. Your guide starts the tour explaining the glassmaking process from the beginning when glass powder (sand, cullet, color) are heated to 2000+ degrees F. in a furnace. Once melted, the molten glass is pulled on a stick and then molded or pressed, fire- glazed and then cooled in a Lehr which uniformly reduces the temperature to prevent shattering. They were making pedestal cake servers the day we were there. They still use many old-time tools and techniques - for example, to frost glass, they dip it in acid. Their warehouse discount prices are great! Fascinating, almost unbelievable, work conditions create an interest for kids.

LAUREL HIGHLANDS RIVER TOURS

Ohiopyle – P.O. Box 107, 15470. *Activity: Outdoors.* (800) 4-RAFTIN or (412) 329-8531, **www.laurelhighlands.com**.

MOUNTAIN STREAMS

Ohiopyle - P.O. Box 106, 15470. *Activity: Outdoors.* (800) RAFT-NOW, **www.mtstreams.com**.

OHIO PYLE STATE PARK

Ohiopyle - P.O. Box 105 Rt. 381 North, Off Rt. 40, 15470. *Activity: Outdoors.* **http://parec.com/state_parks/ohiostpk.htm**. (412) 329-8591. Whitewater. Ferncliff Peninsula Park - trails, flowers, trees, birds and wildlife abound. Visitor Center, Boat Rentals, Mountain Biking, Fishing, Trails, Winter Sports.

WHITEWATER ADVENTURES

Ohiopyle – P.O. Box 31, 15470. Activity: Outdoors. (800) WWA-RAFT. **www.wwaraft.com**.

WILDERNESS VOYAGEURS

Ohiopyle – P.O. Box 97, 15470. *Activity: Outdoors.* (800) 272-4141. **www.wilderness-voyageurs.com**.

SAND CASTLE

1000 Sandcastle Drive (West Route 837), **Pittsburgh** 15120

- ❑ Activity: Amusements
- ❑ Telephone: (412) 462-6666, **www.sandcastlewaterpark.com**
- ❑ Hours: (June - Labor Day); June, 11:00 am - 6:00 pm, July & August, 11:00 am - 7:00 pm
- ❑ Admission: Adults $6.00-$15.00

15 water slides (including "Cliffhangers" pond slide), giant Lazy River, kiddie and adult pools, Boardwalk and the world's largest hot tub. Riverplex Amphitheater.

PITTSBURGH ZOO

One Wild Place (In Highland Park), **Pittsburgh** 15206

- ❑ Activity: Animals & Farms
- ❑ Telephone: (412) 665-3640 or 1-800-4-PGH-ZOO
  http://zoo.pgh.pa.us
- ❑ Hours: Daily, 10:00 am - 6:00 pm (Summer), 9:00 am - 5:00 pm (Winter). Zoo is open year-round.
- ❑ Admission: Adults $6.50, Seniors $4.75 (60+), Children $4.75 (2-13). Parking $2.75.
- ❑ Miscellaneous: Train rides $1.00. Carrousel rides $0.75. Food available.

Over 4000 creatures both great and small. Natural settings with themes like: Tropical Forest, Asian Forest (Siberian Tigers), African Savanna (elephants), Aqua Zoo (penguins and sharks).

- • <u>KIDS KINGDOM</u> - Discovery pavilion of walkthroughs: dark Aquarium Tunnel, Bat Flyway (mesh is the only separation!). Swing-like spiders, Turtle Racers ride, Penguin Slide, Climb through Mole Tunnel.

FRICK ART & HISTORICAL CENTER

Pittsburgh - 7227 Reynolds Street I-376, Exit # 9, 15208. *Activity: The Arts.* 412) 371-0600. *Hours:* Tuesday - Saturday, 10:00 am - 5:30 pm, Sunday, Noon - 6:00 pm. $15.00 fee for "Clayton".

DUQUESNE INCLINE

Pittsburgh - 1220 Grandview Avenue (and West Carlton Street - below), 15211. *Activity: Tours.* **http://trfn.clpgh.org/incline**. (412) 381-1665. *Hours:* Monday through Saturday, 5:30 a.m. - 12:45 a.m. Sundays and Major Holidays, 7:00 a.m. through 12:45 a.m. *Admission:* Adults $1.00, Children $0.50 (6-11) - Fares are each way. One of the few remaining cable cars still in use. Look for the red lights heading up the hill and the wood carved, paneled and trimmed cars. The cars climb and descend 400 ft at a 30 degree angle. Up at the top of the station are momentos and exhibits and the best view of the city.

CARNEGIE SCIENCE CENTER

One Allegheny Avenue (Next to Three Rivers Stadium – off I-279 or I-376), **Pittsburgh** 15212

- ❑ Activity: Museums
- ❑ Telephone: (412) 237-3400, **www.csc.clpgh.org**
- ❑ Hours: Sunday - Friday, 10:00 am - 5:00 pm., Saturday, 10:00 am - 9:00 pm. (Sunday - Friday open until 6:00 pm in Summer)
- ❑ Admission: Adults $4-12.00, Seniors $2-8:00 (65+), Children $2-8.00 (3-18)
- ❑ Miscellaneous: Discovery Store. Restaurant café.

Over 250 hands-on exhibits! Here's a menu of what you can expect at this fun- filled science center:

- OMNIMAX THEATER - Movies that literally make you a PART of the action.
- INTERACTIVE PLANETARIUM - Keeps you on "an edge". Also features laser light shows.
- WW II SUBMARINE - Climb aboard the authentic USS Reguin. See demonstrations on dives, power generators, even touch a real torpedo!
- SCIQUEST LIVE SCIENCE DEMONSTRATIONS - Push a button to create a 4 ft. tornado or learn cooking chemistry.
- SEALIFE AQUARIUM - A large coral reef aquarium and water play table.
- SCIENCE & SPORT - Experience virtual reality basketball and pitching cage.
- SIMULATOR - This is the fun one! Try the dune buggy ride.

NATIONAL AVIARY

Allegheny Commons West (off I-279 - follow signs)
Pittsburgh 15212

- ❑ Activity: Animals & Farms
- ❑ Telephone: (412) 323-7235, **www.aviary.org**
- ❑ Hours: Monday - Sunday, 9:00 am - 5:00 pm (everyday except Christmas)
- ❑ Admission: Adults $5.00, Seniors $4.00 (60+), Children $3.50 (2-12)

See 220 species of birds live in natural habitats like rainforests, deserts, and marshes. The tropical areas have rare, exotic birds in free-flight atriums. Favorites to look for are the live Toucan (so animated, it appears mechanical!), a real cuckoo bird (that sings a loud, sweet sound), and the funny billed marsh birds (boat and spoon shaped, for example).

PHOTO ANTIQUITIES

Pittsburgh - 531 East Ohio Street, 15212. *Activity: The Arts.* (412) 231-7881. **www.photoantiquities.com**. Hours: Monday- Saturday, 10:00 am - 5:00 pm. 19th century photography and equipment. Photo and paper processes, antique cameras, vintage historical print exhibits.

PITTSBURGH CHILDREN'S MUSEUM

10 Children's Way - Allegheny Square (off I-279, follow signs - just blocks from the stadium), **Pittsburgh** 15212

- ❑ Activity: Museums
- ❑ Telephone: (412) 322-5058, **www.pittsburghkids.org**
- ❑ Hours: Monday - Saturday, 10:00 am - 5:00 pm., Sunday, Noon - 5:00 pm. (Closed Monday during the school year)
- ❑ Admission: Adults $5.00, Seniors $4.50, Children $4.50
- ❑ Miscellaneous: Discount Thursdays $3.50. Open until 8:00 pm on Fridays. Pecaboo Café.

A manageable 3 story hands-on museum with the mission to enrich and engage kids. Here are the favorites:

- Jim Henson's creature puppets or Mr. Roger's Neighborhood puppet shows.
- Stuffee - Inside out stuffed huge doll that is designed to teach anatomy and health.
- Mr. Junk - Create artwork from recycled materials.
- Riverscape - Wharf and riverboat - load up your goods, dress up as a sailor.
- Andy Warhol's Myths Studio (best intro exposure to his work) – make your own silkscreen.
- Great Heights – Kids climber (see through tunnel sculpture that you can climb through).
- Ups & Downs – Lift yourself or your kids on these machines using applied physics.

PITTSBURGH PIRATES BASEBALL

Pittsburgh - 400 Stadium Circle (Three Rivers Stadium), 15212. *Activity: Sports.* (412) 321-BUCS or 1-800-BUY-BUCS. **www.pirateball.com**. *Admission:* $3.00 - 18.00. National League Professional Baseball.

PITTSBURGH STEELERS FOOTBALL

Pittsburgh - 400 Stadium Circle (Three Rivers Stadium), 15212. *Activity: Sports.* (412) 323-1200. **www.steelers.com**. *Admission:* Usually seasons are sold out. Call or visit website for details. NFL Professional football team.

CARNEGIE MUSEUM OF ART

Pittsburgh - 4400 Forbes Avenue, 15213. *Activity: The Arts.* (412) 622-3131. **www.cmoa.org**. *Hours:* Tuesday - Saturday, 10:00 am - 5:00 pm. Sunday, 1 - 5:00 pm. Mondays (July/August only). *Admission:* Adults $6.00 , Seniors $5.00, Children $4.00 (3-18).

Paintings, sculpture, film and video projections reflect values and ideas from cultures long ago and today. Hall of Sculpture. Hall of Architecture.

CARNEGIE MUSEUM OF NATURAL HISTORY

4400 Forbes Avenue, **Pittsburgh** 15213

- ❑　Activity: Museums
- ❑　Telephone: (412) 622-3131, **www.clpgh.org/cmnh**
- ❑　Hours: Tuesday - Saturday, 10:00am - 5:00pm., Sunday, 1-5 pm.
- ❑　Admission: Adults $6.00, Seniors $5.00, Children $4.00 (3-18)
- ❑　Miscellaneous: Store, café.

See a world famous dinosaur collection with a T-Rex and 9 other species. Additional sites include Egyptian artifacts, mummies, a Discovery Room, Hall of Geology, Hall of Native Americans, Hall of Minerals and Gems (fluorescent minerals, crystals), and Polar World, an Arctic adaptation.

PHIPPS CONSERVATORY AND BOTANICAL GARDENS

Pittsburgh - One Schenley Park, 15213. *Activity: Outdoors.* (412) 622-6914. **www.phipps.conservatory.org**. *Hours:* Tuesday - Sunday, 9:00 am - 5:00 pm. Hours extended to 9:00 pm on specified dates during seasonal Flower Shows. *Admission:* Adults $5.00, Seniors $3.50, Students $3.50, Children $2.00 (2-12). A historic landmark 13 room Victorian glass house featuring tropical and desert motifs plus one of the nation's finest Bonsai collections. Discovery Garden - hands-on learning for children.

PLAYHOUSE JR.

Pittsburgh - 222 Craft Avenue (Oakland), 15213. *Activity: The Arts.* (412) 621-4445. (November - May). Over 50 years of children's classics and new works like Snow White and The Red Shoes.

SOLDIERS AND SAILORS MEMORIAL MUSEUM

Pittsburgh - 4141 Fifth Avenue, 15213. *Activity: Museums.* http://info.co.allegheny.pa.us/services/soldiers. (412) 621-4254. *Hours:* Monday - Friday, 9:00 am - 4:00 pm., Saturday & Sunday, 1:00 - 4:00 pm. *Admission:* Donations. Veterans Memorial building houses beginning with the Civil War and ending with Persian Gulf activities. Also African-American and Revolutionary War films.

ALLEGHENY OBSERVATORY

Pittsburgh - Riverview Park (US19 in Riverview Park off Perrysville Avenue), 15214. *Activity: Museums.* (412) 321-2400. *Hours:* Thursday - Friday (by appointment - evenings) - (April - October). Free admission. One of the foremost observatories in the world.

GATEWAY CLIPPER FLEET

Pittsburgh - 9 Station Square Dock – Downtown, 15219. *Activity: Tours.* (412) 355-7980. **www.gatewayclipper.com**. *Admission:* Adults $6–8.00, Children $4-5.00. *Tours:* Sightseeing / Theme cruises usually depart around 11:00 am - Noon. *Miscellaneous:* On board gift shops. A "Pittsburgh River Tradition" has sightseeing cruises sailing the three rivers. They are the largest and most successful sightseeing vessels in the America. There are several different boats in their fleet (all climate controlled) and many targeted toward ages 12 and under. These include Family Fun Cruises, Good Ship Lollipop Cruise (meet Lolly the Clown), Bunny Fun, Mother's Day, Firecracker, Thanksgiving, and Santa cruises. Other mascots who frequent kids' cruises are Deckster Duck, and River Rover.

JUST DUCKY TOURS

Station Square – Downtown, **Pittsburgh** 15219

❑   Activity: Tours
❑   Telephone: (412) 928-2489

- ❑ Hours: Wednesday - Sunday (plus Tuesdays in Summer), Mid-April - November
- ❑ Admission: Adults $12.00, Seniors $11.00, Children $8.00 (12 and under)
- ❑ Tours: 10:30 am., Noon, 1:30, 3:00, 4:30, & 6:00 pm., departures. Approximately 1 hour.

Venture aboard fully restored WW II Land and Water Vehicles! On land it uses wheels and conventional steering. On water it uses a propeller and a rudder. By land - narrated tours include Pennsylvania and Lake Erie Railroad, Penn Station, and Ship District. By water - see the Allegheny River and Golden Triangle.

MONONGAHELA INCLINE

Pittsburgh - Carson Street at Station Square, 15219. *Activity: Tours.* (412) 442-2000. *Hours:* Monday - Saturday, 5:30 am - 12:45 am., Sunday, 8:45 am - 12:45 am. *Admission:* Adults $1.00, Children $0.50 (6-11). Fares are each way. Boasting a 35 degree climbing angle and 358 foot elevation, this incline transports tourists and commuters daily from downtown to Mt. Washington. A special note to point out to the kids is that this engineering feat was designed in 1870 - before electric streetcars and the automobile! The trick is that one car climbs while the other descends - look for the green and yellow lights highlighting the track.

PITTSBURGH PENGUINS HOCKEY

Pittsburgh - 1 Chatham Ctr # 400 (office) (Civic Arena), 15219. *Activity: Sports.* **www.pittsburghpenguins.com**. (412)642-PENS. Admission $20 - $75.00. National Hockey League.

FORT PITT MUSEUM

101 Commonwealth Place (Point State Park on the forks of Ohio River), **Pittsburgh** 15222

- ❑ Activity: Pennsylvania History
- ❑ Telephone: (412) 281-9285, **www.state.pa.us/PA_Exec/ Historical_Museum/BHSM/toh/ftpitt/ftpitt.htm**
- ❑ Hours: Wednesday - Saturday, 10:00 am - 4:30 pm., Sunday, Noon - 4:30 pm
- ❑ Admission: Adults $4.00, Seniors $3.50, Children $2.00 (6-12), Family $10.00
- ❑ Miscellaneous: Blockhouse welcome center and gift shop (free to visit). Living history reenactments (Summer-Sunday afternoons)

This was the site of the largest British post in North America until they were forced to leave during the American Revolution. The fort played a pivotal role in the French and Indian War. Exhibits re-create the story of war, trade, and the founding of Pittsburgh. Listen to a taped explanation of the fort while viewing a scale model of Fort Pitt. There's also an 18th century trading post.

PITTSBURGH REGIONAL HISTORY CENTER

1212 Smallman Street (in the strip district), **Pittsburgh** 15222

- ❑ Activity: Pennsylvania History
- ❑ Telephone: (412) 454-6000, **www.pghhistory.org**
- ❑ Hours: Daily, 10:00 am - 5:00 pm
- ❑ Admission: Adults $6.00, Seniors $4.50 (62+), Children $3.00 (6-18)
- ❑ Miscellaneous: Museum shop, café.

The initiative of this museum is to preserve Western Pennsylvania history through intriguing exhibits such as:

- POINTS IN TIME - Emphasis is placed on Steelworkers that are immigrants. Meet Mary, the mother of 5 children and married to a steelworker. Learn why she lost her baby and how she helped raise money in times of poverty.
- GREAT HALL - 1949 restored trolley with audio and a Conestoga wagon.
- DISCOVERY PLACE – Tells a story of 8 real kids from the area – a steel worker, a servant, and an over-privileged child. Children even as young as 12-14 were laborers – learn how some of them did their jobs (ex. packing pickles for Heinz or ironing clothes for pennies). People with a heritage from Pittsburgh should be very proud and touched by this emotional history center!

POINT STATE PARK

Pittsburgh -101 Commonwealth Place, 15222. *Activity: Outdoors.* **http://parec.com/state_parks/pntstpk.htm**.   (412)   471-0235. Historical Center.

SOCIETY FOR CONTEMPORARY CRAFTS

Pittsburgh - 2100 Smallman Street (Strip District), 15222. *Activity: The Arts.* (412) 261-7003. **www.contemporarycraft.org**. *Hours:* Tuesday - Friday, 10:00 am - 5:00 pm. Saturday, 9:00 am - 5:00 pm. Visitors discover latest trends in the gallery, the store and the children's studio.

PITTSBURGH CENTER FOR THE ARTS

Pittsburgh - 6500 5th Avenue (Fifth and Shady Avenues - Mellon Park), 15232. *Activity: The Arts.* (412) 361-0873, **www.pghcenarts.net**. *Hours:* Monday - Saturday, 10:00 am - 5:30 pm. Sunday, Noon - 5:00 pm. Contemporary international, national and regional art exhibits. Sells regional artist's work. Art camp.

BEECHWOOD FARM NATURE PRESERVE

Pittsburgh - 614 Dorseyville Road (SR8 & SR28), 15238. *Activity: Animals & Farms.* (412) 963-6100. **www.aswp.org**. *Hours:* Tuesday - Saturday, 9:00 am - 5:00 pm., Sunday, 1:00 - 5:00 pm. Free admission. Headquarters of the Audubon Society of Western Pennsylvania. 90 acres of fields, woodlands, ponds, and trails. Bird observation room.

CENTER FOR AMERICAN MUSIC

Pittsburgh - Forbes Avenue & Biglow Blvd. (Stephen Foster Memorial - University of Pittsburgh), 15260. *Activity: The Arts.* (412) 624-4100. **www.pitt.edu/~amerimus/museum.htm**. Fee for guided tours. Museum devoted to "American life" music - specifically, materials related to Pittsburgh songwriter, Stephen Foster.

NATIONALITY CLASSROOMS

157 Cathedral of Learning (I-376 west to exit 7A, University of Pittsburgh), **Pittsburgh** 15260

- ❑ Activity: Tours
- ❑ Telephone: (412) 624-6000
  www.pitt.edu/~natnlyrm/countries/natrooms.html
- ❑ Hours: Monday - Saturday, 9:30 am - 3:00 pm., Sunday, 11:00 am - 3:00 pm.
- ❑ Admission: Adults $2.00, Seniors $1.00, Children $0.50 (8+)
- ❑ Tours: 90 minute hour guided or tape recorded tours. Please request a tour that is adapted to younger audiences.

❚❚Tour the World in 90 Minutes!" - Visit 24 classrooms depicting heritages of different ethnic communities. See authentic examples of cultural architecture and décor from Africa, Asia, Middle East, and Eastern and Western Europe including:

- • Gothic Commons. Ukrainian Room – wood carvings on beams and doors, hand painted pottery and tile.
- • German - stained glass fairy tales. African - Sankofa birds.

RODEF SHALOM BIBLICAL BOTANICAL GARDENS

Pittsburgh - 4905 Fifth Avenue, 15260 *Activity: Outdoors.* (412) 621-6566.　**http://trfn.clpgh.org/rodef/garden.htm.** *Hours:* Sunday - Thursday, 10:00 am - 2:00 pm (also from 7 to 9:00 pm on Wednesday - June through August) and from Noon - 1:00 pm Saturday. Most complete garden of biblical plants. More than 100 tropical and temperate species. Free Admission.(June - mid-Sept.)

UNIVERSITY OF PITTSBURGH PANTHERS FOOTBALL

Pittsburgh – 15260. *Activity: Sports.* (412) 648-8300 or (800) 643-7488. **www.pittsburghpanthers.com.**

PITTSBURGH'S PENNSYLVANIA MOTOR SPEEDWAY

Pittsburgh (Carnegie) - (US 22/30, Noblestown Exit), 15106. *Activity: Sports.* **www.ppms.com/pmsindex.htm.** (724) 853-RACE. Saturdays at 7:00 pm (March - September). 1/2 mile dirt track racing.

FRIENDSHIP HILL NATIONAL HISTORIC SITE

Point Marion - (US 119 to PA 166), 15474. *Activity: Pennsylvania History.* (724) 725-9190.　**www.nps.gov/frhi.** *Hours:* Daily, 8:30 am - 5:00 pm. Closed Christmas day only. Free admission. Visit the home of Albert Gallatin (a famous local financier, scholar and diplomat of early republic). "A country, like a household, should live within its means and avoid debt", says Albert Gallatin. He was elected to the US Senate, played a role in the Whiskey Rebellion and served in Congress.

LINN RUN STATE PARK

Rector - Box 50 (Linn Run Road), 15677. *Activity: Outdoors.* (412) 238-6623. **http://parec.com/state_parks/lnrnstpk.htm.** Boat Rentals, Mountain Biking, Sledding, Campsites.

LAUREL RIDGE STATE PARK

Rockwood - R.D. 3, Box 246, 15557. *Activity: Outdoors.* (724) 455-3744. **http://parec.com/state_parks/lrlrstpk.htm**.

WESTERWALD POTTERY

40 Pottery Lane (US 40 - 7 miles east of I-79), **Scenery Hill** 15360

- ❏ Activity: Tours
- ❏ Telephone: (724) 945-6000
- ❏ Hours: Monday - Friday, 8:00 am - 5:00 pm
- ❏ Admission: Free
- ❏ Tours: By appointment.
- ❏ Miscellaneous: Gift shop. Llama herd on site. Discounted pieces of pottery outside.

Potters making their signature country style decorative wears are simply amazing to watch! Watch a pre-measured lump of clay get hand thrown on a wheel and shaped before your eyes. They make pots, plates, mugs, and cute (and useful) applebakers. The Westerwald signature is on every piece and they specialize in personalized giftware. You'll even get to see the drying (hardening kilns bricked up for 3 days) and the artists who glaze and paint each piece by hand. The blue and gray stoneware is reproduction quality of those made in Germany's Westerwald region (thus the company name) as early as the 16th century. Look for a specialized name piece as a souvenir.

LAUREL HIGHLANDS RAILROAD

Scottdale - 25 South Broadway - SR819, 15683. *Activity: Tours.* (724) 887-4568 or (888) STEAMIN. **www.cooksway.com**. *Hours:* Weekends, Noon & 3:30 pm. (May - October). *Admission:* Adults $10.00+, Children $8.00+ (for 2 hour tours - Call for additional prices and events). "The Highlander".

WEST OVERTON MUSEUM

Scottdale - Overholt Drive (West Overton Village - SR819), 15683. *Activity: Museums.* (724) 887-7910. *Hours:* Tuesday - Saturday, 10:00 am - 4:00 pm., Sunday, 1:00 - 5:00 pm. (Mid-May - Mid-October). *Admission:* Small. A 19th Century industrial village with a museum (30 minute film "Pillars of Fire" about coke - for steel making operations), Homestead, Birthplace of H.C. Frick (millionaire by age 30 with steel coke business), barns, and a gristmill.

JENNINGS ENVIRONMENTAL EDUCATION CENTER

Slippery Rock - 2951 Prospect Road, 16057. *Activity: Outdoors.* **www.parec.com/state_parks/jennstpk.htm.** (724) 794-6011. *Hours:* Daily, Dawn - Dusk. Educational Center. Monday - Friday, 8:00 am - 4:00 pm. Free admission. *Miscellaneous:* Hiking trails. Picnic areas. Surviving remnants of a Midwest Prairie. In late July, blooms of blazing star (wild prairie flowers) along with other assorted wildflowers of all varieties. Due to the glacial activity, the ground is mostly clay and only supports growth of thin grasses and plants.

KOOSER STATE PARK

Somerset - 943 Glades Pike (PA Route 31), 15501. *Activity: Outdoors.* **http://parec.com/state_parks/koosstpk.htm.** (814) 445-8673. Beach, Campsites, Rustic Cabins, Fishing, Trails.

LAUREL HILL STATE PARK

Somerset - 1454 Laurel Hill Park Road, 15501. *Activity: Outdoors.* **http://parec.com/state_parks/lrlhstpk.htm.** (814) 445-7725. Beach, Year-round Education & Interpretation Center, Boat Rentals, Campsites, Fishing, Trails.

SOMERSET HISTORICAL CENTER

10649 Somerset Pike (SR601 and SR985), **Somerset** 15501

❑   Activity: Pennsylvania History
❑   Telephone: (814) 445-6077
    www.somersetcounty.com/historicalcenter
❑   Hours: Wednesday - Saturday, 9:00 am - 5:00 pm., Sunday, Noon
    - 5:00 pm. (May - October)
❑   Admission: Adults $3.50, Seniors $3.00 (64+), Children $1.50
    (over 5), Family $8.50.
❑   Miscellaneous: 12 minute film about the history of the mountain
    barrier area.

This center interprets daily rural life in southwestern
Pennsylvania from 1750 - 1950. Isolated because of the
Allegheny Mountains, they had to produce necessities from home -
maple sugar, ginseng, and furs were traded - food was produced on
the farm. With the Industrial Revolution came advances in farming
(hand labor to machines and commercial crops). The site includes
a log house, a smokehouse, a log barn, a covered bridge, a maple
sugar camp, a general store, and various machines (corn husker &
shredder, reaper, buggy). Pioneer and agricultural demonstrations
daily.

TOUR-ED MINE AND MUSEUM

748 Bull Creek Road (SR28 north, exit 14 - Allegheny Valley
Expressway), **Tarentum** 15084

❑   Activity: Tours
❑   Telephone: (724) 224-4720
❑   Hours: Wednesday - Monday, 1:00 - 4:00 pm. (Memorial Day -
    Labor Day)
❑   Admission: Adults $6.00, Children $3.00
❑   Tours: Given by guides who are real miners - approximately 2
    hours.
❑   Miscellaneous: Cool temperatures below - about 50 degrees F. -
    A jacket or sweater is suggested. Gift shop.

Wearing required hardhats and ducking down a little, you'll board a modernized mining car as you travel 1/2 mile underground into an actual coal mine. Original mines began in 1800 when labor was all done by hand. See demonstrations of this plus setting up a new mine area (installing the roof supports to prevent cave ins), and the most modern mining - a continuous miner (robotic). Above ground you can take a stroll to the past again as you view company stores and housing, strip mines, and a sawmill.

SEARIGHTS TOLL HOUSE MUSEUM

Uniontown - US40 west, 15401. *Activity: Museums.* (724) 439-4422. *Hours:* Tuesday - Saturday, 10:00 am - 4:00 pm., Sunday, 2-6:00 pm. (Mid-May - Mid-October). *Admission:* Very small. In 1806, the National Road began construction connecting the East and West. The National Road tollhouse is kept as it once was, with a toll keeper's office, kitchen, and living room.

PENNSYLVANIA TROLLEY MUSEUM

One Museum Road (I-79 to Meadowlands, exit 8), **Washington** 15301

- ☐ Activity: Museums
- ☐ Telephone: (877) PA-TROLLEY, **www.pa-trolley.org**
- ☐ Hours: Daily, 11:00 am - 5:00 pm (Memorial Day - Labor Day), Weekends & Holidays (April, May, September, December)
- ☐ Admission: Adults $6.00, Seniors $5.00 (65+), Children $3.50 (2-15)
- ☐ Miscellaneous: Museum store. In cooler weather, heated trolleys are running. Trolley theatre videos. Air conditioned museum.

Because the kids will be heavy with anticipation once they see the rail yard full of trolleys - plan on taking a ride right away! The trolleys are run on three miles of Pennsylvania rail and each ride takes approximately 30 minutes. Along the rail, you'll learn the history of the vehicle that you are riding on and why it's so special. As you complete your guided or self-guided tour, you'll get to meet CAR #832 - "The Streetcar Named Desire" used in the stage play by Tennessee Williams. By sure to peek in the car shop where volunteers are restoring cars for future use.

WASHINGTON COUNTY MUSEUM

Washington - 49 East Maiden Street (Route 40 - downtown), 15301. *Activity: Pennsylvania History.* (412) 225-6740. *Hours:* Tuesday - Friday, 11:00 am - 4:00 pm., Saturday & Sunday, Noon - 4:00 pm. (February - Mid-December). *Admission:* Adults $4.00, Children $2.00. The LeMoyne House was owned by a leader in unpopular activities such as anti-slavery and herbal health remedies, Dr. F. Julius LeMoyne. See the beds under which runaway slaves hid and the beehive in the herb garden on the roof.

GREENE COUNTY MUSEUM

Waynesburg - P.O. Box 127 (I-79, exit 3 to SR21), 15370. *Activity: Pennsylvania History.* **www.greenepa.net/~museum.** (724) 627-3204. *Hours:* Wednesday - Friday, 10:00 am - 4:00 pm., Saturday & Sunday, Noon - 4:00 pm. (May - August), Thursday - Sunday, Noon - 4:00 pm. (September, October). *Admission:* Adults $4.00, Children $2.00. Young Foundry and Machine Shop - Century old, belt driven machine shop and foundry with 25 fully operational machines. Colonial to Victorian. Gift Shop year-round.

KENNYWOOD PARK

4800 Kennywood Blvd. I-376, Exit 9, **West Mifflin** 15122

❑   Activity: Amusements
❑   Telephone: (412) 461-0500, **www.kennywood.com**
❑   Hours: Mon - Sun, 11:00 am – Midnight (Mid-May - Labor Day)
❑   Admission: General $17 - $20.00, Senior $3.95

A traditional amusement park -- National historic landmark. Home of the world's fastest coaster, 4 roller coasters, live shows, arcades, mini-golf, paddle boats. Also: Lost Kennywood - lagoon, shopping areas and "Pittsburgh Plunge" ride.

GEORGE WESTINGHOUSE MUSEUM

Castle Main - 325 Commerce Street (US30 to SR148 - Fifth
Avenue - Left on Herman Avenue - Left on Commerce),
Wilmerding 15148

❑   Activity: Museums

❑   (412) 823-0500, **www.georgewestinghouse.com**

❑   Hours: Monday - Friday, 10:00 am - 4:00 pm.
     Saturday, 11:00 am - 3:00 pm

❑   Admission: Donation

A tribute to George Westinghouse - the inventor and entrepreneur - plus key people who worked for his companies. The small museum is broken down into three rooms - The Family Room (personal & home belongings), the Inventions and Room of Achievement (highlights of 361 patents, the first radio broadcast in the country - KDKA in Pittsburgh!, time capsules) and the Appliance Room. Highlights for kids are the Spencer switch display where two metals put together in a disc, react differently to temperature. As they heat they jump away from the hot plate, and as they cool, they freely jump back. The principle was used for discs to temperature regulate irons. The kids are greeted by "Saranade" - the first electronic doll, in the Appliance Room, along with other "Every House Needs Westinghouse" inventions. These include washer, dryers, irons, waffle grills, radios, and home entertainment centers.

RYERSON STATION STATE PARK

Wind Ridge - R.D. 1, Box 77 (PA Route 3022), 15380. *Activity: Outdoors.* **http://parec.com/state_parks/ryerstpk.htm.** (724) 428-4254. Pool, Visitor Center, Boat Rentals, Sledding, Campsites, Fishing, Trails, Winter Sports.

Seasonal & Special Events

JANUARY

WINTERFEST

CE - Shawnee on Delaware. Shawnee Mountain Ski Area. (717) 421-7231. Fun activities open to all skiers, snowboarders, and tubers! Product sampling, give-aways, contests, prizes, equipment demonstrations, entertainment, ski party and more. Admission. (3rd Saturday in January)

ENDLESS MOUNTAINS SLED DOG RACES

NE - Estella. Camp Brule. (717) 924-3458. Sled dog teams compete for cash prizes. Mid distance and sprint races. Food, displays. Admission. (Last weekend in January)

WINTER SLEIGH RALLY

NE - Forksville. Montanvale Farm. (717) 946-4160. Antique sleighs compete in various classes. Horse-drawn bobsled rides. Food. Weather permitting: snow is needed. Admission. (3rd Saturday in January or alternate snow date)

WINTER CARNIVAL AND ICE SCULPTURING

NW - Erie. Bayfront. (814) 454-7191.

WINTERFEST

NW - Marienville. M.A.C.A. Park. (814) 927-8218. Ice skating, auction, sleigh rides, snow sculptures, scavenger hunt, food, entertainment, door prizes, games, cake and pie bake-off. No admission. (Last weekend in January)

FEBRUARY

GROUNDHOG DAY

CW - Punxsutawney. (800) 752-PHIL. Join thousands of Phil's faithful followers for his annual prediction. Fun for everyone. Hours vary. (**www.penn.com/punxsycc**) (February 2)

GREATER PHILADELPHIA SCOTTISH AND IRISH MUSIC FESTIVAL AND FAIR

SE - King of Prussia. Valley Forge Convention Center. (610) 825-7268. Scottish and Irish musical entertainment with Highland and step dancing, bands, singers, storytellers, exhibits, craft vendors, Scottish and Irish foods and fraternal organizations. Admission. (2nd weekend in February)

WINTERFEST

SW - Champion. Seven Springs Mountain Resort. (800) 452-2223. Includes ski races, craft show, children's activities, celebrity olympics, torchlight parade and other fun and games. No Admission. (1st weekend in February)

MARCH / APRIL

MAPLE SUGARING

Actual tapping of trees. Syrup making. Demonstrations of coopering and sugaring off in a realistic sugar camp. Pancakes and syrup served.

- ❑ **CE - Turbotville.** Montour Preserve. (570) 437-3131. (March)
- ❑ **CW – Slippery Rock.** Jennings Environmental Education Center. (724) 794-6011. (Mid-March)

Maple Sugaring (cont.)

- ❏ **NE - Troy**. Endless Mountains. Alparon Park. (570) 297-2791. (Last weekend in April)
- ❏ **SE – Philadelphia**. Andorra Natural Area in Fairmount Park. (215) 685-9285. (Late February – Early March)
- ❏ **SW - Somerset**. Historical Center. (814) 445-6077. Admission. (3rd Sunday in April)
- ❏ **SW - Washington**. Mingo Creek County Park. (724) 228-6867. (Last Saturday in March)

ST. PATRICK'S DAY

- ❏ **NE – Moosic**. Lackawanna County Stadium. (800) 22-WELCOME. No Admission. Afternoon. (March 14th)
- ❏ **NE - Scranton**. Downtown. (717) 348-3412.

KIDSFEST

SE - Reading. (610) 376-3811. Child-related services and products with demonstrations, prizes, activities and entertainment. (1st Sunday in April)

EASTER EGG HUNTS

- ❏ **NW - Erie**. Erie Zoo. (814) 864-4091.
- ❏ **SC - York City**. (717) 840-7440.

EASTER BUNNY TRAIN RIDES
- Candy treats.

- ❏ **CE - Jim Thorpe**. (717) 325-4606. Departure Noon and 2 pm. Admission. (Weekend before and of Easter)
- ❏ **NE - Honesdale** Train Station. Stourbridge Line. (717) 253-1960. 1 1/2 hours. Mr. Mouse, too! Entertainment. Admission. (Easter weekend)

- ❑ **NW – Titusville**. OC & T Railroad. Perry Street Station. (814) 676-1733. Departure 2 pm. Admission, (Weekend before Easter)
- ❑ **SC** - (near **Hershey**). Middletown Race Street Station. (717) 944-4435. Live music. Admission. (Easter weekend and weekend after)
- ❑ **SC - York**. Stewartstown Railroad. (717) 993-2936. Admission. (Easter weekend and weekend after)

CHARTER DAY, MARCH 8TH

Commemorates the original charter given to William Penn for the land that is today the Commonwealth of Pennsylvania.

- ❑ **CE - Northumberland**. Joseph Priestly House. (717) 473-9474. No Admission. (Afternoon)
- ❑ **NW - Titusville**. Drake Well Museum. (814) 827-2797. Free, (Afternoon)
- ❑ **SE - Horsham**. Graeme Park. (215) 646-1595. (Afternoon)
- ❑ **SE - Lancaster**. Landis Valley Museum. (717) 569-0401. No Admission. (Afternoon)
- ❑ **SE - Strasburg**. Railroad Museum of Pennsylvania. (717) 687-8628. No Admission. (Afternoon)
- ❑ **SW - Fort Washington**. Hope Lodge. (215) 646-1595. (Afternoon)

MAY

CIVIL WAR ENCAMPMENT

C - Boalsburg. PA Military Museum Parade Grounds. (814) 466-6263. Northern and Southern military units encamped throughout the area. Daily living history demonstrations. Live fire artillery demonstrations. Day-long festivities in nearby Boalsburg. Did you know that this is the birthplace of Memorial Day? Parking fee only. (Memorial Day Weekend)

SPRING CORN FESTIVAL

CE - Allentown. Museum of Indian Culture. (610) 797-2121.
Native American cultural festival with foods, crafts,
demonstrations, and family fun outdoors. Bring your own seating.
Admission. (1st Sunday of May)

AMBRIDGE NATIONALITY DAYS

CW - Ambridge. Merchant Street from 4th to 8th Street. (724)
266-3040. A celebration of ethnic pride offering tasty foods from
all over the world plus entertainment, crafts, and special children's
attractions. (Mid-month - May)

UNIVERSAL SOLDIER AND PIONEER DAYS

CW - Hanover Township. Raccoon State Park. (724) 899-2200.
A living history encampment presenting pioneer craft and musical
entertainment. Demonstrations and drills by Revolutionary, Civil,
World I and II, and modern military. No admission. (3rd weekend
of May)

FISHING DERBY

CW – Sigel. Clear Creek State Park Beach. (814) 752-2368.
Annual kids' fishing derby for ages 15 and under. No Admission.
(1st weekend of May)

BLOSSBURG COAL FESTIVAL

NC - Blossburg. Island Park. (717) 638-2527. Crafts, coal
museum, carnival, car show, general store. Parade Saturday
morning. No Admission. (Wednesday-Saturday, Mid-month- May)

BLACK BEAR ROUND-UP

NC - Denton Hill. Susquehannock State Forest. Annual family
activity - search for black bear silhouette cut-outs in state forest
lands. Bring bear cut-outs back to PA Lumber Museum to win
prizes. Admission. (4th Saturday of May)

MIFFLINBURG BUGGY DAYS

NC - Mifflinburg - SR45 - Downtown, 17844. (570) 966-1355. Explore the actual home, carriage house, and workshop of the Heiss Coach Works, the only operation rescued from almost 50 different buggy works in the area (early 1900's). It looks as it did before the Heiss family left. Working demonstrations and buggy rides. (Memorial Day Weekend)

APPLE BLOSSOM FESTIVAL

SC - Arendtsville. South Mountain Fairgrounds. (717) 677-7444. Live entertainment, orchard tours, delicious apple foods, plus! (1st weekend of May)

MAY DAY FAIRIE FESTIVAL

SC - Glen Rock. Glen Rock Farm. (717) 235-6610. Fairie tale-telling, fairie market place, come in costume, May pole dancing. (1st Saturday of May)

NATIONAL ROAD FESTIVAL

SC - 26 Municipalities. (412) 329-1560. 90 miles of fun, food, entertainment, crafts, wagon train reenactments, historic tourism. Family reunions on the road commissioned by Jefferson that opened travel to the West. (Mid-month - May)

NATIVE AMERICAN POW-WOW

SC - Wrightsville. Sam Lewis State Park. (717) 432-5011. Crafts, story-telling, dancing, songs, and food. No Admission. (3rd weekend of May)

MERCER MUSEUM FOLKFEST

SE - Doylestown. Mercer Museum. (215) 345-0210. Traditional artisans make the skills and trades of early America come to life during this nationally acclaimed festival. Entertainment, militia encampment, and full picnic fare. Admission.(2nd weekend - May)

RHUBARB FESTIVAL

SE – Intercourse. (800) 732-3538. Kitchen Kettle Village. Annual festival that teaches us that rhubarb (a red-stalked vegetable) is no longer just for pies. Kids can play games (even build mini-racecars – The Rhubarb Race Car Derby). Food and games. No admission. (Mid-May - on Saturday).

REVOLUTIONARY ROCKFORD

SE - Lancaster. Historic Rockford Plantation. (717) 392-7223. Gigantic Revolutionary War Encampment featuring over 1000 costumed re-enactors. Enjoy 18th century music and demonstrations at the historic home of Edward Hand, George Washington's Adjutant. Admission. (3rd weekend of May)

ANNUAL KITE DAY

SE - Langhorne. Core Creek Park. (215) 757-0571. Celebration of art and leisure kite flying activities. Kite demonstrations, petting zoo, Belgian horses, hayrides, pony rides, face painting, and kite vendors. No Admission. (1st Sunday of May)

JAPANESE HOUSE & GARDEN CHILDREN'S FESTIVAL

SE - Philadelphia - (Fairmont Park - Horticulture Center - off Montgomery Drive), 19103. www.libertynet.org/jhg. (215) 878-5097. See a traditional tea ceremony along with Japanese folk tales and music. Try Japanese food (small samplings) or hands-on learn about Japanese dolls, dress or origami (try one). Also open May - October for regular hours. (Festival in May)

INTERNATIONAL CHILDREN'S FESTIVAL

SW - Pittsburgh. Allegheny Center and West Park. (412) 321-5520. Indoor main stage performances by world class professional theater companies along with outdoor stages, strolling performers, workshops, and recreational, educational, and cultural activities. Admission. (2nd week of May)

ST. NICHOLAS GREEK ORTHODOX CATHEDRAL GREEK FOOD FESTIVAL

SW - Pittsburgh (Oakland). St. Nicholas Cathedral Community Center, 419 S. Dithridge St. (412) 682-3866. People from all over enjoy authentic Greek cuisine. (1st full week of May)

MOTHER'S DAY SPECIALS (1/2 OFF PRICES)

- ❑ **CE - Jim Thorpe** River Adventures. (800) 424-RAFT.
- ❑ **CE - Pocono** Whitewater. (800) WHITEWATER
- ❑ **SC - Middletown.** Race St. Station. "TAKE MOTHER TO DINNER TRAIN. The M & H Railroad offers a two-hour dinner train ride in vintage coaches along the Swatara Creek. Narration and live music. Pre-paid reservations required. (717) 944-4435.
- ❑ **SW - Avella.** Meadowcroft Museum of Rural Life. (724) 587-3412.
- ❑ **SW – Washington.** PA Trolley Museum. (724) 228-9256.

JUNE

STRAWBERRY FESTIVALS

Sample strawberry treats like fresh strawberry shortcakes and strawberry ice cream or sundaes. Entertainment. Kids' activities.

- ❑ **SC - Loganville.** Brown's Orchards. (717) 428-2036. Amish hayrides, live musical entertainment, strawberries and ice cream, children's activities, games, demonstrations, contests and prizes. No Admission. (1st weekend of June)
- ❑ **SC - McConnellsburg.** McConnell Park. (717) 485-4064. Entertainment, strawberry goodies.
- ❑ **SW - Finleyville.** Trax Farms. (724) 835-3246. Strawberry desserts. Watch them make strawberry jam. Pick your own. Children's activities. (2nd weekend of June)

FATHER'S DAY SPECIALS (1/2 OFF PRICES)

❑ **NE - Scranton**. Steamtown National Historic Site. Fathers FREE with family. (717) 340-5200. (3rd Sunday of June)

❑ **SC - Middletown**. Race St. Station. "TAKE FATHER TO DINNER TRAIN". The M & H Railroad offers a two-hour dinner train ride in vintage coaches along the Swatara Creek. Narration and live music. Pre-paid reservations required. (717) 944-4435.

❑ **SE - Kutztown**. Train Station. (610) 683-9202. All Dads and Grandpas ride half-fare. Noon - 2:00 pm. Admission.

❑ **SW - Avella**. Meadowcroft Museum of Rural Life. (724) 587-3412.

❑ **SW – Washington**. PA Trolley Museum. (724) 228-9256.

INDIAN POW WOWS

❑ **NC - Ludlow**. Wildcat Park. (814) 362-4068. Native American singing and dancing. Iroquois social dancing. Arts and crafts. Native food storytelling and much more! Admission. (3rd weekend of June)

❑ **NE - Forksville**. Sullivan County Fairgrounds. Rte. 154. Eastern Delaware Nations' Pow Wow. (717) 924-9082. (3rd weekend of June)

❑ **SE - Media**. Ridley Creek State Park. (610) 566-1725. Native Americans of the Delaware Valley present a Pow Wow at Colonial Pennsylvania Plantation with crafts, food, legend tellers, and dancers. Admission. (1st weekend of June)

FESTIVALS / OTHER

RAYSTOWN REGATTA

C - Huntingdon - Seven Points Recreation Area. 16652. (800) 269-4684 or 1-888-RAYSTOWN. **www.raystown.org**. Boat racing, concerts, kid's activities, fireworks. (Early June weekend)

KIDS ART FESTIVAL

C - **Johnstown** - 1217 Menoher Blvd. (Community Arts Center). 15905. (814) 255-6515. (Last weekend in June)

THUNDER IN THE ALLEY MOTORCYCLE RALLY

C - **Johnstown** - (Johnstown and Cambria County Area). Hill climbs, dirt drags, dual sport ride, Heritage ride, parade. (Last full weekend in June).

CANAL FESTIVAL

CE - **Easton**. Hugh Moore Park. (610) 559-6613. Annual canal festival featuring canal boat rides, 19th century living history encampments and reenactments, Locktender's House tours, continuous music and entertainment, food. Parking $5.00. (Last Sunday of June)

KID'S FEST

CE - **Shawnee on Delaware**. Shawnee Mountain Ski Area. (717) 421-7231. Annual Kid's Fest with special events, entertainment, and activities geared for children and their parents - plus Shawnee Place Play and Water Park. Admission. (last Saturday of June)

ORIGINAL PENNSYLVANIA DUTCH FOLK FESTIVAL

CE - **Summit Station**. Schuylkill County Fairgrounds. (610) 683-8707. An annual celebration of the Pennsylvania Dutch lifestyle with demonstrating craftsmen, entertainment, food, nature center, antique farm museum and much more. Admission. (Last Saturday, June and first Saturday, July)

CAMELBACK FIREFIGHTERS COMPETITION

CE - Tannersville. Camelbeach at Camelback. Exit 45, I - 80. (717) 629-1661. See firefighters compete in Bucket Brigade, Keg on a Wire, and much more. Apparatus displays. vendors, food. Over 10 companies compete. No Admission. (3rd Saturday of June)

FOREST FEST

NC - Bradford & Kane. Allegheny National Forest. (814) 362-4613. Fishing tournament, guided nature walks, interactive programs, fish hatchery tours, open houses, a festival that highlights the operation and beauty of the forest. No Admission. (3rd weekend of June)

AMERICAN FOLKWAYS FESTIVAL

NW - Clintonville. I - 80, Exit 415. (814) 385-6040. Pioneer theme show set in rustic woods. Demonstrations, music, food. No Admission. (Last 2 weekends in June)

HERSHEYPARK CIVIL WAR FEST

SC- Hershey. Hershey Park. (717) 534-3090. Journey back to the days of the Civil War and observe battle reenactments, artillery and infantry demonstrations, and authentic arts and crafts. Free to public. (2nd weekend in June)

NATIONAL STREET ROD ASSOC. NATIONALS

SC – York. 17401. *Activity: Sports.* (717) 848-4000. Admission. Over 4500 pre-1949 street rods, games, live entertainment, food. (First full weekend in June).

STAHL'S POTTERY FESTIVAL

SC - Zionsville. Stahl's Pottery. (610) 965-5019. Tour historic, early 20th century wood-fired kiln and pottery site. Potting techniques demonstrated. Over 15 contemporary potters display and sell their wares. Light lunch available. No Admission. (3rd Saturday of June)

BERRY FESTIVAL

SE - Intercourse. Rain or Shine, Kitchen Kettle Village. (717) 768-8261. Our old-fashioned berry festival includes an abundance of different foods made from a range of different summer berries. No Admission. (3rd weekend of June)

GERMAN SUMMERFEST

SE - Lancaster. Salunga Exit off 283. (717) 898-8451. Family-oriented. Includes German music, dancing, kids' area. No Admission. (1st weekend of June)

ELFRETH'S ALLEY DAYS

SE - Philadelphia - 2nd Street (between Arch & Race Streets), 19106. (215) 574-0560. Tour the oldest residential street in America. Once a year, privately owned homes (almost all 30) that line this old town alley are open to visit. The Museum (Number 126) is open year-round and once served as a seamstress store. Most homes were also shops for carpenters, printers and such. These crafts are demonstrated (basket weaving, broom making, candle dipping, needlework) by locals either on the streets at tables and chairs, or within the storefronts. Tours are available throughout the year, however children must be extremely behaved since these homes are private residences. (1st weekend in June).

CHERRY FAIR

SE - Schaefferstown. Alexander Scdhaeffer Farm Museum. (717) 949-2244. Celebrating Cherry Season with food, games, traditional period craftsmen, musical entertainment, cherry quilt raffle, and homemade cherry pies, fritters, and ice cream. No Admission. (Last Saturday of June)

APPLE DUMPLING FESTIVAL

SE - West Wyomissing. Owls Grove. (610) 678-5399. Berks County's number one summer family event featuring a variety of great food, games, rides, musical entertainment, pageants, and apple dumplings by the thousands! No Admission. (Mid-June)

RODEO

SW - Monongahela - Rt. 481 (Circle X Arena), 15063. (724) 258-3322. 7:30 pm. IPRA World Championship sanctioned. Admission. Bull riding, bareback, saddle, barrel, steer wrestling, clowns and entertainment. (Last weekend in June)

GREATER PITTSBURGH RENAISSANCE FESTIVAL

SW - West Newton. Renaissance Festival Village. (724) 872-1670. Sixteenth century European village atmosphere with combat jousting, crafts, theater, food and Lords/Ladies. Eat with your hands. Admission. (Last weekend of June, every weekend of July)

JULY

JULY 4TH CELEBRATIONS

Parades, music, food, fireworks & contests.
- ❑ **C - Martinsburg**. Morrison's Cove Memorial Park. (814) 793-2176. Rides, too! (Weeklong)
- ❑ **CW - Butler**. Memorial Park. (724) 285-7639. Frog jumping contest.
- ❑ **CW - New Wilmington**. Westminster College. Lawn of Brittain Lake. (412) 946-7354. (July 3rd)
- ❑ **CW - Volant**. 50's theme, music, costumes and dance.
- ❑ **NC - Galeton**. (814)435-2321. Firemen's competition. (July 3rd and 4th)
- ❑ **NW - Sharon**. Three by the River. (412) 981-3123. Small Ships Revue (anything that floats) regatta. (July 3rd)

- ❑ **SC - Hershey.** (717) 534-3090. Admission.
- ❑ **SC - Middletown.** Near Hershey. Race St. Station. (717) 944-4435. UNCLE SAM VISITS THE M&H RAILROAD. Uncle Sam rides all trains and passes out American flags to children during the 1 ¼ hour train ride. Narration and live music. Admission.
- ❑ **SC - York.** Fairgrounds. (800) 372-7374.
- ❑ **SE - Doylestown.** Fonthill Museum. (215) 348-9461. Pony rides, contests. Admission.
- ❑ **SE – Kutztown.** Fairgrounds & Railroad Station. (888) 674-6136. Pennsylvania Dutch culture and food. Folk artists, children's activities, farmyard zoo. Meet Uncle Sam with patriotic sing-a-longs on the railroad . (Admission, call (610) 683-9202. (Week of July 4th)
- ❑ **SE - Nottingham.** County Park. (610) 932-2589. Admission.
- ❑ **SW - Avella.** Meadowcroft Museum of Rural Life. (724) 587-3412. Historical patriotic activities. Admission.
- ❑ **SW - Canonsburg.** (724) 745-4518.
- ❑ **SW - Latrobe.** Downtown. (412) 537-8417.

REVOLUTIONARY WAR DAYS

C - Altoona. Fort Roberdeau Historic Site. (814) 946-0048. Experience danger on the 1778 frontier when British Rangers and Iroquois from Niagara attack patriots and ruin bullet making at General Roberdeau's lead mine fort. Admission. (2nd weekend in July)

PEOPLE'S CHOICE FESTIVAL OF PENNSYLVANIA ARTS

C - Boalsburg. Pennsylvania Military Museum Parade Grounds. (814) 466-6263. Annual four day Arts & Crafts Festival featuring over 140 artists, food, family entertainment, and children's activities. Come and see the best of central Pennsylvania. Parking fee. (2nd long weekend in July)

CENTRAL PENNSYLVANIA FESTIVALS OF THE ARTS

C - State College - (Downtown & PSU Campus), 16802. (814) 237-3682. The first day is usually Children and Youth Day featuring art creations of local kids ages 8-18. Art and mask parade with costumed characters, storytelling, marionettes, and concerts. (2nd Full Week of July, Monday - Friday)

"GO WILD" WEEKEND

CE - Allentown. The Game Preserve. (610) 799-4171. Featuring "Zoolympics", a chance for children to test their physical abilities as they learn about animals. Annual Mascot Party, family activities, entertainment. Admission. (Last weekend of July)

RODEO

CE - Benton - (I-80, Exit 35 to 487 North). (717) 925-6536. No Admission. Bull riding, bareback, saddle, barrel, steer wrestling, clowns and entertainment. (2nd weekend in July)

BLUEBERRY FESTIVAL

CE - Bethlehem. Burnside Plantation, Schoenersville Rd., (610) 691-0603. Enjoy blueberry delights galore on a 250 year old restored Moravian farm. Crafts, demonstrations, children's activities, and special tours are featured. Admission. (Last weekend of July)

CHILDREN'S FESTIVAL

CW - New Castle - 124 East Leasure Avenue (Hoyt Institute of Fine Arts), 16101. (412) 652-2882. Art workshops and displays. (July)

FIREWORKS CAPITAL OF AMERICA FIREWORKS FESTIVAL

CW – New Castle. Downtown area. (724) 654-8408. Children's activities, street dancing, musical entertainment, "Ducky Derby", Ice Cream Social, plus a Fireworks Spectacular. No Admission. (2nd Saturday of July)

BARK PEELER'S CONVENTION

NC - Galeton. Pennsylvania Lumber Museum. (814) 435-2652. Annual woods festival. Events include crafts, music, saw milling, woodhick demonstrations. Contests: birling, fiddling, tobacco spitting, frog jumping. Admission (July 4th and 5th)

ARMED FORCES SHOW

NE–Scranton/Wilkes-Barre. Wilkes-Barre/Scranton International Airport. (717) 655-3077. Best Air Show in the East. World-class aerobatics. Top Gun fighter demonstrations. Parachuting, Vintage Warbirds and classics. Over 100 aircraft and exhibits on display. Admission. (2nd weekend of July)

AIR SHOW

NW - Erie. (814)833-4258. (Mid July weekend)

GREEK FESTIVAL

NW - Erie. 4376 West Lake Road. (814) 838-8808. Greek food and pastries, Greek music and dancing. No Admission. Free parking and church tours. (2nd weekend of July)

PIONEER AND ARTS FESTIVAL

NW - Jamestown. Pymatuning State Park. (724) 932-3141. Displays, demonstrations, arts and crafts, Indian dancers, frontier activities, encampment, historical program, tour of the Gatehouse, food and live entertainment. No Admission. (Last weekend in July)

OIL HERITAGE WEEK

NW - Oil City. Justus Park and throughout town. (814) 676-8521. Heritage festival celebrating the history of oil. Festival includes sporting events, concerts, parades, children's events, historic tours, and a stagecoach robbery. No Admission. (Last full week of July)

INVASION OF NASCAR

SC - York - (Center City), 17401. Raceways (717) 849-2301. *Hours:* 9:00 am - 8:00 pm. Free. Features race cars and drivers - especially, NASCAR. Food and novelty vendors. Kid's area. (4th week in July)

KEYSTONE NATIONAL RIB COOKOFF AND MUSIC FEST

SC - York. York Interstate Fairgrounds. (610) 767-5026. Summer's hottest event, four days of ribs to feast on, lots of musical entertainment, pig races, special children's area, carnival midway, fun time. Admission. (Last long weekend of July)

CIVIL WAR ENCAMPMENT

SE - Berks County. Berks County Heritage Center. (610) 374-8839. The year is 1863, and Pennsylvania Federal Regiment try to enlist new recruits and demonstrate military life. Free. (2nd weekend in July)

SCOTTISH HERITAGE FESTIVAL

SE - Horsham. Graeme Park. (215) 343-0965. Explore the Scottish Heritage of the Keith and Graeme families through music, dance, exhibits, food and more. See Scottish games and crafts. Admission. (3rd Sunday of July)

INTERNATIONAL BASEBALL INVITATIONAL

SW - Freeport - 16629. They come from around the world (15 to 19 year-olds, that is) to compete. Also, Pittsburgh Pirates Alumni participate in an "Old Timers" game mid-week. Fireworks. No Admission. For more information contact: (724) 353-9426 **www.fortheloveofthegame.org**, or Freeport International Baseball Invitational, 233 Bear Creek Road, Sarver, PA 16055. (Late July)

VINTAGE GRAND PRIX

SW – Pittsburgh. (412) 471-7847. Racing and car shows. Run by volunteers with proceeds benefiting mentally retarded and autistic children and adults. (3rd weekend in July)

GREATER PITTSBURGH RENAISSANCE FESTIVAL

SW - West Newton. Renaissance Festival village. (724) 872-1670. 16th century European village atmosphere with combat jousting, crafts, theater, food, and Lords/Ladies. Admission. Free parking. (Last weekend of June/Every weekend of July)

AUGUST

ALL-AMERICAN AMATEUR BASEBALL ASSOCIATION TOURNAMENT (AAABA)

C - Johnstown - Point Stadium. 15901. (814) 536-7993. Major League Scouts are in attendance to watch sixteen teams of 18-20 year-olds compete for the championship. Also, visit the AAABA Hall of Fame featuring tournament legends who made it to the "big leagues". (2nd weekend in August)

ROASTING EARS OF CORN FOOD FEST

CE - Allentown. Museum of Indian Culture. (610) 797-2121. Native American cultural festival with foods, crafts, dancing, demonstrations, and family fun outdoors. Bring your own seating. Admission. (2nd Sunday of August)

MUSIK FEST

CE - Bethlehem. More than 650 FREE performances indoor and outdoors. All styles of music, children's activities, fireworks, international foods. (2nd weekend of August)

CROOK FARM FAIR

NC - Bradford. (814) 368-9370. 1800's restored buildings including a farmhouse, one-room schoolhouse, blacksmith's shop, carpenter's shack, a barn and candle-making shop. Carnival, entertainment, tours, old-fashioned cooking and craft demonstrations Admission. (Weekend before Labor Day)

CHERRY SPRINGS WOODSMAN SHOW

NC - Galeton. Cherry Springs State Park. (814) 435-2907. Lumberjack competition and horse pulling contest. Entertainment, displays, food. No Admission. (1st weekend of August)

MT. JEWETT SWEDISH FESTIVAL

NC - Mt. Jewett. (814)778-5701. A community-wide festival celebrating Swedish heritage. Highlights include a parade, fireworks, Swedish smorgasbord. Entertainment for all ages. (3rd weekend of August)

ARMED FORCES AIR SHOW

NE - Avoca - (Wilkes-Barre / Scranton International Airport), 18641. (877)-2-FLYAVP. **www.flyavp.com**. *Admission:* Adults $10.00, Children $4.00 (6-12). Premier air shows in the Northeast.

Formation flying, aerial acrobatics, parachutes, and in-ground aircraft exhibits. (Mid-August Weekend)

STEAM SHOW

NW -Portersville. Northwest Pennsylvania Steam Engine & Old Equipment Show Grounds. (412) 452-9545. All types of steam engines in operation. Homemade ice cream machine, shingle mill threshing, bailing, sawmill, train rides, and many shade trees. No Admission. (1st weekend of August)

HANS HERR HERITAGE DAY

SE - Lancaster - US222 to 1849 Hans Herr Drive, 17584. (717) 464-4438. *Hours:* Monday - Saturday, 9:00 am - 4:00 pm., *House Tours.* (April - early December), Admission. Tour the oldest Mennonite meeting house in America. Site includes stone house, farm, orchard, and picnic areas plus a Visitor's Center. During this farm festival see demonstrations of 18th and 20th Century farm activity. Wagon rides, food. (1st Saturday in August)

LANCASTER FEST

SE - Lancaster. (717) 399-7977. Cultural celebration of music, dance, food, crafts, and performing arts. 30 acts on 4 main stages. International food court. No admission.

PENNSYLVANIA RENAISSANCE FAIRE

SE - Manheim. Mount Hope Estate. (717) 665-7021. Hundreds of costumed merrymakers create a fantasy of bygone days and knights. Admission. (weekends)

AG PROGRESS DAYS

SE - Rock Springs. Larson Ag Research Center - SR45, (814) 865-2081. Ag museum (open mid-April to Mid-October). One of the largest agricultural shows in the country features a petting zoo, live animal expos, games and food, and farming technology demos. Free admission. Tuesday – Thursday, (Mid-August)

CIVIL WAR ENCAMPMENT

SE - **Sinking Spring**. The American House. (610) 670-8880.
Living history event. Civil War re-enactors display authentic camp
life, cavalry drill demonstrations, and cannon firings. A National
Civil War Discovery Trail Suite. Food and shopping. Admission.
(3rd weekend in August)

ANNIVERSARY OF THE BATTLE OF BUSHY RUN

SW - **Harrison City**. Bushy Run Battlefield. (412) 527-5584.
Live re-enactment of the Battle of Bushy Run, 1763. Period British
and Native American campsites, and a variety of other programs.
Admission. (1st weekend in August)

RODEO

SW - **North Washington** - 16048. (724) 894-2968. Tuesday -
Saturday, 8:00 pm. PRCA sanctioned. Admission. Bull riding,
bareback, saddle, barrel, steer wrestling, clowns and entertainment.
(3rd week of August)

PONY LEAGUE WORLD SERIES BASEBALL

SW – **Washington.** Lew Hays Pony Field. 15301. (800) 531-4114
or (724) 222-9315. **www.ponyworldseries.com**. The world's best
13 and 14 year-old Pony League players meet. (3rd week of
August)

SEPTEMBER

JOHNSTOWN FOLKFEST

C - Johnstown. Cambria City National Historic District. (888) 222-1889. Free traditional music, festival held in historic neighborhood. Nationally recognized performers, over fifty ethnic food vendors and church tours. (Labor Day weekend)

WOODHICK WEEKEND

C - Penfield. Parker Dam State Park. (814) 765-0630. A hands-on competition in old logging events to see who is the best woodhick of the year. X-cut sawing, log rolling, shoe pitching, seed spitting, and more. No Admission. (1st Sunday of September)

CELTIC CLASSIC HIGHLAND GAMES & FESTIVAL

CE - Bethlehem. Historic Downtown Area. (610) 868-9599. Exciting and educational weekend celebrating the cultures of Ireland, Scotland, and Wales. Music, dance, bag piping, athletic competition, children's activities, and authentic vendors. **www.celticfest.org.** No admission. (Last weekend of September)

FUNFEST

CE - Hazelton. Downtown Hazelton. (800) OKF-FEST. Family-oriented community festival featuring street fair, free entertainment, parade, fireworks, huge craft show, children's activities, teen street party, and ethnic food. No Admission. (2nd weekend of September)

SCOTTISH & IRISH FESTIVAL

CE - Shawnee on Delaware. Shawnee Mountain Ski Area. (717) 421-7231. Non-stop Irish and Scottish music, Scottish and Irish dance exhibitions, bagpipe bands and Highland athletic demonstrations, Scottish & Irish vendors, food, Shawnee Mountain chair lift rides, and more! Admission. (Mid-September)

SHAWNEE ON DELAWARE RODEO

CE - Shawnee on Delaware. Shawnee Mountain Ski Area. (717) 421-7231. *Hours:* Noon - 5:00 pm. Bull riding, bareback, saddle, barrel, steer wrestling, clowns and entertainment. PRCA sanctioned. (Last weekend in September)

KINZUA BRIDGE "FESTIVAL OF THE ARTS"

NC - Mt. Jewett. Kinzua Bridge State Park. (814) 778-5608. Features local arts and crafts vendors and food concessions. Native American village and crafts, live family-oriented entertainment, children's games, antique cars. No Admission. (3rd weekend of September)

LABOR DAY REGATTA

NE - Lock Haven. Susquehanna River. (717) 748-6388. *Hours:* Noon - 11:00 pm. Boat races, midway rides, live entertainment, nightly fireworks. No charge. Monday night - (Labor Day weekend)

LA FESTA ITALIANA

NE - Scranton. Courthouse Square. (717) 346-6384. Italian style festival features delicious ethnic food, crafts and live entertainment to suit young and old. Great fun for the whole family. No Admission. (Labor Day weekend)

OIL REGION RIVER ROMP

NW – Oil City. Along Allegheny River. (800) 483-6264. Catfish and carp fishing contests. Triathlon: (canoe, run, bike). Kid's casting activities, jet boat rides, educational displays, food vendors and more! (2nd Weekend of September)

CIVIL WAR RE-ENACTMENT

SC - Bedford. Old Bedford Village. (800) 238-4347. Admission. (Labor Day weekend)

HERSHEY POLKA FEST

SC - Hershey. Hershey Park. (717) 534-3090. Enjoy live Polka music, dancers, and traditional German food. Admission. (2nd Sunday of September)

POLISH AMERICAN FESTIVAL

SE - Doylestown. Ferry Road. (215) 345-0600. Polish folk song dance ensembles, polka bands, entertainment shows, Polish and American foods, and amusements. Admission. (1st two weekends of September)

MUSHROOM FESTIVAL

SE - Kennett Square - US-1 (Downtown area). (800) 932-6963. **www.mushroomfest.com**. Parade, entertainment, cooking contest, tours of Mushroom Museum at Phillips Place with film, slides, and mushroom growing exhibits. Varieties of every mushroom for sale. (3rd weekend in September)

SCARECROW COMPETITION & DISPLAY

SE - Lahaska. Peddler's Village. (215) 794-4000, Unusual and delightful bird-chasing creations compete for over $1400 in prizes. Vote for your favorite traditional, contemporary, whirl-a-gig and amateur. Displayed throughout the village. Pumpkin painting, square dancing. Make one workshop. (Mid-September to Mid-October)

INTERNATIONAL DAY FESTIVAL

SE - Langhorne. Core Creek Park. (215) 295-6567. Performances, food, crafters, and other activities of an ethnic nature. Admission. (2nd Sunday of September)

MT. PLEASANT GLASS & ETHNIC FESTIVAL

SE - Mt. Pleasant. Washington Street & Veterans Park. (724) 547-7738. Over 100 arts, crafts and ethnic food booths. Two stages of national and regional entertainment. Parade, contests, rides and glass blowing demonstrations. No Admission. (Last weekend of September)

PENNSYLVANIA DUTCH BALLOON FESTIVAL

SE - Strasburg. Historic Strasburg Inn. (717) 687-7691. 20 hot air balloons, food, live music, helicopter rides, petting zoo. Admission. (Early September)

HIGHLAND GAMES

SW - Ligonier. Idlewild Park. (412) 851-9900. Scottish Fair. Massed bagpipe bands on parade, Highland dancing, athletics, Scottish breed dog exhibit, genealogy services. children's games. Admission. (2nd weekend of September)

PITTSBURGH IRISH FESTIVAL

SW - Pittsburgh. I.C. Amphitheater, Station Square. (412) 422-5642. Entertainment, food, marketplace, cultural and educational children's activities, bingo, Irish dogs, customs. Admission. (2nd weekend of September)

COVERED BRIDGE FESTIVAL

SW - Washington. (800) 531-4114. Enjoy the rich heritage of Washington and Green Counties' 9 different covered bridges during this festival. Old time fiddlers, country style foods, petting zoo, wagon rides. No Admission. (3rd weekend of September)

SEPTEMBER / OCTOBER

FALL PLAYLANDS

Petting zoo, refreshments, pumpkin patch, pony or wagon rides.

- ❑ **CE - Breinigsville**. Grim's Corny Maze. (610) 395-5655. 4 acre maze. Straw maze and corn box. Free. (Weekends, last week of August - last week of October)
- ❑ **CE - Catawissa**. Pumpkin Fall Festival. Rohrbach's Farm Market. (717) 356-7654. (2nd weekend in October)
- ❑ **CE - Coplay**. Strawberry Acres. (610) 262-3674.
- ❑ **CE - Leighton**. Fall Pumpkin Patch. Walker's Tree Farm. (610) 377-1829. (October weekends)
- ❑ **CE - Nescopeck**. Mazeland U.S.A. Zehrer Bros. Farm. (717) 752-8820. World's Largest Maze Tour.
- ❑ **NE - Uniondale**. Fall Festival. Elk Mountain Ski Resort. (717) 679-4400. Scenic chair lift rides, entertainment. (1st weekend in October)
- ❑ **NW - Cambridge Springs**. Pumpkinville. Finney's Farm. Rte. 99 South. (814) 398-4590. Pumpkin characters out in the field.
- ❑ **NW - Spartansburg**. Country Halloween. Holly Hill Belgians (800) 438-8112. Admission. (Mid through late October)
- ❑ **SC - New Park**. Maize Quest. Maple Lawn Farm. (717) 382-4846. 10 acres of corn maze with fountains and bridges. Admission.

Fall Playlands (cont.)

- ❑ **SE - Monocacy**. UFO Corn Maze. SR 724. (610) 404-UFO MAZE. Enter the largest UFO ever spotted, explore Area 51, see crop circles. Then, can U Find Out? Admission. (Friday-Sunday)
- ❑ **SE - Ronks**. Amazing Maize Maze. Cherry Crest Farm. (717) 687-6845. Different design each year. (i.e. Noah's Ark). Also 3 smaller mazes on property. Admission.
- ❑ **SW - Champion**. Autumnfest. Seven Spring Mountains Resort. (800) 452-2223. Scenic chair lift rides, Alpine slide, open-spit cooked foods. (Last weekend in September. All October weekends)
- ❑ **SW - Clinton**. Fall Festival. Hozak Farms. (724) 899-2400. Admission. (October weekends)

FALL HARVEST FESTIVALS

Tractor pulls, antique steam engines, parades, food (made with steam), threshing, baling, cider and apple butter making, hayrides, children's activities, petting zoo & fall crafts.

- ❑ **C - Centre Hall**. Nittany Antique Steam Engine Days. Penn's Cave Grounds. (814) 364-1664. Admission. (2nd week of September)
- ❑ **CE - Summit Station**. Schuylkill County Fall Festival. (570) 754-3150. Admission. (1st weekend in October)
- ❑ **CE - Stroudsburg**. Harvest Festival. Quiet Valley Living Historical Farm. (570) 992-6161. Admission. (2nd weekend in October)
- ❑ **NE - Forksville**. Endless Mountains Flaming Foliage Show. Sullivan County Fairgrounds. (570) 247-7625. (1st weekend in October)
- ❑ **NE - Hawley**. Harvest Hoedown. Keystone Street & Main. (570) 226-3191. (1st Saturday in October)
- ❑ **NW - Portersville**. Fall Fling. NW PA Steam Engine & Old Equipment Show Grounds. (412) 452-9545. Admission. (1st weekend in October)

- ☐ **SC - Bedford**. Fall Foliage Festival. (800) 765-3331. No Admission. (1st & 2nd weekend in October)
- ☐ **SC - Harrisburg** - Fort Hunter Day. (717) 599-5751. (3rd Sunday in September)
- ☐ **SC - McConnellsburg**. Fall Folk Festival. Fulton County Fairgrounds. (717) 485-4064. Admission. (3rd weekend in October)
- ☐ **SC - Mechanicsburg**. Williams Grove Historical Steam Engine Association Show. (717) 766-4001.
- ☐ **SE - Harleysville**. Apple Butter Frolic. Indian Creek Haven Farm. (215) 256-3020. Admission. (1st Saturday in October)
- ☐ **SE - Lancaster**. Harvest Days. Landis Valley Museum. (717) 569-0401. Admission. (2nd weekend in October)
- ☐ **SE – Philadelphia**. Fairmount Park. Andorra Natural Area. (215) 685-9285. (October)
- ☐ **SE - Schaefferstown**. Harvest Fair. Alexander Schaeffer Farm Museum. (717) 949-3235. Admission. (2nd weekend in September)
- ☐ **SW - Avella**. Maize Days. Meadowcroft Museum of Rural Life. (724) 587-3412. Admission. (2nd weekend in October)
- ☐ **SW - Somerset**. Harvest Day. Somerset Historical Center. (814) 445-6077. (3rd Sunday in October)

OCTOBER

BURNSIDE PLANTATION ENCAMPMENT

CE- Bethlehem. (610) 868-5044. Three Revolutionary period regiments. Admission. (2nd weekend in October)

APPLE HARVEST FESTIVAL

CE - Catawissa. Krum's Orchards. (717) 356-2339. Free hayrides, entertainment, apple cider, baked goods, door prizes, chicken dinner, Marily's Apple Dumpling Special, carmel apples, scarecrow making, crafts, apple butter, barbecue, etc. (2nd weekend in October)

COVERED BRIDGE AND ARTS FESTIVAL

CE - Elysburg & Forks. Knoebels Amusement & Twin Covered Bridges. (717) 784-8279. Crafters, demonstrations, entertainment, food, rides. See the only twin-covered bridges and the fall foliage that awaits your family. (2nd weekend in October)

FALL FOLIAGE FESTIVAL

CE - Jim Thorpe. ASA Packer Park. (888) 546-8467. Crafts, ethnic food, bands, barber-shop quartets, and 3-hour train excursions. Tour the Old Jail and Home. (2nd weekend in October)

SHAWNEE FALL FOLIAGE

CE - Shawnee on Delaware. Shawnee Inn & Golf Resort. (717) 424-4000. Crafters, food, music, amusement rides, children's shows, animals, Fall foliage in full bloom. Admission. (3rd weekend in October)

SHAWNEE LUMBERJACK FESTIVAL

CE - Shawnee on Delaware. Shawnee Mountain Ski Area. (717) 421-7231. As seen on Outdoor Life TV, Eastern Ironjack Competition. Birling, pole climbing, buck sawing, skunk races, pony rides, chair lift rides, chainsaw carving and more! Admission. (2nd weekend in October)

CIVIL WAR RECRUITMENT DRIVE

CW - Clarion. (814) 226-4450. Authentic home town recruitment. (3rd weekend of October)

SULLIVAN COUNTY. FLAMING FOLIAGE FESTIVAL & WOODSMEN'S ACTIVITIES

NE - Forksville. Fairgrounds, Rt. 154. (717) 946-4160. Horse-drawn wagon rides, horseshoe pitching contest, children's activities, apple butter making, woodsmen's activities, entertainment and food. Admission over age 12. (2nd weekend in October)

NATIONAL APPLE HARVEST FESTIVAL

SC - Arendtsville. South Mountain Fairgrounds. (717) 677-9413. An Old time festival of apple products, live country music, hundreds of arts and crafters, antique autos and tractors, steam engines, orchard tours and food. Admission, (1st & 2nd weekend in October)

ARTS OCTUBAFEST

SC - Carlisle. Downtown. (717) 245-2648. Scarecrows, Kids Alley, entertainment, tuba finale, crafts.

HERSHEYPARK BALLOONFEST

SC - Hershey. (800) HERSHEY. See 50 colorful and unusually shaped hot air balloons at the 10th annual Hersheypark Balloonfest. Includes several launches, balloon glows, rides, entertainment, crafts and food. Parking fee. (4th weekend in October)

CIVIL WAR LIVING HISTORY ENCAMPMENT

SE - Drexel Hill. (610) 789-2324. (1st Sunday in October)

1777 ENCAMPMENT RE-ENACTMENT

SE - Fort Washington. (215) 646-1595. Admission. (Late October, early November)

HAY CREEK APPLE FESTIVAL

SE - Morgantown. Historic Joanne Furnace. (610) 286-0388. Homemade apple specialties. Scarecrows, pumpkin paintings, hay and pony rides. FREE. (2nd Saturday in October)

BATTLE OF GERMANTOWN RE-ENACTMENT

SE - Philadelphia - Germantown Avenue on Market Square, (215) 844-1863. Free Admission. This historic district is home to Cliveden (family homestead with original furnishings and bullet marks still visible) plus a museum with an overview of America's first German settlement. This land was the scene of a Revolutionary Battle of Germantown, the birthplace of writer Louisa May Alcott, and the site of the Underground Railroad. What some kids may feel are boring museums, become more interesting during a festival as history is relived. (1st Saturday in October)

PUMPKIN PATCH TROLLEY

SE - Washington. PA Trolley Museum. (724) 228-9256. Ride orange-colored trolleys and the kids get to pick a pumpkin, too! (2nd and 3rd weekend in October)

SNITZ FEST

SE - Willow Street. Hans Herr House & Museum (717) 464-4438. Fall celebration of the harvest, especially the apple harvest. See cider being pressed, apple "schnitzing", taste historic apple varieties. Games for children. Admission. (1st Saturday in October)

FORT LIGONIER DAYS

SW - Ligonier. (724) 238-4200. Commemorates the key battle of the French and Indian War. (2nd weekend of October)

PUMPKIN FESTIVALS

Pumpkin painting and carving, pie-eating contests. Pumpkin patch (wagon rides out there). Refreshments.

- ❑ **CE – Mount Pocono.** Appletree Farm. SR611. (717) 839-7680. Admission. Daily, all month long.
- ❑ **CW - Plumville.** Wells Fruit Market. (724) 397-2847. Live bands, storytelling. (1st weekend)
- ❑ **CW - Volant.** Main Street. (724) 523-2591. (2nd Saturday)
- ❑ **NW - Conneaut Lake.** Downtown. (800) 332-2338. (2nd weekend)
- ❑ **SC - Bedford.** Bedford Village. (800) 238-4347. Admission. (Last weekend)
- ❑ **SE - Chadds Ford.** (610) 388-7376. (Last weekend)
- ❑ **SE - Doylestown.** Fonthill Park. (215) 345-6644. Admission. (Last weekend)
- ❑ **SE - Lancaster.** Landis Valley Museum. (717) 569-0401. (Last weekend)
- ❑ **SE - Media.** Tyler Arboretum. (610) 566-9134. (3rd weekend)
- ❑ **SE- Norristown.** Elmwood Park Zoo. (610) 277-3825. Admission. (3rd weekend)

OCTOBERFESTS

German music, dance, foods & cultural exhibits. "Um-pah-pah" bands & cloggers.

- ❑ **C - Johnstown.** Bottle Works Ethnic Arts Center. (814) 536-5399. (1st Saturday)
- ❑ **CE - Allentown.** Cedar Beach Park. (610) 437-6900. (2nd weekend)
- ❑ **CW - Ambridge.** Old Economy Village. Erntefest. (724) 266-4500. Admission. (1st Saturday)
- ❑ **SC - Bedford.** Old Bedford Village. (800) 238-4347. Admission. (3rd weekend)

Octoberfests (cont.)

❑   **SE - Lancaster**. Salunga Exit off Rte 283. (717) 898-8451.
    (Late September/Early October weekends)

NOVEMBER

HERSHEYPARK CHRISTMAS CANDYLANE

SC - Hershey. Hersheypark. (717) 534-3090. More than 1,000,000
lights, unique shops, holiday entertainment, great food and rides.
Look for Santa and his live reindeer! Admission for rides. Hours
may vary. (Mid-November - New Year's weekend)

ANNIVERSARY OF LINCOLN'S GETTYSBURG ADDRESS

SC - Gettysburg. Daytime, Gettysburg National Cemetery. (717)
334-6274. The annual observance of President Abraham Lincoln's
famous address with brief memorial services and noted speakers.
(3rd week as announced in November)

REMEMBRANCE DAY

SC - Gettysburg. Daytime, Albert Woolson Monument. (717)
334-6274. An annual event held in conjunction with the parade of
Civil War troops and a wreath-laying ceremony. (3rd week as
announced in November)

CHILDREN'S THANKSGIVING CELEBRATION

SE - Lancaster. Landis Valley Museum. (717) 569-0401.
Children of all ages will enjoy an afternoon of fun and games and
learn about the celebration of Thanksgiving in the 19th century.
(4th week as announced in November)

PEDDLER'S VILLAGE ANNUAL APPLE FESTIVAL

SE - Lahaska. Peddler's Village. (215) 794-4000. Live music, marionettes, pie-eating contests. Apples served up in fritters, pastries, butter, dipped in chocolate and caramel, or enjoyed plain. (1st weekend in November)

TAFFY PARTIES

SW - Avella. Meadowcroft Museum. Taffy pulling party in log house, holiday programs in one-room schoolhouse. Make an ornament. (Late November and early December weekends)

PITTSBURGH MODEL RAILROAD MUSEUM

SW - Gibsonia - 5507 Lakeside Drive, 15044. (724) 444-6944 **www.fyi.net/~moose**. Holiday Miniature railroad displays the transportation systems in Pittsburgh during the 1950's. Accent on coal, steel, and steam production in use. (Late November - Early January)

SPARKLE SEASON - PITTSBURGH'S CELEBRATION OF THE HOLIDAYS

SW - Pittsburgh. Downtown area. (888) PGH-FEST. Celebrate the holiday season in downtown Pittsburgh! Over 1,000 displays, performances, activities and events - many free! Includes Parade Holly Trolley. (3rd week November - 1st week of January)

NOVEMBER / DECEMBER

FESTIVAL OF LIGHTS

Glistening lights. Visit with Santa. Hot chocolate. Freshly baked cookies. Toy/gift shops. Weekend entertainment. (Evenings - late November through New Year's Day unless noted otherwise)

- ❑ **C - Altoona**. Lights on the Lake. Lakemont Park. I-99 Frankstown Rd. Exit. (800-434-8006)
- ❑ **CE - Allentown**. Lights in the Parkway. (610) 437-7616.
- ❑ **NW - Erie**. Zoolumination. Erie Zoo. (814) 864-4091. Walk-thru. Admission. Mid - to - late December only.
- ❑ **SC - York**. Christmas Magic. Rocky Ridge County Park. (717) 840-7440. Walk-thru. Admission.
- ❑ **SE - Bernville**. Koziar's Christmas Village. Off SR 183. (610) 488-1110. Top 10 PA Travel Attractions. Walk-thru. Admission.
- ❑ **SE - Strasburg**. Christmas Spectacular. Village Greens Mini-Golf, Rte. 741. (717) 687-6933. Admission.
- ❑ **SW - Greensburg**. Overly's Country Christmas. Westmoreland Fairgrounds. (412) 925-3539. Admission.
- ❑ **SW - Indiana**. "It's A Wonderful Life". Blue Spruce Park. (724) 463-7505. Jimmy Stewart's home town. See "Blue the Spruce Ness Monster". Drive-thru. Admission.
- ❑ **SW - Pittsburgh**. Zoo Lights. (412) 665-3640. Walk-thru. Admission. Begins mid-December.

TRAIN RIDES WITH SANTA

Sing songs and eat treats as you ride the train with Santa aboard. (Thanksgiving - December weekends)

- ❑ **CE - Jim Thorpe**. (717) 325-4606. Heated cars. Admission. (1st two weekends)

- ❏ **NE - Honesdale**. (800) 433-9008. Mrs. Claus and Rudolph, too! Admission. (1st two weekends in December)
- ❏ **NE - Scranton**. Steamtown National Historic Site. (888) 693-9391. Toys for Tots Train (Thanksgiving weekend only). Face painting, live music. FREE with new toy donation.
- ❏ **NW - Titusville**. OC & T Railroad. Perry Street Station. (814) 676-1733. (2nd weekend in December)
- ❏ **SC - Middletown**. Race Street Station. (717)944-4435. Admission. Dinner with Santa on 1st Saturday in December.
- ❏ **SE - Kutztown**. (610) 683-9202. Elves ride too! Toy train display. Admission.
- ❏ **SE - West Chester**. Brandywine Service Railroad. (610) 793-4433. (Thanksgiving - Christmas)
- ❏ **SW - Washington**. PA Trolley Museum. (724)228-9256. Toy train lay-out. Admission.

DECEMBER

"THE NUTCRACKER" AND CHRISTMAS MUSICALS

- ❏ **C - Altoona**. Mishler Theater. (814) 946-9944.
- ❏ **CE - Allentown**. Allentown Symphony Orchestra with the Repertory Dance Theatre. (610) 432-6715.
- ❏ **CE - Bethlehem**. Live Bethlehem Christmas Pageant. Community Arts Pavilion. (610) 867-2893.
- ❏ **CE - Easton**. American Repertory Ballet Company. (610) 252-3132.
- ❏ **CW – New Castle**. Parou Ballet Company. (412) 652-1762.
- ❏ **CW - Uniontown**. State Theatre Center for the Arts. (724) 439-1360.
- ❏ **NE - Pittsburgh**. Pittsburgh Ballet. Benedum Center. (412) 456-6666.
- ❏ **NE - Susquehanna** Choral. "Candlelight Christmas". (717) 533-7859.

"The Nutcracker" And Christmas Musicals (cont.)

❏ **NW - Franklin**. A Christmas Carol. World Premiere Musical. Barrow Theatre. (814) 437-3440.

❏ **SC - Chambersburg**. A Christmas Carol. Caledonia Theatre Company and Thunderbird Ltd. Capitol Theatre. (717) 352-2164. (Month-long)

❏ **SC - Hershey**. Christmas with Dickens - A Christmas Carol by Gerald Charles Dickens, great-great-grandson of Charles. Hotel Hershey. (800) HERSHEY.

❏ **SE - Lancaster**. American Music Theatre. (800) 648-4102.

❏ **SE - West Chester**. Brandywine Ballet Company. (610) 696-2711.

❏ **SW - Pittsburgh**. Pittsburgh Pops and Mendelsohn Choir. Heinz Hall. (412) 392-4900.

CHRISTMAS OPEN HOUSES

Tours of decorated, historical buildings. Refreshments.

❏ **C - Altoona**. Baker Mansion Museum. (814) 942-3916. Admission. (Thanksgiving weekend plus 1st two weekends in December)

❏ **C - Altoona**. Railroaders Memorial Museum. (888) 425-8666.

❏ **C - Lewisburg**. Packwood House Museum. (570) 524-0323. (3rd Saturday in November thru mid-January)

❏ **C - State College**. Centre Furnace Mansion. (814) 238-4779.

❏ **CE - Emmaus**. Downtown. (610) 965-6279. (1st long weekend in December)

❏ **CE - Bethlehem**. (800) 360-8687. Admission. (Thanksgiving weekend thru weekend after New Year's)

❏ **CW - Ambridge**. Old Economy Village. (724) 266-4500. Admission. (1st weekend in December)

❏ **CW - Butler**. Butler County Shaw House. (724) 283-8116.

❏ **CW - Butler**. The Old Stone House. (724) 738-2408.

❏ **CW - Clarion**. Sutton-Ditz House Museum. (814) 226-4450. (Day after Thanksgiving)

- ❏ **NC - Ridgway.** Elk County Museum. (814) 834-3723.
- ❏ **NE – Milford.** Grey Towers. (717) 296-9630. Home of Gifford Pinchot, the founder of USDA Forest Service. Admission.
- ❏ **SC - Bedford.** Old Bedford Village. (814) 623-1156. Admission. (1st & 2nd weekend in December)
- ❏ **SC - Fayetteville.** Paul-Corbett House. (717) 352-8468. (Mid-September - days before Christmas)
- ❏ **SC - Gettysburg.** Downtown. (717) 334-6274. Admission. (1st & 2nd weekend in December)
- ❏ **SC - Harrisburg.** Fort Hunter Mansion. (717) 599-5751. Admission. (December 1st-23rd)
- ❏ **SE – Dublin.** Pearl S. Buck House. Green Hills Farm. (215) 249-0100. Admission. (Tuesday – Saturday)
- ❏ **SE - Fort Washington.** Mather Mill. (215) 646-1595. Admission. (Weekend after Thanksgiving)
- ❏ **SE - Lancaster.** Landis Valley Museum. (717) 569-0401. (1st Wednesday - Saturday and 3rd Saturday in December)
- ❏ **SE - Lancaster.** Wheatland. (717) 382-8721. Admission. (1st & 2nd weekend in December)
- ❏ **SE - Morrisville.** Pennsbury Manor. (215) 946-0400. Admission. (2nd weekend in December)
- ❏ **SE - Philadelphia.** Elfreth's Alley. (215) 574-0560. Admission. (2nd Saturday in December)
- ❏ **SE - Kennett Square.** Longwood Gardens. (800) 737-5500.
- ❏ **SE - Reading.** Centre Park. (610) 649-4300. Admission. (2nd Sunday in December)
- ❏ **SE - Schwenksville.** Pennywalker Mills. (610) 287-9349.
- ❏ **SE - Strasburg.** Railroad Museum of Pennsylvania. (717) 687-8628. Admission. (2nd Sunday in December)
- ❏ **SE - Wyomissing.** Gring's Mill. (610) 374-8839. (December)
- ❏ **SW - Farmington.** Nemacolin Woodlands. (724) 329-8555. (Saturday after Thanksgiving)
- ❏ **SW - Indiana.** Jimmy Stewart Museum. (800) 83-JIMMY. Admission. (Thanksgiving weekend thru December)

Christmas Open Houses (cont.)

- ❑ **SW - Laughlintown**. Compass Inn Museum. (724) 238-4983. Admission. (1st Saturday in November thru 2nd Saturday in December - weekends only)
- ❑ **SW - Pittsburgh**. Cathedral of Learning. (412) 624-6000. Admission. (Month of December)
- ❑ **SW - Clayton**. The Henry Clay Frick Estate. Pittsburgh (412) 371-0600. Admission. (3rd Thursday in November - mid-January, (Tuesday - Sunday)
- ❑ **SW - Washington**. LeMoyne House. (412) 225-6740. (1st weekend in December)

FESTIVAL OF TREES

Indoor display of 50+ artificial decorated trees. Gift shop. Snacks. Entertainment. Santa and Christmas/Winter characters. Arts and crafts.

- ❑ **C - Huntingdon**. (814) 643-3577.
- ❑ **C - Johnstown**. Community Arts Center. (814) 255-6515. Admission. (Mid-November to early December)
- ❑ **C - State College**. Penn State Ag Arena. (800) 350-5084. (2nd week of December)
- ❑ **CW - Lucinda**. (814) 226-7288.
- ❑ **NE - Scranton**. Steamtown National Historic Site. (888) 693-9391. Admission. (Mid-December through New Year's weekend)
- ❑ **SE - New Hope**. Parry Mansion. (215-) 862-5652
- ❑ **SW - Ligonier**. Ligonier Valley Library. (724) 238-6818. Admission. (2nd week of December)

DECEMBER

BLUE KNOB RESORT WINTER FESTIVAL

C - Claysburg. Blue Knob Resort. (814) 239-5111. Activities include sleigh rides, ski race, snowboard race, tug-of-war, live entertainment, entrance fee charges, prizes awarded. (Last weekend in December)

KAWANZA CELEBRATION

C - Johnstown. Bottle Works. (814) 536-5399. (Early December in December)

WALKER'S CHRISTMAS HOLIDAY

CE - Leighton. Walker's Tree Farm. (610) 337-1829. Wagon ride across the 100 acre farm to choose and cut your special tree. Meet Santa and friends. Snacks, gift shop, trains. (First 2 weekends in December)

COCK 'N BULL RESTAURANT'S COLONIAL DINNER

SE - Lahaska. Peddler's Village. (215) 794-4000. Observe preparation of foods colonial-style over an open hearth. Enjoy a four-course meal from colonial era. Keepsake menu. Historical characters, live music. Perfect for families, schools and groups. (Early December – Late March)

SANTA FAMILY FUN CRUISES

SW - Pittsburgh. Gateway Clipper Fleet (412) 355-7980. (1st weekend in December)

NEW YEAR'S EVE - FIRST NIGHT

An alcohol-free, family-oriented celebration for New Year's Eve. Music, dance, theatre, comedy, poetry. Giant ice sculptures. Fireworks. Arts and crafts, storytellers and puppets.

- ❏ **C - State College**. Downtown and Penn State Campus. (800) 358-5466.
- ❏ **CE - Bloomsburg**. Downtown. (717) 784-5530.
- ❏ **NC - Bradford**. Downtown.
- ❏ **NW - Erie**. Downtown.
- ❏ **SC - Harrisburg**. Downtown.
- ❏ **SC - York**. Downtown. (717) 854-1587.
- ❏ **SE - Bristol**. Downtown.
- ❏ **SE - Philadelphia**. Delaware River. (215) 636-1666.
- ❏ **SW - Pittsburgh**. Downtown. (888) PGH-FEST.

GROUP DISCOUNTS AND FUNDRAISER OPPORTUNITIES!

Dear Coordinator:

We're excited to introduce our new book to your group! This new guide for parents, grandparents, teachers and visitors is a great tool to discover hundreds of fun places to visit around Pennsylvania. **KIDS ♥ PENNSYLVANIA** is one resource for all the wonderful places to travel either locally or across the state.

We are two parents who have researched, written and published this book. We have spent over 1000 hours collecting information and, very often, visiting every site listed in this guide. This book is kid-tested and the descriptions include great hints on what kids like best!

After you have reviewed your copy of **KIDS ♥ PENNSYLVANIA**, please consider the following options: *(Please visit* **www.kidslovepublications.com** *for latest information)*

❑ **Group Discount/Fundraiser** – Purchase the book at the price of $10.00 and offer the 23% savings off the suggested retail price to members/ friends. Minimum order is ten books. Greater discounts (up to 38%) are available for fundraisers. Call for details.

❑ **Available for Interview/Speaking** – The authors have a treasure bag full of souvenirs from favorite places in Pennsylvania. We'd love to share ideas on planning fun trips to take children while exploring Pennsylvania. The authors are available, by appointment, at (614) 898-2697. The minimum guaranteed order is 50 books. There is no additional fee involved.

Call us soon at (614) 898-2697 to make arrangements!
Happy Exploring!

Attention Parents:

All titles are "Kid Tested" (*the authors and kids personally visited all of the most unique places*) and wrote the books with warmth and excitement from a parent's perspective. Find tried and true places that children will enjoy. No more boring trips! Listings provide: Names, addresses, telephone numbers, <u>internet addresses</u>, directions, and descriptions.

KIDS LOVE INDIANA ™

❖ **Discover places where you can "co-star" in a cartoon or climb a giant sand dune.** Almost 600 listings in one book about Indiana travel. 10 geographical zones, 193 pages.

KIDS LOVE MICHIGAN ™

❖ **Discover places where you can "race" over giant sand dunes, climb aboard a lighthouse "ship", eat at the world's largest breakfast table, or watch you favorite foods being made.** Over 600 listings in one book about Michigan travel. 8 geographical zones, 200+ pages.

KIDS LOVE OHIO ™

❖ **Discover places like hidden castles and whistle factories.** Almost 1000 listings in one book about Ohio travel. 9 geographical zones, 291 pages.

KIDS LOVE PENNSYLVANIA ™

❖ **Explore places where you can "discover" oil and coal, meet Ben Franklin, or watch you favorite toys and delicious, fresh snacks being made.** Over 900 listings in one book about Pennsylvania travel. 9 geographical zones, 268 pages.

ORDER FORM

Kids Love Publications

7438 Sawmill Road, PMB 500
Columbus, OH 43235
(614) 898-2697

Visit our website: **www.kidslovepublications.com**

Quantity	Title	Price (ea.)	Total
	"Kids Love Indiana"	$12.95	
	"Kids Love Michigan"	$12.95	
	"Kids Love Ohio"	$12.95	
	"Kids Love Pennsylvania"	$12.95	
Special Combo Pricing - Please Indicate Quantity & Titles Above			
	Combo #2 - Any 2 Titles	$21.95	
	Combo #3 - Any 3 Titles	$29.95	
	Combo #4 - All 4 Titles	$36.95	
Note: All Combo Pricing is for different titles only. For multiple (10+) quantity discounts <u>of one title</u> please refer to the Group Sales information page in this book.	Subtotal		
	Sales Tax (Ohio Residents Only) - 5.75%		
	Shipping	FREE	
	TOTAL		

(Please make check or money order payable to: KIDS LOVE PUBLICATIONS)

Name_____

Address_____

City_____State_____

Zip_____Telephone_____

All orders are shipped within 2 business days of receipt by U.S. Mail. Your satisfaction is 100% guaranteed or simply return your order for a prompt refund. If you wish to have your books personally autographed (for a special gift, etc.) please include a legible note indicating what you wish to be written in your book(s). Thanks for your order and Happy Exploring!

George ♥ _Michele_